THE CENTURY
OF CALAMITY

THE CENTURY OF CALAMITY

ENGLAND IN THE LONG ELEVENTH CENTURY

T. D. Asch

AMBERLEY

First published 2021

Amberley Publishing
The Hill, Stroud
Gloucestershire, GL5 4EP

www.amberley-books.com

Copyright © T. D. Asch, 2021

The right of T. D. Asch to be identified as
the Author of this work has been asserted in
accordance with the Copyright, Designs and
Patents Act 1988.

ISBN 978 1 3981 0123 4 (hardback)
ISBN 978 1 3981 0124 1 (ebook)

British Library Cataloguing in Publication Data.
A catalogue record for this book is available
from the British Library.

1 2 3 4 5 6 7 8 9 10

Typesetting by Aura Technology and Software
Services, India. Printed in UK.

CONTENTS

Introduction   7

Prologue   11

1 Old England   13

2 Downfall   43

3 Edmund Ironside   74

4 Good King Edward   121

5 Twilight   154

6 Brothers in Arms   180

7 Conquest   206

8 Colonisation   224

Epilogue   257

Appendix I   Archbishops   259

Appendix II   Ealdormen & Earls   260

Appendix III   The Edict When the Great Army
                Came to England   262

Appendix IV   The Sermon of the Wolf to the English   264

Appendix V   The Penitential Ordinance   273

Bibliography   277

Index   280

INTRODUCTION

In the beginning were the Vikings.[1]

The first recorded Viking attacks on what was to become the kingdom of England happened at the end of the eighth century. For a while the perpetrators were happy to raid and return to Scandinavia to enjoy the fruits of their banditry. However, by the middle of the ninth century the Great Heathen Army (as it was known to its victims) had launched an invasion with the intention of conquering the country, and establishing permanent settlements.

There was no kingdom of England for the Great Heathen Army to invade. Instead, there were four smaller realms, each ruled by its own king: Northumbria, Mercia, East Anglia and Wessex. By 878 Northumbria, Mercia and East Anglia had

---

[1] The peoples of Scandinavia were collectively known as the Norse. The Norsemen who attacked England between the end of the eighth century and the middle of the eleventh century, the period known as the Viking Age, were mainly Danish. Strictly speaking, the term 'Viking' is only correct when referring to raiders, not to Scandinavians in general.

been utterly eclipsed, and the Danish invaders controlled all of England except for a western rump of the kingdom of Wessex. They were on the point of defeating this last redoubt of English rule when they were stopped by Alfred the Great, whose victory at the battle of Edington in the spring of that year turned the tide.

The next fifty years saw Alfred, his son Edward, and his grandson Æthelstan gradually win back the lost territory, and by the time Æthelstan died in 939 he was generally recognised as king of all England, which covered roughly the same territorial area it does today. The House of Wessex had become England's ruling dynasty, and it was to remain so for as long as England was ruled by Englishmen.

The threat from the Danes had dissipated, but it never disappeared: the Vikings were and are justly famous for their military prowess, and England was always a tempting target. They would, in the end, be back.

They did not, though, trouble the country while Alfred's great-grandson Edgar, who became king in 959, was on the throne. By then England had become powerful, and in 973 Edgar held two ceremonies, one at Bath and one at Chester, to demonstrate and emphasise this power. At Bath, fourteen years after he became king, and shortly after his thirtieth birthday, Edgar was crowned. The coronation was an 'imperial' one, at which he was anointed not just as King of England but as the overlord of the kings of the rest of Britain. Then, at Chester, these other kings, including the King of Scots, the King of Strathclyde, and several Welsh kings, formally recognised his greater status by rowing him on the River Dee.

It was not to last. Just two years after the ceremony at Chester, at the height of his powers, and at just thirty-two years of age, Edgar died, so far as we can tell of natural causes, leaving two young sons as his heirs.

PROLOGUE

In the spring of 1066 an elderly monk looked up at the night sky.[1]
What he saw terrified him.

'So you are come,' he said to himself. 'The cause of lamentation
to many a mother, you are come. I saw you a long time ago. But
now I behold you more terrible, Ready to hurl devastation on
this country.'

At the time people called it a 'hairy star'. Now we know it
to have been Halley's Comet, which passed by our world in the
autumn of 989, and then again in the spring of 1066.

---

1 Eilmar was his name; he was a monk of Malmesbury, where this tale
became part of the abbey's folklore when it was written down by William
of Malmesbury, a monastic historian from the same religious house, in the
twelfth century.

ENGLAND AT THE TURN OF THE ELEVENTH CENTURY

I

OLD ENGLAND

It is always a temptation for a rich and lazy nation,
To puff and look important and to say: –
'Though we know we should defeat you,
we have not the time to meet you.
We will therefore pay you cash to go away.'

And that is called paying the Dane-geld;
But we've proved it again and again,
That if once you have paid him the Dane-geld
You never get rid of the Dane.

Rudyard Kipling

England's was an elective monarchy. The principle of primogeniture, that the king's eldest son would automatically inherit the Crown, had not been established. Instead, when a king died, the *witenagemot* – the meeting of the *witan*, the 'wise men' of the kingdom, which normally operated as a royal council – would assemble and elect his successor.

By convention, only æthelings – that is, princes of the blood royal – were eligible for election. Edgar's two sons, Edward and Æthelræd, were both potential successors. Both were still children: Edward was at most thirteen in 975, and Æthelræd around eight or nine.[1] Edward was therefore the obvious choice, but his accession was not uncontested.

There may have been several reasons for the witan to have been wary of Edward. He and Æthelræd were half-brothers, and whereas Æthelræd's mother was Edgar's queen, the identity of Edward's mother is now unclear. Presumably it wasn't unclear at the time, but no contemporary record of her survives, and perhaps it may have been the cause of some embarrassment. There were, for instance, later rumours that she had been a nun. Alternatively, and less scandalously, she may have been an earlier wife of Edgar's: were that the case, she may have died before Edgar replaced her, or she may have been set aside in favour of Ælfthryth, Æthelræd's mother. We don't know for sure, but that we don't know suggests that there may have been something which some people found unsatisfactory.

It has also been suggested that the division over the succession reflected a division in the country at large. King Edgar may not have lived an impeccably Christian life himself. But his Archbishop of Canterbury, Dunstan, took his Christianity very seriously indeed, and was later to be canonised. While Dunstan was archbishop, he reformed the monasteries, expelling monks who had disregarded their vows of poverty, chastity, and obedience, and replacing them with holier men: in particular, men who were not married. This had not pleased everyone, and when Edgar died there was what

---

1 Births, even of royal children, were not recorded, at least not in a form which has survived, so we don't know their exact ages.

historians have sometimes described as an 'anti-monastic reaction'. There was chaos, yes, but there were also some deliberate reversals of Edgar's, or Dunstan's, approach: Ælfhere, the ealdorman of Mercia, had taken advantage of Edgar's death to expel these new monks from Mercian monasteries and replace them, presumably with their original inhabitants or men related to them.[2]

Why? Because while monks, theoretically at least, secluded themselves from worldly concerns, they, and particularly their abbots, were nonetheless usually from notable families. Monasteries mattered regardless of how observant their inmates were: they were centres of social, cultural and economic life as well as religious houses.

There is no direct evidence that the divisions over which of his sons was to succeed Edgar had anything to do with this. There is no surviving contemporary record of anyone being described, never mind describing himself, as part of an anti-monastic reaction. Still, there was clearly a division between those who wanted to see Dunstan's reforms maintained (such as Æthelwin, the ealdorman of East Anglia, who raised an army to defend the monasteries in that region from those who might have sought to 'purge' them of their new inhabitants) and those who wanted to see them reversed, and although the two æthelings were probably too young to have taken sides themselves, that doesn't mean they couldn't have acted as figureheads. Both Dunstan and Oswald, the Archbishop of York, supported Æthelræd, whereas Ælfhere supported Edward. It may have been chaotic and anarchic, but among the chaos and the anarchy the outlines of rival factions can be discerned.

---

2 An ealdorman was a royal official representing the king in a shire or a group of shires. Ealdormen were responsible for carrying out the king's government: this included, for instance, defence, law and order, and tax collection.

If religious concerns didn't make people support the younger brother, perhaps it was a question of character. Edward does seem to have been a rather disagreeable young man. In Byrhtferth of Ramsey's *Life of Oswald of Worcester*, written shortly after Oswald's death in 992 to celebrate a holy clergyman who had served as Archbishop of York for twenty years, the ætheling is reported as having worried some of the ealdormen: he 'hounded them not only with tongue-lashings, but also with cruel beatings'. There is no compelling reason to believe that Byrhtferth wasn't telling the truth, and assuming he was, then perhaps the witan had understandable reservations about electing such a man as their king.

Even so, Edward was elected. He was young, but his brother was younger. His parentage was more dubious, but he might be relied on to allow powerful and influential people – the sort of people who would sit in the witan and choose Edgar's succesor – to reverse some of Dunstan's more controversial reforms. If a deal was struck, no record of it has survived; perhaps his (probable) 'designation' by the dying Edgar sealed the decision.[3]

The most important surviving source for this period of English history is the *Anglo-Saxon Chronicle*. Originally compiled at the end of the ninth century at the instigation of Alfred the Great, and written in (Old) English, this document was then frequently updated at several different monasteries with records of major events. There are enough similarities between the entries in the different versions of the *Chronicle* that it is clear that there was some sort of master copy being distributed, but the entries are not identical: sometimes this is because chroniclers at different monasteries included

---

3 Kings could 'designate' their successors, or they could try to: the witan would decide whether or not to respect their wishes once they were dead.

material which was important to that monastery; sometimes it is because some chroniclers included more details about events than others; and sometimes it is because different chroniclers have different interpretations of those events. The versions which cover this period were compiled at the abbeys of Abingdon, Worcester, and Peterborough, and are therefore sometimes referred to by those names. Sometimes the records appear to have been made more or less contemporaneously, but it seems that the entries for Æthelræd's reign were written up all at once, shortly after its end.

Sometimes the records are detailed: the events of 1016 and 1066 cover several pages. The entry for 976, though, reads simply, 'This year there was a great famine in England.' Edward's reign had got off to a bad start. And things soon went from bad to worse. A year later, at Calne in Wiltshire, there was another disaster, when the floor of the upstairs chamber in which a meeting of the witan was taking place collapsed. 'Some were dreadfully bruised,' commented the Chronicler, 'and some did not escape with life.' Luckily, the Archbishop of Canterbury survived unscathed: he 'stood alone upon a beam'.

Neither of these events were Edward's fault, but even so the surviving members of the witan may well have asked themselves if they had made the right decision in selecting so unsuitable a king: those so inclined could easily discern a demonstration of divine displeasure. But if Edward was shaping up badly, he was about to encounter a sudden boost to his reputation, when in March 978 he was murdered.

According to Byrhtferth of Ramsey, Edward was on his way to visit Æthelræd when he was dragged off his horse and killed on the spot. The account of the murder in the *Anglo-Saxon Chronicle* is restrained. 'This year King Edward was slain,' it starts. 'He was buried at Wareham without any royal honour,' it goes on, before launching into a tirade. 'No worse deed than this was ever done by the English nation,' and then:

> Men murdered him but God has magnified him. He was in life an earthly king: he is now after death a heavenly saint. Him would not his earthly relatives avenge, but his heavenly father has avenged him amply. The earthly homicides would wipe out his memory from the earth, but the avenger above has spread his memory abroad in heaven and in earth. Those who would not before bow to his living body, now bow on their knees to his dead bones.

The two bare statements of fact (the treatment of Edward's body and the failure to avenge his death) are fairly damning in and of themselves, even if no individual was explicitly blamed. This, though, was as far as the Chronicler was prepared to go. Perhaps he was unwilling to point the finger directly at the perpetrator without proof; perhaps doing so was too dangerous. John of Worcester, though, who began his *Chronicle of Chronicles* early in the twelfth century, and completed it in 1140, was less circumspect. 'Edward was foully murdered,' he wrote, 'at the instigation of his stepmother.'

The *Chronicle of Chronicles* is an invaluable complement to the *Anglo-Saxon Chronicle*, on which its structure, outline, and content is based, because John of Worcester usually adds explanatory detail gleaned from other sources, some of which are now lost, to what can sometimes be a rather bare account. When that information can be cross-referenced with other sources, it usually turns out to be accurate, which means that in so far as anyone can be trusted to tell the truth about the eleventh century, John of Worcester can be.

A year after his death, the dead king was exhumed and re-interred in grander circumstances more fitting to a martyred monarch in Shaftesbury Abbey. His remains were reportedly found incorrupt, and a cult grew up around him; a cult which was vigorously supported by his younger brother. Edward was never formally canonised, but he quickly came to be regarded in England as a saint, and both Æthelræd and his mother made sure that they were seen 'bowing on their knees to his dead bones'.

The first half of the twelfth century was a little golden age of history writing, with several renowned historians producing some remarkable works. As well as John of Worcester there was William of Malmesbury, who wrote *Deeds of the English Kings* in 1125, Orderic Vitalis, whose *Ecclesiastical History* was compiled between 1123 and 1141, and Henry of Huntingdon, whose *History of England* was completed in or shortly after 1154.

The extent to which they can be trusted is, of course, debatable, perhaps especially so when it comes to events which were not within living memory. These historians undoubtedly had access to sources which are now lost. But there is an unavoidable and unanswerable question over their histories, which is whether, when material appears in a twelfth-century account but does not appear in any contemporary document, it is because the author used a reliable source which has not survived, or whether, instead, it is the product of someone's imagination, be it the historian whose work survives, or the unknown writer of the original source material which he used. Still, it is not as though contemporary accounts can be wholly trusted either. So little survives from the eleventh century that there is not much about this period that can be proved beyond reasonable doubt.

Often it is just a question of judgment. That the dying King Edgar designated Edward as his successor is not recorded in any contemporary document; we are dependent on John of Worcester for it. It seems unlikely to have been made up: the succession of the elder son didn't necessarily need an explanation, and so there is no reason to think that John chose to 'tidy up' the story by adding a royal designation for which he had no evidence. On the balance of probabilities, he probably did have access to another source, which is now lost, which indicated that Edgar had indeed officially endorsed Edward as his successor.

It may also have been that John of Worcester had access to impeccable sources which convincingly indicted Ælfthryth of her stepson's murder. But it seems very unlikely that such sources ever existed.

Was Ælfthryth responsible? She is certainly the prime suspect. There are always people who benefit from the removal of a monarch, and in Edward's brief reign he had alienated plenty of families, but the clearest and most obvious beneficiary was her son Æthelræd, who, being aged between ten and twelve, was probably too young to have been involved in plotting the murder himself. What is very suspicious is that nothing appears to have been done to pursue the murderers. It was the moral duty of a slain man's kin to avenge his death: Æthelræd should, with the help of his mother, have been hunting down and taking revenge on his brother's killers. That was the ancient principle of the 'blood feud'.[4]

His embrace of the cult of his half-brother may have been cynical, or it may have been desperate, or he might have regretted

---

4　The only way to avoid being involved in a blood feud was for the killer to pay the dead man's 'wergild', or 'blood price', which depended on his social status: the greater the man, the greater the wergild.

what was done in his interest. It was certainly no substitute for pursuing justice.

The witan elected Æthelræd to succeed his brother. According to the *Anglo-Saxon Chronicle* they did so 'very readily, and with great joy'. Perhaps, despite the circumstances in which it had happened, they were relieved to be rid of Edward. No doubt Æthelræd's mother, and a number of ealdormen, were pleased at the accession of a new king, especially one so young and easily manipulated. At around eleven years of age, he was old enough to reign but not old enough to rule, and so the government of the kingdom fell on others' shoulders: Ælfthryth's, and those of the country's senior ealdormen and clergymen.

If William of Malmesbury is to be believed, Æthelræd's reign was doomed from the start. Even as a baby, he had appalled Dunstan, because 'as he was immersed in the baptismal font, he defiled the sacrament by a natural evacuation'. Now, at his coronation, the Archbishop of Canterbury prophesied that he and his people would suffer for the circumstances of his accession. 'Such evils,' he said, 'shall come upon the English nation as they have never suffered.'

William of Malmesbury was a serious historian, and Dunstan was by this time an old man who had always been quite happy to speak truth to power. That the Archbishop of Canterbury would have voiced these thoughts during a coronation service seems inherently unlikely, but that he and many others might have had them, and might have voiced them at other times, does not.

These were particularly inauspicious circumstances for whoever was in charge. As the country adapted to having a boy king, the problem which had plagued England in the past came back. In 980, with the king just entering his teens, Viking armies raided the Isle of Thanet, Southampton, and Chester; the next year a force landed in Devon and Cornwall and ravaged that corner of the country. Then, in 982, it was the turn of Portland and Dorset; in the same year, 'London was destroyed by fire'.

Why did the Viking raids start again? It must have been at least partly because, in its unstable condition and with a child on the throne, England was weaker than it had been for generations. It's not difficult to imagine the Scandinavian warriors smirking at the thought of the English differences over what should happen in those monasteries: they had other plans for them.

Still, this was not yet a crisis. The raids were local calamities, but on the national scale they were, at this stage, only a nuisance. These were not attempts at conquest. The Vikings who plundered Southampton came in seven ships; those who attacked Portland came in three. The *Anglo-Saxon Chronicle* distinguishes between 'the pirate army' and 'the pirate army of the north', which attacked Chester: evidently these were different raiders from different parts of the Viking world, which at this time included settlements in Ireland, the Isle of Man, the west coast of Scotland, Orkney and Shetland, as well as the original Norse homelands in Scandinavia. These were indeed pirates, rather than conquerors: they were opportunists looking to capitalise on the mess into which England had got itself.

In 983 Ælfhere, the ealdorman of Mercia, died. He was succeeded by his brother-in-law, Ælfric, but Ælfric did not last for very long: a couple of years after being appointed he was banished for treason, following a meeting of the witan at Cirencester; and no ealdorman of Mercia appears to have replaced him for over a decade. By now the king had reached the age of majority, and although no chronicler supplies an explanation for

Ælfric's removal, this is probably significant: Æthelræd was now old enough to take his own decisions, and he was overturning one which had been taken in his name just two years previously, quite possibly against his judgment. Perhaps the king considered that the ealdormanry of Mercia was too large, and that its ealdorman therefore had too much power. It wasn't just Ælfric who couldn't be trusted to do the job: no one could. Better not to have an ealdorman of Mercia at all; and evidently the royal government could function without one.

Soon after the banishment of Ælfric, Æthelræd picked a fight with the Bishop of Rochester. The details are far from clear. All that the *Anglo-Saxon Chronicle* says is 'This year the king invaded the bishopric of Rochester', which is almost tantalising in its bareness. John of Worcester says that it was 'because of some quarrel'. (Even William of Malmesbury, who is usually quick to attack Æthelræd, and who was not above adding memorable details on occasion, simply says 'from some unknown cause'.)

For a king to attack a settlement in his own kingdom was not unprecedented, but nor was it normal, everyday policy, and the *Anglo-Saxon Chronicle*'s silence as to the reasons why is therefore surprising. There must have been a story there, but it is now probably lost to us. One relatively obscure chronicler, Sulcard of Westminster, writing almost a century after the event, supplies an explanation so banal that it might well be the truth: the Bishop of Rochester had evicted a soldier in Æthelræd's service from his land. The most we can say is that the king will have had his reasons.

(This, by the way, is part of the reason why we trust certain twelfth-century historians. They took the art of writing history seriously. They didn't know any more than we do why Æthelræd 'invaded' Rochester. A century and a half later, with no one around to contradict them, there must have been a temptation to ascribe a reason. Given how Æthelræd's reign developed, all sorts of potential explanations would have been plausible and could have helped to build a picture of the man and his rule. But no such illustration was supplied: not by John of Worcester, nor by any of his contemporaries. They didn't know why he did it, and they didn't pretend that they did.)

If Sulcard was right, the Bishop of Rochester only removed the royal servant from his land because 'he was ignorant of this donation'. Besieging the city might seem rather an excessive reaction to what was, after all, just a misunderstanding. Might it have been that conspicuously exercising his authority was Æthelræd's principal aim? It's certainly possible. He was acutely aware, as were all those around him, that he should not really have been king at all. The promotion of the cult of St Edward the Martyr, which mourned the murder from which he had benefited, must have been particularly humiliating for him, but he participated in it, presumably because he felt that he ought to, or that he had to. If he felt simultaneously guilty and angry about his situation, it would be no surprise; if he was looking for an opportunity to remind his subjects that he was their king, perhaps a minor misunderstanding with the Bishop of Rochester provided him with one.

But the attempt to punish Rochester did not go according to plan. The royal forces besieged the city, but, according to John of Worcester, 'finding the difficulty in reducing it, ravaged the lands of St Andrew the Apostle'.[5] A city in Æthelræd's own kingdom had successfully defied him, and although he may have inflicted

---

5 That is, the lands of the diocese of Rochester.

considerable damage on the diocese in retaliation, this was hardly the clear message he might have wanted to have sent to his people. And what followed was to weaken England still further. A disease which brought diarrhoea and fever and death swept through the country, alongside another which afflicted cattle. At the best of times, early medieval life was tough: infant mortality was high, life expectancy was low, disease was irresistible, and for ordinary people hunger was common. The *Anglo-Saxon Chronicle* does not go into detail, but that it mentions it at all indicates that this was serious, and significantly worse than usual.

And England wasn't only plagued by natural afflictions. Viking activity began to step up. A raid on Watchet in Somerset was followed by what appears to have been a more serious incursion into Devon in 988: not only was a thegn slain, but several of his followers too.

A thegn was an important man. He owned, theoretically, at least five 'hides' of land, and so could fully equip himself for war, with good-quality horses, armour, and weapons.[6] There were roughly 5,000 such men, and thegnly families therefore constituted the top 1 per cent of Anglo-Saxon society. Their privilege, ultimately, rested on their doing military service for their king. They were required to follow him into battle and fight alongside him at all costs, up to and including their own lives; in return, he shared the spoils of war with them. When a thegn reported for military duty he would bring with him men who owed him a similar loyalty, in return

---

6 Exactly what constituted a hide seems to have varied, but it appears, at least in theory, to have been regarded as the amount of land needed to support one household headed by a free man who was liable for military service. The geographical size of a hide varied depending on the value of the land: a hide in Northumbria, where farmland was less productive and rents lower, was significantly larger than a hide in Wessex.

for a similar obligation. This relationship was fundamental to the country's armed forces: it was how the king got his men on to the field of battle, or indeed into his ships.

In that same year, Dunstan, who had been Archbishop of Canterbury for nearly thirty years, and who was in his late seventies, died. Soon afterwards, Halley's Comet appeared in the night sky.[7] There was no shortage of signs that this was to be a bad time.

* * * *

A couple of years after the comet's return, yet another Viking force arrived in eastern England. This was a serious army, and its purpose was more than a smash-and-grab raid: the ealdorman of Essex, Byrhtnoth, had enough warning of the invasion that he could summon an army to meet it in battle. The events of the battle were recorded, or immortalised, in a poem, *The Battle of Maldon*, which was composed soon afterwards. It is unlikely, though, that it accurately portrays what actually happened: this was an heroic poem, intended to celebrate the honour of the men who died around the body of their lord.

According to the poet, the Viking army was stationed on an island, almost certainly Northey, just off the coast of Essex near Maldon. Byrhtnoth's men were opposite them on the mainland. At low tide the water could be crossed on foot, but the causeway was narrow, and after the Vikings attempted to force their way across

---

7 The *Anglo-Saxon Chronicle* makes no reference to a comet in 989, but does record one in 975 and another in 995. Perhaps the Chronicler, writing a quarter of a century later, got his date wrong. The alternative, that Halley's Comet was not visible from England in 989, but that two different comets were seen, one fourteen years earlier, and another six years later, seems less likely.

without success, their commander asked Byrhtnoth to allow them to make the crossing unimpeded before the two armies engaged in battle, a request to which Byrhtnoth acceded.

This may seem extraordinary. It evidently seemed extraordinary at the time too. The poet describes Byrhtnoth as being 'ofermod', which is difficult to translate from the Old English: sometimes rendered as 'arrogant', perhaps 'overconfident' might be closer to its original meaning. In any case, it does suggest that Byrhtnoth was sufficiently confident of victory that he allowed the enemy to land and prepare for battle. And this is why it is an unconvincing explanation: whatever the character of the ealdorman of Essex, by 991 the idea that an English commander would assume that his men would easily defeat a Viking army seems unlikely.

But if it wasn't through overconfidence, why would Byrhtnoth have made such an elementary mistake? Well, it's quite possible that he was diligently adhering to the spirit of his duty as an ealdorman, especially the ealdorman of a coastal shire: to defend it from foreign invasion. He did not have to allow the invaders to land. But the alternative was not an easy victory. The Viking position on Northey was just as difficult to attack as the English position on the mainland: it would have been recklessly irresponsible for him to have tried. The most likely outcome of a refusal would have been the Vikings sailing away, landing elsewhere, and wreaking havoc there instead. Someone would have to meet them in battle: Byrhtnoth was the man on the spot, so Byrhtnoth it was going to have to be.

Many of Byrhtnoth's men fought valiantly. But some did not. The villains of the poem are not Vikings but the Englishmen who fled the field of battle, in particular a certain Godric, who took Byrhtnoth's horse and rode away on it. The heroes are those who stayed and fought to the death. One of them, perhaps surprisingly, was Ælfwin, the son of the aforementioned (and disgraced) Ælfric. In the poem, he reminds those around him that 'boasts on the benches' are all very well, but being 'heroes in the hall' was not good enough. On the field of battle he announces that 'now we can find out who is brave'.

Ælfwin's motivational lines must be the product of artistic licence. But in a way, Maldon was a wholly representative battle: some, perhaps because they had no opportunity to escape, did indeed fight to the last man. Others did not. In theory, the men of Byrhtnoth's force were supposed to fight alongside him to the death. In practice battles did not end in such a way. This celebration of the men who adhered to the warrior code with which they had grown up was also a condemnation of those who did not, and this was a message which was becoming increasingly important.

There has always been a tension between soldiers and their leaders. For both, military victory and the soldier's survival is the best possible outcome; for both, military defeat and the soldier's death is the worst. However, whereas a ruler or a general prefers to sacrifice individual soldiers, those individual soldiers would prefer defeat and survival to victory and death.

There are various ways in which armies, or indeed societies, have tried to mitigate this. One is through military training. A well-drilled, well-disciplined soldier knows what he is expected to do on the battlefield and is therefore more likely to be able to concentrate on his task, and less likely to panic in the face of the enemy. An experienced professional soldier spends his life learning the skills of soldiering and the habit of obedience; he also forms bonds of comradeship with his peers, which can counterbalance his natural instinct for self-preservation.

Leaders can, of course, provide incentives and disincentives. Men who fight bravely are usually rewarded; men who desert are usually punished. But there is a limit to how effective this can be. It is difficult to devise material incentives which are greater than the difference between life and death. And so societies often discourage ordinary cowardice in less tangible and sometimes more mystical ways: social disgrace for those who succumb to it, reverence, and possibly spiritual rewards in the next life, for those who don't.

This is what *The Battle of Maldon* was all about. It was composed to be performed: it was almost certainly recited in front of groups of men sitting on benches in halls boasting about their bravery. This was not subtle indoctrination: it was an explicit statement to such men that England expected them to do their duty, that they ought to be like Ælfwin, and not like Godric.

That such a statement was considered necessary is revealing. Under pressure from the Vikings, the bonds which held English society together were fraying.

****

Byrhtnoth's crushing defeat might have been heroic, but England was now facing a national emergency. The Vikings were marauding along the coastline unopposed, spreading terror as they went. In response, taking the advice of the witan, Æthelræd decided not to raise another army to challenge them, but to raise money to pay them off instead.

It is easy to criticise this decision as having been motivated by cowardice. And of course Æthelræd was being cowardly. He did not wish to fight against an intimidating and formidable enemy. But there were good reasons for this. The record of his armies against the Vikings had been a miserable one, and the defeats had been getting more and more serious. And if, as *The Battle of Maldon* implies, English warriors were becoming increasingly inclined to abandon the field of battle if their cause appeared to be lost, fighting was even riskier.[8] Yet more defeats would only weaken the English position further. It is therefore wholly understandable that Æthelræd's counsellors should have advised him to make peace. The Vikings were offered, and accepted, £10,000 in return for an end to their raiding.[9]

'Paying the Dane-geld' may not have seemed as unwise at the time as it did to Rudyard Kipling, composing his poetry 900 years later. England was, by the standards of the time, rich: that was the reason the Danes were raiding it. The southern part of the country in particular was full of fertile agricultural soil. Trade, both within the country and with foreigners, was healthy. And because England was a stable country, with a relatively sophisticated system of government, the king was able to tap

---

8 It is possible that the poem was composed significantly later, and if it dates to the end of Æthelræd's reign it may be that the poet overstated the significance of Godric's behaviour: with hindsight what could actually have been a minor incident might have looked like an incident of immense importance in tracing the origins of the sort of unreliability with which Æthelræd had to cope. It is also possible that Godric was nothing more than a dramatic device, a contrast for Byrhtnoth's heroism. But it is rather more likely, especially in the light of what we know to have happened soon after Maldon, that a lot of men did indeed flee the field of batle well before they should have.

9 Trying to 'translate' monetary values from one age to another is never easy, and especially for early medieval England. Very roughly, a hide of land was valued at around £1, so £10,000 was the equivalent of 10,000 free households' property. (Estimating the population of eleventh-century England can also only be done very roughly: the lowest estimates are of around a million-and-a half people, while the highest put it at 3 million.) £10,000 was a great deal of money.

that wealth. He could levy taxes, and his subjects throughout the realm would pay up.[10]

Fighting aggressive wars could be profitable, but only if those wars were fought on enemy territory: a successful army could 'live off the land', looting and pillaging to keep itself supplied, and return home with the spoils of war. This was what Vikings had been doing for centuries. But for a king trying to defend his country there could be no prospect of this sort of success: for Æthelræd's armies, trying to protect their homeland against invasion, even success would be costly. The appeal of paying the invaders off instead is clear. Rather than raising an army, which might or might not have been victorious (and which would be expensive either way), the king could raise a tax, use it to pay tribute to the enemy, and thereby guarantee peace.

It was taking this sort of advice which gave Æthelræd his famous soubriquet, the 'Unready'.[11] Of course the king could not be everywhere at once, and there was nothing wrong with relying on ealdormen as a first line of defence, especially against raiders who might appear anywhere along the coastline. Even so, the defence

---

10 There were royal officials and royal courts all over England. The country was divided into shires; each shire was divided into 'hundreds', which were, at least theoretically, comprised of a hundred 'hides'. There were hundred courts and shire courts, and, as well as earldormen like Byrhtnoth, there were 'reeves' in every hundred, ensuring that the orders of the king, and the decisions of his courts, were enforced and upheld. There were town-reeves, port-reeves, and indeed shire-reeves, or sheriffs. This was not the case in other countries. The King of France, for instance, reigned over a greater population and land area. But the King of France did not have these courts or officials throughout his territory. Instead he was the 'overlord' of powerful hereditary magnates, such as the Duke of Normandy. These magnates owed their allegiance to their sovereign, but otherwise they governed their own lands without interference: the King could demand military service, but he could not impose laws or levy taxes on them.

11 The Old English word 'unraed', from which the nickname derives, did not mean 'ill-prepared', but 'badly-advised'.

of the realm was one of the king's greatest responsibilities, and Æthelræd did not even attempt to discharge his duty to his people by summoning an army and leading it into battle against that enemy himself.

Why not? He was now in the prime of life. There is no suggestion anywhere that he was suffering from any disability. The question is now unanswerable, but his absence from the battlefield cannot have impressed his contemporaries, who no doubt asked it themselves. Nor can it have impressed the Vikings. Having been paid tribute, they would, of course, be back.

Sometimes, appeasement is the only practical policy. If there is no prospect of victory, then it is wiser to avoid battle, and sometimes the only way to do that is to make concessions. It may not be glorious; it may not be fertile source material for heroic poetry; there may even be something embarrassing or shameful about it. But to rule it out as a last resort is just as bad as defaulting to it as a first resort. Even Alfred the Great, during the Danish onslaught that nearly destroyed Wessex, had paid off the Danes, preserving his precarious position for the time being. A government that resorts to appeasement, though, should use the breathing space to prepare for next time.

And that is just what Æthelræd's government proceeded to do. It should not have allowed itself to get into such a mess in the first place. Paying tribute should never have been necessary: there had been plenty of warning. A decade of Viking activity had preceded Maldon. There had been some internal turmoil, but nothing so serious that it should have impeded a coherent national response. Still, Æthelræd had been shaken out of any complacency, and now he began to ready the country for the Vikings' inevitable return.

Internationally, he went in search of an alliance. He didn't have far to look.

Normandy was, formally, a French province. Charles the Simple, who had been King of France at the beginning of the tenth century, had granted it to Rolf, a Viking leader, in 911. This was a step further than paying money, but it did provide a neat solution to the Viking problem. Rolf was no longer just a Norse chief; he was a French aristocrat, the Count of Normandy (the territory of the *normands*, or Norsemen): in return for the land, he had become Charles' vassal.[12] He would fight to defend that territory because it was his; and in doing so he fought to defend the territory of the King of France, even if, in reality, the King of France could forget about exercising any real power over Normandy. Richard, Rolf's grandson, governed the duchy autonomously, and this autonomy, in practice if not in theory, extended to negotiating treaties with foreign powers.[13]

By the end of the tenth century, the Normans had converted to Christianity and were speaking French, or at least a Norman dialect of French. The founder of the dynasty was being referred to by the French version of his name, Rollo. It is possible that

---

12 At its most basic, the relationship between a vassal and his lord required service on the part of the vassal and protection on the part of the lord. It could be personal (as was more common in England before the Conquest) or it could be the basis of landholding (as was more common in continental Europe), in which case the vassal held land from the lord in return for military service. The ceremony at which this relationship was formalised was known as 'homage'.

13 It was around this time that Normandy stops being described as a county ruled by a count and starts being described as a duchy ruled by a duke. Richard 'the Fearless' was the Count of Normandy for over fifty years until his death in 996; his son, also named Richard, was the first to call himself Duke. This promotion may have been bestowed on him by the King of France, but there is no record of it; it may be that the younger Richard simply decided that he was sufficiently grand to merit the greater title, and in effect awarded it to himself.

their ethnic origin may have made the Normans sympathetic to Scandinavians, and that this explains why they were welcome in Norman ports; but it is just as likely that, faced with Vikings simultaneously threatening violence and offering to spend their money in the marketplaces of Normandy, they were simply following a pragmatic policy.

Certainly this seems to have been the source of some tension between Æthelræd and Richard of Normandy: the treaty between the two of them, brokered by the Pope, John XV, and agreed in the spring of 991, stipulates that neither would assist the other's enemies. The text itself implies that the treaty was a papal initiative, but the Pope may well have been alerted to the issue by the new Archbishop of Canterbury, Sigeric 'the Serious', who visited to Rome to collect his pallium in 989 or 990.[14]

Æthelræd also prepared a naval force to meet the Vikings when they next returned. Warships from all around the country were ordered to assemble at London, and were put under the command of Ælfric, ealdorman of Hampshire, described by the *Anglo-Saxon Chronicle* as 'one of those in whom the king had most confidence', and Thored, ealdorman of Northumbria.[15] They were soon to be put to the test: in 992, just a year after Maldon, the longships returned. The English had a plan ready: the newly assembled navy was to catch the Vikings unawares, blockade their ships in a harbour, and destroy or capture them.

---

14 The pallium is a ceremonial vestment worn around the shoulders. It was bestowed in person by the Pope as part of the formal ordination of an archbishop.

15 Not to be confused with Ælfric of Mercia, who disappeared from the historical record after his banishment in 985.

The plan worked up until the night before it was supposed to be implemented. The Viking fleet was spotted as it made landfall. The English navy set sail to carry out their mission. But Ælfric, in the words of the *Anglo-Saxon Chronicle*, 'skulked away from the army, to his great disgrace' and warned the enemy. Having been tipped off, they just about managed to get out of the harbour before the English arrived, 'except for the crew of one ship, who were slain on the spot'. Chased out into the open sea, there was a battle, 'and there a great slaughter was made'.[16] The ship carrying Ælfric was taken, but the man himself somehow escaped capture. Unable, therefore, to take action against the ealdorman personally, Æthelræd responded by ordering his son to be blinded.

We don't know what happened to Ælfric next. But, extraordinarily, he appears to have remained an ealdorman and remained in the king's service. Had Ælfric perhaps been carrying out a royal command, which the chroniclers had misunderstood (or misinterpreted or misreported)? Had he carried out that command honestly but incompetently? This would explain why he was allowed to remain in office, but it would not explain why his son was blinded. Could that have been for an entirely unrelated offence? It's certainly possible. The *Anglo-Saxon Chronicle* does not explicitly connect the father's actions with the son's punishment, and it is conceivable that this is because they weren't connected.

Even if Ælfric himself was not guilty of it, the habit of succumbing to treachery was becoming widespread. The Vikings

---

16 The location of the harbour, or the battle which followed, is not recorded. However, as the royal navy, which had originally gathered at London, was assisted in the battle by ships from East Anglia, it was most probably somewhere in or around the Thames estuary.

now turned their attention to the north, first attacking Bamburgh, and then raiding along the North Sea coast, rampaging through Northumbria and Lincolnshire. The men charged with defending the country are named and shamed in the *Anglo-Saxon Chronicle*, and by John of Worcester, who supplies an explanation for their behaviour: they 'betrayed their followers and gave the signal for flight', he wrote, because they were 'Danes by their father's side'.

From the 850s to the 920s, Northumbria and large parts of eastern England had been ruled by Danes. By the time these regions had been reconquered, they had become collectively known as the Danelaw, the territory where Danish law applied, and several generations of Danes had controlled it. Northumbria, which briefly fell back under Norse control in the years around 950, when it was ruled by Erik 'Bloodaxe', was particularly difficult to govern from the distant heartland of the West Saxon royal dynasty. There had been significant immigration from Scandinavia, at least among the upper echelons of society. And English kings tended to spend most of their time in Wessex and rarely went that far north, preferring to leave government in the hands of their ealdormen.

This might sound like a combination of circumstances which could have encouraged disloyalty on the part of leading Northumbrians. But John of Worcester's allegation should be treated carefully. It may well be that the men concerned were of Norse origin. But correlation is not causation. Thored was probably at least partly Norse by blood, but he appears to have been rather more loyal to his king than Ælfric, a West Saxon ealdorman with a very English name. By 993 several generations of Northumbrian thegns had been subjects of the King of England, and even if there were still family ties, or looser kinship affinities, between Northumbrians and their Scandinavian cousins, it is not as though the inhabitants of the former Danelaw had any reason to think fondly of the Vikings who were pillaging their way through their country. It seems rather more likely that their Danish heritage was irrelevant: the thegns who fled the battlefield were making exactly the same calculations as many other Englishmen.

The collapsing reputation of England's armed forces had by now attracted the attention of the highest authorities in Scandinavia. In the late summer of 994 Sweyn Forkbeard, King of Denmark, accompanied by Olaf Tryggvason of Norway, brought ninety-four longships' worth of warriors with them and sailed up the Thames to London. They intended to sack the city, but according to the *Anglo-Saxon Chronicle* 'they sustained more harm and evil than they had ever supposed that any citizens could inflict on them'.

Attacking a fortified city was difficult, as Æthelræd had found at Rochester. One of the reasons for Alfred's successful defiance of the Great Heathen Army had been the establishment of 'burhs', or walled towns, which could not be broken into, and in which people, animals, and supplies could be sheltered. London, bounded by rivers (the Fleet to the west as well as the Thames to the south) and with well-maintained city walls, was impregnable, and could resist the Danes, just as the burhs of Wessex had resisted them a century previously.

London's hinterland was to pay for the city's resistance. Sweyn's army, furious at their failure, marauded its way through Essex, Kent, Sussex, and Hampshire, with even more savagery than usual: they stole horses, looted anything of value, burned anything which could not be looted, and slaughtered the inhabitants, including children. In desperation, Æthelræd offered them a significantly more generous payment than had been made just three years previously. He would hand over £16,000; in addition to this, rather than sail home immediately, the Danes would spend the winter at Southampton, with all their costs being paid by the people of Wessex.

The last quarter of 994 was not just a tragedy for the people who found themselves at the literal sharp end of the Danes' wrath. It was also a national humiliation, and a personal humiliation for Æthelræd too. The King of England found himself sending hostages to a Norwegian warlord in the service of the King of Denmark as security for his own good behaviour while he negotiated the next stage of the capitulation.[17]

And yet Æthelræd seems to have managed to rescue something out of the dire situation. He concluded a treaty with Olaf, in which the Norwegian was brought to Andover and baptised, with Æthelræd standing as his godfather. Olaf also pledged never to attack England again, and he never did.

Was this a diplomatic success? Remarkably, it seems as though it might have been. Firstly, Olaf agreed to be baptised, and for Æthelræd to be his sponsor. It is easy to dismiss this as essentially meaningless, especially for a follower of traditional Norse religious practices, but nonetheless of course Olaf knew its significance for Æthelræd, and was willing to give him what he wanted.[18]

---

17 Hostages were usually close family members. A father might hand over his son as a guarantee that he was acting in good faith: the risk to the son's life was intended to discourage any duplicity on the part of the father.

18 This is partly because, for a non-Christian, a baptism ceremony is of no importance. But only partly. Many of the nuances of what is sometimes described as paganism are now lost and can't be recovered, but it may well have been that Christians and pagans interpreted such ceremonies in different ways. For a Christian, it involved the repudiation of all other gods and all other faiths. But for a pagan the natural way to interpret an agreement to worship the Christian God might have been to add Him to the already-existing pantheon.

Secondly, Olaf kept his promise. Why?

Most probably it was because when he returned to Norway he was able to seize control of that country and have himself declared king, before spending the next four or five years fighting to keep it. Before their voyage, Olaf was Sweyn's subordinate. Thereafter they were enemies, until Olaf was killed in battle at the hands of Sweyn in the last year of the tenth century. For that half-decade, neither was attacking England. Æthelræd was no diplomatic genius: for a few years he got lucky.

Still, the possibility that Olaf's conversion contributed to his keeping his word should not be dismissed. In so far as any windows can be made into any men's souls, it seems that he genuinely embraced his new faith; and if he did, then perhaps Æthelræd can take some of the credit for what followed. As King of Norway Olaf introduced Christianity to the country, building its first churches and indeed persecuting those who were unwilling to repudiate their old religious practices. And in standing as his spiritual sponsor, Æthelræd could possibly have been posing, however unconvincingly, as some kind of imperial overlord. When Olaf returned to Scandinavia and claimed the Norwegian crown, he did so as the King of England's godson. This did not confer any secular authority, but for a Christian it was not completely without significance.

Æthelræd hadn't only made peace with Olaf, he had thrown his weight behind him. (Sweyn does not appear to have participated in any peace treaty: perhaps, having achieved what he'd set out to do, he returned home sooner than Olaf did.) It might not have made much difference, but if it was wholly irrelevant, why would Olaf have agreed to a treaty in which he acknowledged the King of England as his godfather? Clearly he thought he had *something* to gain from it, and it wasn't just the treasure that was coming his way: that would have been handed over anyway, with or without a baptism.

It does seem inexplicable: Æthelræd might have held a heavyweight title, but he was not exactly held in the highest regard. It's easy to see how he might have wanted to invoke the image of Alfred the Great, who had baptised his Danish enemy, Guthrum, as part of the treaty they concluded in 878. That, though, had been after a significant English victory (at the Battle of Edington). It is less easy to see why Olaf wanted or needed Æthelræd. And yet evidently he did.

For a while there was calm. The conflict between Sweyn and Olaf kept the leading Scandinavians occupied with Scandinavian affairs; the English government went about its business. Once more, Æthelræd seemed to take advantage of the opportunity to prepare for the inevitable onslaught from the north. And once more, events would conspire to undo him.

* * * *

The term 'Dane-geld' is somewhat misleading. Æthelræd actually levied two different taxes to deal with the Vikings. One, the *gafol*, was to fund tribute payments. The other, the *geld* or *heregeld* ('army tax'), was to pay for the soldiers and sailors in the king's own service, including mercenaries. As many of those mercenaries were themselves of Scandinavian origin, both *gafol* and *geld* involved the transfer of money from English taxpayers to Danish warriors, so it may appear to be excessively pernickety to insist on the distinction, but there was one, and it mattered: the *geld* was what one might reasonably expect a king to do, whereas the *gafol* was only levied because of the country's military difficulties.[19]

These taxes were a significant burden. Some landowners found themselves having to sell some of their property in order to pay, which can only have further damaged Æthelræd's reputation among his subjects. The English taxpayer appears to have tolerated the policy, but men of property cannot have been delighted at the prospect of sacrificing it in order to pay for their king's ineptitude. Similarly, while it is dangerous to try to find causes of the régime's collapse in events, which happened twenty years previously, it would be unreasonable to say that the implosion of the régime in 1013 was without long-term causes. The people of England suffered the depredations of the Vikings, followed by those of their own rulers. A reluctance to fight, and an indifference to the régime which had failed to protect them and then further punished them for that failing, is exactly what might be expected; and that, eventually, is precisely what happened

In the last years of the last decade of the last century of the first millennium, that was far in the future. Æthelræd was trying to prepare for the next campaign, whenever it might come. These preparations were not helped by continued Viking raids,

---

19 Both *geld* and *gafol* appear to have been paid in cash. English coinage was much admired in northern Europe, where so much of it ended up (many more English coins have been found in Scandinavia than in England). The moneyers whose craftsmanship so impressed the Scandinavians were tightly controlled. In a law code, probably issued in the late 990s, Æthelræd reminded his moneyers that they could only work for him. He also forbade them to work 'in the wood or elsewhere': they were only allowed to operate from towns and cities where they could be monitored. A moneyer who broke these laws, or who manufactured counterfeit coins, was liable to be executed. (There were compensatory benefits though. Designs were changed every few years, and obsolete coins were supposed to be exchanged for the latest versions. These exchanges enabled moneyers to make a profit, from which the king took a cut, by exchanging fewer coins of the new style for those handed in of the old style.)

which exposed fundamental and ongoing difficulties in England's system of national defence. The *Anglo-Saxon Chronicle* records raids on every south-coast county between 997 and 1000, and also grumbles at the ineffective response. These were not on the same scale as that launched by Olaf and Sweyn: they were similar to the raids of the previous decade, smash-and-grab affairs in which the Vikings would land, loot, and leave before any force to oppose them could be gathered. Still, the *Anglo-Saxon Chronicle* makes it clear that there was also a malaise in the country's military organisation. It was not wholly clear what was wrong: armies were 'through something or other put to flight', or 'had not the aid which they should have had'. These deficiencies extended to the navy as well: 'As soon as the ships were ready, then arose delay from day to day.'

We can't quite be certain why this was. But clearly there was a crisis of leadership. England could raise money, and England could raise armies. The structures were sound. But the country's resources were being used badly. It is certainly tempting to attribute this to Æthelræd's own reluctance to take to the field of battle himself, but perhaps this wasn't the whole story: the country does not appear to have been blessed with talented commanders, and this can't have been wholly the fault of its king.

'Thus,' concluded the Chronicler, in his last entry for the tenth century, 'in the end these expeditions by land and by sea served no other purpose but to vex the people, to waste their treasure, and to strengthen their enemies.'

2

DOWNFALL

A bad man and a bad king.

E. A. Freeman

The new century appears to have galvanised Æthelræd and his government. Having stumbled from crisis to crisis, veering from embarrassment to humiliation along the way, it was time to take the initiative.

His first proactive measure was a raid on Cumbria, which was then part of the Norse kingdom of Strathclyde. Was this targeted retaliation for particular raids? Quite possibly. It probably wasn't difficult to distinguish the origins of Vikings, whether by appearance, dialect, equipment, or in some other way. The raiders of the late 990s may well have come from those regions: they weren't sent by the King of Norway, because we know that he kept his promise to Æthelræd, and they're unlikely to have been sent by the King of Denmark, because Sweyn's priority at this point was his campaign against Olaf.

It is, of course, possible that these Vikings were freelancing Danes or Norwegians. But attempting to exact retribution across the North Sea against Denmark or Norway was far too risky for Æthelræd. Not only was it a long journey, it would provoke a furious and devastating reaction. Cumbria, by contrast, was rather more accessible, and rather less intimidating. Æthelræd needed a victory. As their king he was entitled to his subjects' loyalty, but he had given them no other reason to continue to support him, and the circumstances of his own accession can have left him in no doubt that being anointed with holy oil at his coronation would not be enough to secure his position for ever. In more than twenty years there had been no glorious victories to boast about and no spoils of war to enjoy. A lack of commitment to his cause was already conspicuous.

Æthelræd seems to have led the army himself, for once, and the operation against Strathclyde was a qualified success. It has been suggested that, as there is no further hint in the chronicles of further raids from the Norse parts of the British Isles, it achieved what it set out to do; it has also, less plausibly, been suggested that Æthelræd was emulating his father in exerting his imperial authority over the other kingdoms in the archipelago. Even here, though, in a campaign intended to boost morale by producing an easy victory against a weaker enemy, there was a debacle. The royal fleet failed to rendezvous with the army as planned, probably because it was caught in storms; rather than abandon the plan altogether, the fleet attacked the Isle of Man instead. It wasn't a total failure, but nor was it a glorious achievement.

It seems that Æthelræd may well have also sent a task force against Normandy at around this time. One Norman historian,

William of Jumièges, who wrote his *Deeds of the Dukes of the Normans* in or around 1070, includes a fairly lengthy account of the raid. The objective was to 'harry' the duchy, capture Duke Richard, and bring him back to England in chains.[1] It turned out to be a complete fiasco: the English made landfall successfully, but were soon met in battle by a force consisting of some knights supported by the local population, including women using agricultural equipment as weaponry. Only one Englishman survived, plus the few who had stayed behind to guard their ships; they sailed back across the English Channel duly chastened.

It is not a particularly credible tale, and it is the only account of the expedition to have survived. At times it reads like crude boasting: Æthelræd was 'full of shame and sorrow', and the moral of the story was that Norman military power should be respected. William of Jumièges is vague about the reasons for the operation, saying only that the King of England and the Duke of Normandy had fallen out 'on a number of matters'. There is nothing to test it against. But it cannot be assumed to be pure fiction. No doubt some of the details are wrong. But evidently the English fleet was sent on such missions, and certainly there was a complicated diplomatic relationship between England and Normandy.

In the spring of 1002, Richard's sister Emma was dispatched to England to marry Æthelræd. Now Æthelræd had already been married, and perhaps still was, though there is no record of his first wife, Ælfgifu, the daughter of Thored, ealdorman of Northumbria, after 1001. Perhaps she was set aside to make way for Emma, or perhaps she had died: we don't know, and there is no way

---

1 The term 'harrying' meant seizing and destroying property as well as attacking and killing people.

of knowing. Ælfgifu had given Æthelræd at least nine children, six of them boys.[2] Richard was well aware that whatever promises might be made (none are recorded) any boys born to his sister would have serious competition for the English crown when the time came. Even so, he clearly thought an alliance was worth trying. Æthelræd may have been an unimpressive figure, but there was more to England than its king: perhaps Emma would be able to exert some influence, and perhaps the prestige of having a member of the ducal family marry into English royalty was worth something. Æthelræd, meanwhile, would, in theory, gain an ally, or at least a neighbour who would be a little more reluctant to welcome Vikings into his ports.

The marriage was not a great success, but nor was it a catastrophic failure. In the early years of their marriage, Emma gave birth to two sons, Edward and Alfred, and a daughter, Godgifu, but it does not appear to have been a particularly happy union.[3] According to William of Malmesbury, Æthelræd was reluctant to do his conjugal duty, but 'degraded the royal dignity by his intercourse with harlots'. This, not surprisingly, did not impress the new queen who, 'conscious of her high descent, became indignant at her husband, as she found herself endeared to him neither by her blameless modesty nor by her fruitfulness'.

There is another source which, by its silence, confirms that Emma and Æthelræd did not enjoy a fairy-tale romance.

---

2 The eldest son, Æthelstan, was named after his great-grandfather's brother, the grandson of Alfred the Great. The second son, Egbert, was named after the first West Saxon king to be acknowledged as overlord of all the other kings in England. Thereafter the boys were named, in order, after Æthelstan's successors as King of England: the third son was Edmund, the fourth Eadred, the fifth Eadwig, and the sixth Edgar.

3 Godgifu married into French aristocracy. Her first husband was Drogo of Mantes, Count of the Vexin; after his death she married Eustace of Boulogne.

The *Encomium Emmae Reginae*, written by an anonymous author in the early 1040s 'in praise of Queen Emma', while she was still alive, does not mention their marriage at all, and goes to some lengths to pretend that it had never happened.[4] It seems, by then, to have been an embarrassment to her, which, if William of Malmesbury was telling the truth, is wholly understandable. Still, we know that she was an important figure. She had a far higher profile than her predecessor, who is never even mentioned in the *Anglo-Saxon Chronicle* and whose role appears to have been limited to the production of æthelings.

Confusingly, William of Jumièges states that the raid happened after the marriage, which would suggest that whatever agreement was reached almost immediately broke down. This isn't, of course, impossible: it is not difficult to imagine that Richard agreed not to harbour Æthelræd's enemies and then, faced with a Viking fleet, went back on his word. However, it seems more likely that the raid, if it happened at all, happened before the marriage. Richard probably didn't consider himself bound by the treaty to which his father had agreed, and so had no reason not to break it; but Æthelræd, whether he considered this reasonable or not, preferred Normandy not to assist the Danes' war effort, and sent a fleet to emphasise this.

If that's what happened, though, the raid cannot have been the total disaster that William of Jumièges, writing seventy years after the event, says it was. Perhaps the only surviving account is misleading: perhaps it had been moderately successful after all, and had indeed achieved what its instigator had intended by inducing Richard to renew his father's treaty.

---

4 The encomiast was probably a monk of St Bertin's Abbey in St Omer, which was then in Flanders and is now in the far north of France.

Whatever the truth, this diplomatic accomplishment was to be eclipsed by another military catastrophe.

* * * *

In 1001 there was another large-scale Viking assault, and again it consisted of raids all along the south coast of the country. The English response was characteristic. The fyrd (the militia in which all free men were liable to serve) was raised, and fought a pitched battle against them: according to the *Anglo-Saxon Chronicle* eighty-one Englishmen died, and a larger number of Danes, but it was the Danes who 'had possession of the field of slaughter' and who were thereafter able to continue to harry their way through Wessex. They were joined by Pallig, a Dane in Æthelræd's service. Pallig appears to have been more than just a mercenary soldier: as well as gold and silver, 'the king had also well gifted him with homesteads'. William of Malmesbury describes him as 'a powerful nobleman' who was married to Sweyn Forkbeard's sister Gunhild. Another army was raised from the men of Devon and Somerset, but 'as soon as battle was joined the English fyrd gave way', and thereafter there was no further opposition. Eventually the Vikings withdrew to the Isle of Wight. Æthelræd summoned the witan, which agreed that again the Danes should be paid tribute, this time £24,000, in return for peace.

By the autumn of 1002, Æthelræd had been utterly humiliated. Even before the money was handed over, the man who had conducted the negotiations on his behalf, Leofsige, the ealdorman of East Anglia, killed a reeve and was banished. The cause of their dispute is not known, but if it had nothing to do with the king's policy it would be quite some coincidence, and if the king's policy had not caused any tensions at court it would be remarkable.

Unable to protect his people, and unable to punish those who had destroyed them, Æthelræd lashed out in anger against people he could attack instead. Having been warned that there was a Danish plot to kill him and his witan, and to seize the throne, he issued an order that on St Brice's Day, 13 November, 'all the Danes in England' be killed.

The words 'all the Danes in England' are those of the *Anglo-Saxon Chronicle*. Later historians add more detail. John of Worcester clarifies that the victims were 'all the Danes of every age and both sexes'. English government was efficient, and it is not too much of a stretch to imagine Æthelræd's scribes issuing writs (that is, official letters containing instructions) to his reeves, ordering them to take Danish men of fighting age by surprise on a specified date and kill them. That is exactly what Henry of Huntingdon, who began *The History of the English People* in the 1120s, and finished it in 1154, says happened. 'Concerning this crime,' he wrote, 'in my childhood I heard very old men say that the king had sent secret letters to every city, according to which the English either maimed all the unsuspecting Danes on the same day and hour with their swords, or, suddenly, at the same moment, captured them and destroyed them by fire.'

This appears to have been exactly what happened in Oxford. In a charter issued to the Priory of St Frideswide confirming a grant of land there is a brief account of what happened in that city: the Danes were driven into the church, which was then set on fire; they tried to fight their way out, and were slaughtered as they did. There is, in the same document, a brief and now infamous justification: the Danes were 'the cockle in the wheat', a Biblical analogy comparing them to a disease, which would affect the rest of the country, were they not cut out.

William of Malmesbury includes Pallig and his family among the victims. He describes Gunhild, 'who possessed considerable beauty', seeing her husband and son killed in front of her. 'She bore her death with fortitude, and she neither turned pale at the moment, nor, when dead, and her blood exhausted, did she lose her beauty.' Meanwhile John of Wallingford, an Oxfordshire chronicler writing in the second-half of the twelfth century, had a memorable explanation. Englishmen, he wrote, were displeased that their countrywomen seemed to prefer the company of Danish men: their habits of regularly washing and combing their hair made them more appealing.

John of Wallingford does not appear in many serious histories, because much of the information in his chronicle is inaccurate. As an explanation for the massacre this is entirely unconvincing, even if in some way it taps into a popular memory of Viking masculinity eclipsing native Englishmen. What it does reveal, though, along with the other histories and chronicles, is that this was a big deal. It needed justifying at the time and it needed explaining later.

It is not altogether clear who the victims were, or who they were intended to be. 'The Danes' cannot have encompassed everyone of Danish ancestry throughout England. There were far too many such people, especially in what had been the Danelaw, many of them in positions of authority. However, both John of Worcester and William of Malmesbury confirm explicitly that women and children were killed, and the account of Gunhild's death makes it clear that, at least in her case, she was the victim of a deliberate, calculated act intended to punish her husband's treachery.

Still, it seems more plausible that Gunhild was an exception, and that the massacre was aimed not at Danes in general, however that be defined, but at young Danish men. The obvious cockles in the wheat were mercenaries such as Pallig, who had taken Æthelræd's money and then betrayed him. Presumably other Danish mercenaries, who had not yet betrayed him, were also massacred; so too, probably, were young Danes of military age, such as merchants, who found themselves in English towns on St Brice's Day 1002. It has been suggested that two mass graves, one discovered at St John's College, Oxford in 2008, another at Ridgeway Hill in Dorset in 2009, might supply some archaeological evidence to support this argument. In both graves were found the remains of dozens of young men, carbon-dated to around this period. While those found in Dorset appear to have been conventionally executed, those in Oxford seem to have been burned and hacked at. It is always immensely tempting to connect a rare piece of archaeological evidence with a rare piece of written evidence, and although it's certainly possible that these were the men who were killed at St Frideswide's, it is also possible that they were some other group of men who were killed at some other time for some other reason.

Historians of our own age are rather less exercised about the massacres. There is almost a consensus that the Danes had it coming. Some of them had no doubt been warriors themselves, and had perpetrated atrocities every bit as bad as those that were inflicted on them. And if the victims included those who had never taken up arms, well, that can be justified too. Their loyalty was suspect; they might well pass on all sorts of information to England's enemies.

So Æthelræd was justified in exacting vengeance. Some take it further, and suggest that while of course he gave the order, in doing so he was leading his subjects just as they wished to be led.

There was, so the speculation goes, plenty of enthusiasm for the massacres: they could not have taken place without the support of the population at large, and it isn't difficult to see why, after all that had happened in the preceding twenty years, the English would support their king in committing mass murder.

It is probably fair to assume that there was even less sympathy for the Danes in the England of 1002 than there is today. Even so it is interesting that there is very little nodding in approval from historians who were close enough in time to the event that they could talk to people who had talked to people who could remember it. And however popular the policy might have been while it was taking place, however strong the feeling that the Danes had had it coming, those who participated in the massacres, and those who witnessed them, must have known deep down that they were sowing the wind, and would in their turn reap the whirlwind.

They did not have long to wait.

* * * *

Sweyn Forkbeard responded to the news entirely predictably. The longships were assembled, the warriors were summoned, and as the dark Scandinavian winter melted away, ushering in the campaigning season, a Danish force once more set sail for England.

They first made their way to Devon. England's new queen had received lands in England, including Exeter, and she had appointed a Norman, Hugh, to represent her there. When the Danes arrived, he was not equal to the task of defending the city. 'Exeter was taken by storm,' laments the *Anglo-Saxon Chronicle*, 'through the fault of a certain French ceorl.' John of Worcester describes him as a count, but says that it was 'through contrivance, negligence, or treachery', that the Danes were able to sack the city.

To describe Hugh as a 'ceorl', or 'churl', was probably a calculated insult rather than a mistake. Most men in England could be described as ceorls: some were prosperous citizens, burgesses, or country landowners, while some, while legally not slaves, were not exactly free either. They might, for instance, own little or none of their own property; they might be legally required to work on a lord's land for part of the week or at certain times of year or both; they might well not be paid for that work, but instead be permitted to occupy a cottage on that land. To group a Norman nobleman with such people was intended to disparage either him personally, or the society in which he was regarded as an aristocrat, or both.

Hugh might have been inept, but his failing was more than matched by one of England's grandest ealdormen. As the Danes marched into Hampshire and Wiltshire, Ælfric of Hampshire was given command of the fyrd. But when he saw the enemy, Ælfric literally found he had no stomach for the fight. He retched and vomited, and declared himself too ill to lead his men into battle.

It is tempting to sympathise with Ælfric here. The prospect of a battle against the King of Denmark was surely enough to cause such a physical reaction, especially in the circumstances of 1003. But no one seems to have considered the possibility that his symptoms were genuine. The *Anglo-Saxon Chronicle* denounces him as 'up to his old tricks', and accuses him of feigning his sickness. Seeing their commander retreat from the field of battle, the rest of the army decided not to go through with it either, and slunk away, leaving Wiltshire at Sweyn's mercy. This particular quality was in even shorter supply than usual, and both Wilton and Salisbury were sacked before the Danish headed back to their ships.

There can be no doubt that Sweyn led a formidable army. But it is also clear that Danish warriors were not invincible. They found, in Æthelræd's England, a particularly weak enemy, and acquired for themselves an intimidating aura. Nonetheless, when they came up against decent commanders, they sometimes struggled, and that is what happened when they targeted East Anglia in 1004.

East Anglia did not have an ealdorman: Æthelræd had not appointed a replacement for Leofsige after his banishment. However, a local thegn, Ulfcytel, appears to have been regarded as the leading figure in the region, and when the Danes sacked Norwich and began plundering the surrounding countryside, it was Ulfcytel who summoned the local notables and persuaded them that, as they were unprepared to fight, they should pay tribute straight away, before too much damage was done.

So far Ulfcytel's reaction had been similar to that of his West Saxon contemporaries: he had been a little quicker to recognise the reality of the situation, perhaps, and to take steps to minimise the damage. But his abilities were made clear in what happened next. The Danes, having agreed a truce, proceeded to disregard it, and marched to Thetford. But Ulfcytel had kept them under careful surveillance. He had also used the period of truce wisely: he had quietly gathered an army, and he had positioned them to intercept the Danes on their return to their ships. (Thetford is and was some way from a navigable river, and so they had left their ships behind and proceeded on foot; in their absence Ulfcytel ordered the ships to be destroyed, but the order was not carried out.) This time, there was no panicking: the East Anglians stood and fought, and there were heavy losses on both sides. The Danes managed to get back to their ships, and thence, eventually, to Scandinavia, but both English and Danish authorities agreed that Ulfcytel's men had been their toughest English adversaries: indeed, in Scandinavia he became known as 'Snilling', or 'the Bold'.

If he received similar recognition in England, other than from chroniclers, it is difficult to discern. He does not appear to have been given the title of ealdorman, nor to have been given military responsibilities outside of East Anglia. It is almost as though Æthelræd had finally come across one man whom he could trust, and decided not to trust him.

The Danes did not campaign in England in 1005, but this was not because of any English military resurgence. It was because the country was suffering from a devastating famine, the worst in living memory, and there wasn't enough food to supply an army.

****

'The redeeming feature of war,' wrote a German philosopher centuries later, 'is that it puts the nation to the test.' By 1006 England and Denmark had been at war for fifteen years, and it had brutally exposed the weaknesses of Æthelræd's régime. However, it had also shown some of the resilience of the system. The government of England, under immense pressure, had continued to function as it was supposed to. It wasn't just the minting of coins and their collection as taxes which carried on despite the incessant raids. There was a manifest lack of confidence in the king, yet still respect for the Crown seems to have been maintained. When the fyrd was summoned, it appeared; when it was led into battle, it fought. When ships were ordered, they were built. Laws were promulgated and royal courts throughout the land upheld them. Individuals and institutions carefully guarded the charters and diplomas which recorded grants of land: they did not expect the Vikings to

respect their property rights, but they expected their fellow natives
to do so. For all Æthelræd's personal inadequacy, society did not
collapse into anarchy.

Nor, perhaps surprisingly, did it descend into rebellion. By the
turn of the century there were several prominent æthelings who
could have succeeded their father, but there is no record of any of
them having been involved in any plots to overthrow him. This
might have been because Æthelræd was rather good at managing
his magnates, or at least effective in ensuring that none were able
to become strong enough to challenge his position. The refusal
to promote Ulfcytel to the position of ealdorman of East Anglia
after his encounter with the Vikings might appear odd, but it is
consistent with his reluctance to appoint an ealdorman of Mercia
for twenty years: creating over-mighty subjects was asking for
trouble. Moreover, while Æthelræd was reluctant to confront the
Danes, he was not at all apprehensive about taking on his own
subjects. Leofsige of East Anglia was, as it were, bang to rights:
to kill a reeve, a royal official, was to invite the wrath of the king.
But history has not preserved any details of the nature of Ælfric of
Mercia's alleged treason, and nor have the charges against the next
victims of Æthelræd's purges been satisfactorily identified.

These victims included Ælfhelm, ealdorman of Northumbria,
and his sons. The *Anglo-Saxon Chronicle* describes Ælfhelm as
having been 'slain'. John of Worcester explains how the slaying
took place:

The crafty and treacherous Eadric Streona, insidiously plotting
against the noble ealdorman Ælfhelm, prepared a great
entertainment at Shrewsbury, to which he invited him. Ælfhelm,
accepting the invitation, was welcomed by Eadric as his

intimate friend, but on the third or fourth day of the feast he took him to hunt in a wood where he had an ambuscade; and when all were engaged in the chase a ruffian ... who had long before been bribed by the profuse gifts and promises of Eadric to commit the crime, suddenly sprang from his ambush and basely assassinated the ealdorman Ælfhelm.

Eadric 'Streona' (the 'Acquisitive') may have orchestrated the actual killing, but it must have been done at the king's command: Æthelræd's reaction to the murder of one of his ealdormen was to order the victim's sons to be blinded, and, a year later, to elevate the perpetrator to the ealdormanry of Mercia, which is an inconceivable reaction if the assassination had not been officially authorised.

It isn't clear what Ælfhelm had done to earn his fate. It is possible that it was connected with a Scottish incursion into that region in that year: the Scots besieged Durham, and were eventually repelled not by Ælfhelm but by Uhtred, the son of the aged ealdorman of Bernicia (the territory which is now the county of Northumberland). Æthelræd rewarded Uhtred by appointing him as successor both to his father and to Ælfhelm, giving him an enlarged ealdormanry of Northumbria to govern.

So perhaps it was Ælfhelm's failure to defend the north vigorously enough which cost him his life. The reasoning behind Æthelræd having him assassinated, rather than having him brought before the witan, as had happened to Ælfric of Mercia nearly a quarter-of-a-century before, is similarly unclear. Perhaps Æthelræd feared that the witan would be less cooperative this time; perhaps he feared that Ælfhelm, if he was summoned to his own trial, might refuse to attend, or even raise the north in rebellion. Or perhaps he was seduced by Eadric Streona whispering in his ear that he only had to give the order, and the whole problem would be dealt with. Whatever the reason, the incident gives the impression that Æthelræd's government was now somewhat more arbitrary than it had been when he first took control of the country.

In the same entry, the *Anglo-Saxon Chronicle* records a further dispossession, of a man simply named as Wulfgeat. Again, John of Worcester fills in the gaps. 'King Æthelræd stripped Wulfgeat, the son of Leofsige, the king's principal favourite, of his estates and honours, on account of his unrighteous judgments and arrogant deeds.' Whether Wulfgeat was guilty of these charges or not is impossible to tell, and in a way it doesn't matter. Æthelræd was exercising his authority and issuing a stern warning: he would not hesitate to crush anyone who lost his favour.

Whether or not Eadric was involved in this, there can be no doubt that he had become an influential man. He was, in John of Worcester's words, 'of low origin, but his smooth tongue gained him wealth and high rank, and, gifted with a subtle genius and persuasive eloquence, he surpassed all his contemporaries in malice and perfidy, as well as in pride and cruelty'. He was, in short, the ideal man to do the king's dirty work. Eadric's relatively humble background may also have recommended him: if he genuinely had come from nowhere, he owed his position entirely to royal patronage. Such a man might, Æthelræd may well have reasoned, be more likely to be loyal than the head of a great family with extensive lands and connections upon which to draw.[5]

---

5 By 'low origin', John of Worcester did not mean to imply that Eadric was actually a ceorl; he was from a thegnly family, just not a prominent or particularly rich one. And even in this context, the lowliness of his origins might be overstated. Eadric was allowed to marry one of Æthelræd's daughters and therefore become part of the royal family, which certainly suggests that his lineage was deemed acceptable enough for such an honour.

When it came to protecting his own position from potential threats, Æthelræd knew what he was doing.

In the summer of 1006, the Danes announced their return with a raid on Sandwich. In response, Æthelræd called out the fyrd from Wessex and Mercia, but for once it was the Danes who preferred to avoid a pitched battle, launching instead lightning raids in which they gathered booty, and retreated to their ships before the English could engage them. Towards the end of autumn, they returned to the Isle of Wight, as they had done four years previously; Æthelræd, no doubt relieved that they had gone, disbanded the fyrd. The campaigning season was over: if there were commanders who had been keen to fight the Danes they were to go home disappointed, but they might have told themselves that at least there had been no crushing defeat, no national humiliation, and no reason for despair. They might even have told themselves that the Danish reluctance to fight was a good sign, and that the worst might be over.

And then, just a few weeks later, now that the coast was literally clear, the Danish warriors sailed back across the Solent. They marched up through Hampshire, and Berkshire, to Wallingford, just a few miles south of Oxford. Then they followed the ancient Ridgeway track westward to Cuckamsley Hill, and, as the *Anglo-Saxon Chronicle* records, 'waited there out of bravado, for oft it is said, that if they reach it, they should never again get to the sea'.

This is an interesting legend. Clearly it was familiar both to the Danes and to the English, but it isn't clear whether, in occupying the site, the Danes were defying their own superstition or that of the English. Cuckamsley Hill is a long way inland; there is no evidence of it having been of any particular national or spiritual significance, though maybe it was. It is probably fair to say that under normal circumstances a foreign army which found itself there might be unusually vulnerable: it would be relatively easy to surround and cut off. It was certainly much riskier than raiding coastal settlements. Quite how the myth came into being, though, is more difficult to answer. John of Worcester does not repeat it, but includes Cuckamsley Hill on the Danish itinerary (a rare example of his supplying less detail than the *Anglo-Saxon Chronicle*). Maybe it wasn't really a superstition at all. An English commander during the previous summer could have formulated a strategy to encircle the Danes when they reached that landmark, and that plan could had been revealed to the Danes. (If that's what happened, the importance of the site may be no more than that it is near the River Thames, the traditional boundary between Wessex and Mercia, and within striking distance of several potential assembly points for an army comprised of Mercians and West Saxons: Oxford, say, or Wallingford.) In occupying it a few months later, therefore, the Danish warriors were mocking their enemies, not the gods.

And well they might. They carted their loot all the way back to the south coast where it could be loaded onto their ships. They were intercepted by an English force near Reading, which they crushed. Then they marched unopposed through Wessex, from Cornwall to Kent, plundering as they went. For the people of Wessex, the midwinter was very bleak indeed. Nothing like this had happened for well over a century, not since the 870s, when King Alfred had been chased into the marshes of Somerset by the Great Heathen Army. Not only did nothing seem able to stop the rampaging hordes; no one seemed interested in trying.

While all this was going on, the king was skulking in Shropshire. He summoned the witan, and the only course of action they could come up with was the one which had failed the country twice already: they agreed to pay £36,000 to the Danes in return for peace.

The Danes, having gorged themselves, agreed. And so, one more time, the English people had to stand by and watch as their property was seized, this time by royal officials, so that it might be handed over to the men who had just been harrying their land. No one can have persuaded himself that this would be an end to it. But then there seemed to be no alternative. And with all the benefits of hindsight it remains very easy to denounce the decision to appease the Danes yet again, but a viable alternative is still very difficult to identify.

****

It was in these circumstances that Æthelræd summoned the witan to Eanham, in Hampshire. He presented the assembly with a document drawn up by Wulfstan, the Archbishop of York, for their approval. It was quite clear that England had fallen out of divine favour, and the solution too was clear: the people needed to acknowledge and confess their sins, ask forgiveness of the Lord, and resolve to go and sin no more. The law code which emerged is a remarkable statement of what a Christian country ought to be.

It establishes some protections for the 'Christian men' of England. They were forbidden to be sold into foreign slavery, 'and especially not among the heathen people', and they were 'not to be condemned to death for all too small offences'. In return, the code demanded that 'God's dues are to be readily paid every year', and specified several fees to be paid to the Church: these included 'plough-alms fifteen days after Easter, and the tithe of young animals by Pentecost, and of the fruits of the earth by All Saints' Day, and "Rome-scot" by St Peter's Day.'

The country was enjoined to observe festivals (that of St Edward the Martyr is specifically included) and fasts, confession and atonement, and Holy Communion. Priests were caustically reminded that 'they know full well that they may not rightly have sexual intercourse with a woman', but the laity as well as the clergy was urged 'zealously to avoid illegal intercourse'.

Towards the end, the code outlines some of the faults which had brought the wrath of God down upon the English. The use of 'false weights and wrong measures and lying witnesses and shameful frauds' had been compounded by 'horrible perjuries and devilish deeds of murder and manslaughter, of stealing and spoliation, of avarice and greed, of over-eating and over-drinking'.

Better Christian behaviour would appease an angry deity. But practical measures were required too. The requirement to do military service, to provide ships, and to maintain fortifications were emphasised. And the English were sternly reminded that 'if anyone deserts without leave from an army which the king himself is with, it is to be at the peril of his life and all his property'.

The code ended on a desperate note. 'We must all love and honour one God,' it read, 'and entirely cast out every heathen practice. And let us loyally support one royal lord, and all together defend our lives and our land, as well as ever we can, and pray Almighty God from our inmost heart for his help.'

That one royal lord knew that he needed to improve England's defences. He had learned the hard way that an approach based on defeating Danish armies in the field was unlikely to succeed. And so, in 1008, he came up with another defensive strategy, this time focussed on the sea.

He gave the order for the construction of a brand-new navy. The whole country would be involved, but not through paying tax to fund the project: instead, every 300 hides were to provide a ship. This implies co-ordination on the level of the shire, with each shire being allocated a certain number of ships to provide on the basis of its size; the ealdormen and reeves would ensure that the ships were built and supplied. When it assembled at Sandwich it was the largest fleet England had ever seen. Its task was simple: to patrol the coast and intercept the Vikings before they could land.

It was never tested. In the early summer of 1009 Brihtric, Eadric Streona's brother, denounced Wulfnoth, the ealdorman of Sussex and one of the naval commanders, to the king. The chronicles are silent as to the nature of the accusation, but (perhaps mindful of the recent treatment of Ælfhelm) Wulfnoth did not want to take his chances with royal justice. He commandeered twenty ships and, now a fugitive, began harrying the coastal areas. Brihtric saw an opportunity. Motivated, according to the *Chronicle*, by the desire for personal prestige, he took eighty ships and set off in pursuit, but was then caught in a storm and shipwrecked just off the south coast. Those ships which managed to make landfall were gleefully burned by Wulfnoth, of whom, like Brihtric, nothing further is heard.

This fiasco deprived England of a hundred ships; all the work that had gone into the fleet was destroyed by bad weather and bad men. The remaining ships sailed forlornly up the Thames to London, while Æthelræd withdrew from what was now an unprotected danger zone. Everyone knew that the news of the latest catastrophe would soon arrive in Scandinavia, and that the longships would soon set sail, ready to exploit the situation.

Sure enough, it was not long before they were sighted off the coast of Kent. The Vikings landed near Sandwich and made their way inland to Canterbury, where the inhabitants of the city were waiting for them, not with arms, but with £3,000, which was offered to the Danish commander, Thurkill 'the Tall' in return for his leaving the people of East Kent unmolested. Thurkill accepted the payment, returned to his ships, and sailed on to the Danes' preferred offshore base on the Isle of Wight, from where they harried the coastal areas of Sussex and Hampshire. Æthelræd called out the fyrd and marched towards the enemy. Whereas three years previously it had proved impossible to pin down the Danes and engage them in battle, this time it appears that the geographical range of their raiding was rather more limited. On one occasion they went too far inland, and the English were able to intercept them on their way back to their ships. 'All the folk were ready to attack them,' reports the *Anglo-Saxon Chronicle*, and according to John of Worcester, the royal army was 'resolved either to conquer or die'.

Enter Eadric Streona. 'It was prevented,' grumbles the Chronicler, 'by Eadric, as always.' John of Worcester explained in a little more detail. 'The traitorous ealdorman,' he wrote, 'used every effort, by insidious and perplexing counsels, to prevent a battle and persuade the king, for that time, to let the enemy pass. His policy prevailed, and like a traitor to his country, he rescued the Danes from the hands of the English, and suffered them to escape.' There is something a little unconvincing about this. Was Eadric, in 1009, in the pay of the Danes? By the twelfth century this appears to have become the conventional wisdom. William of Malmesbury described him as 'the refuse of mankind', and went on to accuse him of treason. 'This artful dissembler,' he wrote, 'capable of feigning anything, was accustomed, by pretended fidelity, to scent out the king's designs, that he might treacherously divulge them.'

There is, of course, no proof of Eadric having been a Danish spy. It is also rather unlikely. His advice to Æthelræd may have been unwise and unhelpful, and contemporaries as well as later commentators might characterise this incident as another example of 'unræd'. Still, it is worth remembering a few things about the circumstances in which Eadric suggested that battle be avoided. Firstly, the king may not have been difficult to persuade: indeed, Eadric may well have been telling him what he wanted to hear. (This is, of course, far from ideal in a royal counsellor, but it is also far from uncommon, and it is not the same as treason.) Æthelræd appears to have been in personal command of the army, and Æthelræd did not like being in personal command of armies. Secondly, to imply that if only they had engaged the Danes in battle the English would have emerged victorious is perhaps wishful thinking. (If victory really would have been more or less guaranteed, the disparity in numbers must have been notable; but no one seems to have noted it. In any case, while avoiding a confrontation in those circumstances does seem inexplicable, and perhaps hints at skulduggery, it can't have been of decisive importance to the campaign as a whole if there was only a small Danish force.) And thirdly, while Eadric's conduct up until this point does seem to have been fairly dubious, the king was the beneficiary rather than the victim of his duplicity. Accusing 'wicked counsellors' of deception and betrayal is safer and sometimes more appealing than blaming a king for his own decisions, but there is little to suggest that Æthelræd's approach fundamentally changed when his new ealdorman of Mercia emerged. What seems to have happened instead is that the king found someone in whom he had confidence, and so empowered him to act on his behalf. His ruthlessness was a recommendation: and if the magnates of the realm didn't like it, well, they shouldn't have been so disloyal.

It might therefore be worth considering the possibility that Eadric knew something, about the weaknesses of the fyrd or about the strengths of the Vikings, which the chroniclers didn't. Perhaps he wanted to deny a rival the glory of leading an army to victory against the Danes, but perhaps he was in a position of command, and would have got that prestige for himself.

Eadric's loyalty did have its limits, as became clear at the end of the régime; he was essentially a scoundrel, which was clear significantly earlier. Still, at this point it seems that he was a faithful servant of the king.

* * * *

The king, and his advisers, were now in a state of palpable panic. Another edict was issued, this time purely religious in character, calling on the people to pray, to fast, to confess their sins, and above all to repent. Another tax was introduced, of a penny per household, to be spent on defence; and a new coin was introduced with which to pay it. Earlier coins had shown Æthelræd as a warrior king, wearing a helmet, with a cross on the reverse; this new issue had the Lamb of God on one side, and a dove of peace on the other.

But God was not ready to intercede on behalf of the English people.

After spending the second half of 1009 harrying the coastal region opposite the Isle of Wight, the Danes sailed back past Sandwich to the Thames Estuary, and set up camp on the south bank of the river. In the late autumn they turned their attentions to London, the one part of the kingdom which had never succumbed to them, and despite several attempts they found impossible to enter.

Enraged, they proceeded up the Thames, and took their frustrations out on Oxford. Thurkill's failure to take London was, of course, mainly due to the city's defensive fortifications, but the Danes evidently had some respect for the fighting men of the city, because when they learned that a force had been sent out to meet them on their way back from Oxford, they slipped back over the river so as to avoid an encounter.

The Danes spent the winter and early spring in Kent, and then, in May 1010, crossed the river and landed at Ipswich. This time, they were looking for a decisive battle. Ulfcytel had gathered an army to oppose them, and Thurkill led the Danes straight towards him. The men of Cambridgeshire stood firm, but the men of East Anglia did not, and after some hard fighting the Danes were victorious. Ulfcytel was not killed, but the slaughter was such that the fighting strength of the eastern counties was broken. Thurkill, lamented the *Anglo-Saxon Chronicle*, 'held sway in East Anglia, and harried and burned the land for three months'. Yet again, where there should have been resistance there was utter despair. 'At last there was no chief who would gather a fyrd, but each fled as he best might; nor at the last would even one shire assist another.' Once they had finished pillaging East Anglia they turned westward and marched, for the first time, into Bedfordshire, Buckinghamshire, and Northamptonshire. For a second successive winter, they did not return to Scandinavia. Thurkill, so it appeared, was here to stay.

Æthelræd's government had run out of ideas years before. Again, the English asked for peace and offered tribute. The amount of money demanded increased again, while the breathing space afforded by its payment decreased. This time, the Danes wanted £48,000, and the promise to deliver it was not enough: they continued to ravage the countryside throughout 1011, while the English authorities gathered the funds from the exhausted people. The *Anglo-Saxon Chronicle* expresses the country's despair thus:

> All these misfortunes befell us through unræd, that neither tribute nor battle was offered to them at the right time, but when they had done the most evil, then truce and peace were made with them. And nevertheless for all this truce and peace and tribute, they fared everywhere and harried our wretched folk and captured and slew them.[6]

Normal constitutional propriety, though, continued to be observed. On every occasion that tribute was paid, the *Anglo-Saxon Chronicle* records carefully that it was the witan, and not only the king, who made the decision to pay it. This really seems to have mattered. The king, it appears, needed to get the approval of his leading counsellors before he was allowed to tap the nation's resources: it looks as if he might not have had the authority to impose a national tax at will.

---

6 It also lists the counties which the Danes had overrun. East Anglia, Essex, Middlesex, Oxfordshire, Cambridgeshire, Hertfordshire, Buckinghamshire, Bedfordshire, 'half Huntingdonshire and much in Northamptonshire', Kent, Sussex, Surrey, Berkshire, Hampshire, and 'much in Wiltshire'. William of Malmesbury, writing after the Norman Conquest, was of what might today be called 'dual heritage': his father was Norman and his mother was English. He did not approve of the *Anglo-Saxon Chronicle*'s author listing them all: 'That I may not be tedious in mentioning severally all the counties which the Danes laid waste,' he wrote, 'let it be briefly understood that out of thirty-two counties, which are reckoned in England, they had already overrun sixteen, the names of which I forbear to enumerate on account of the harshness of the language.' Was using the native tongue beneath an educated man of the twelfth century? (William, like the other historians of his age, wrote in Latin.) Did William share that disdain, despite his ancestry? Or did he feel like he ought to conspicuously distance himself from it, given his origins? The *Anglo-Saxon Chronicle* was still being produced while he was writing his *Chronicle of the Kings of England*: was this some kind of dig at what he might have considered a relatively unsophisticated work and its authors?

It is deeply unfashionable to see the Old English witenagemot as some sort of ancestor of Parliament, though when the *Anglo-Saxon Chronicle* describes the institution as being made up of 'ecclesiastical and lay' members, as it does in the entries both for 1012 and for 1014, it is difficult not to hear a distant echo of the 'lords spiritual and temporal' who still constitute the House of Lords today. If being mentioned in the *Chronicle* is an indication of importance, it is worth noting that none of the entries for Cnut's reign mention the institution: perhaps the witan was at its strongest when the crown was at its weakest.

Certainly by now royal authority was very weak indeed. In September 1011, just two years after receiving that payment of £3,000 from the city, Thurkill's men besieged Canterbury. For twenty days the city held out, before Ælfmær, the abbot of St Augustine's Abbey, committed what must be the greatest single instance of betrayal even of Æthelræd's age, and started a fire in the cradle of English Christianity, the place where, more than 400 years before, the country's first cathedral had been built. In the panic and confusion, the Danes swept in. John of Worcester takes up the story:

Some of the townsmen were put to the sword; others perished in the flames; many were thrown headlong from the walls; some were hung by their private parts until they expired; matrons were dragged by their hair through the streets of the city, and then cast into the fire and burned to death; infants, torn from their mothers' breasts, were caught on the point of spears or crushed in pieces under the wheels of waggons.

Then, he says, the adult male citizens were decimated. But John of Worcester's description of decimation suggests something more brutal than the classical practice. Instead of slaughtering every tenth man, Thurkill allowed every tenth man to live, with the other nine being put to death.

Vikings did take prisoners, and Thurkill's men were no exception. All those in holy orders, women as well as men, were captured. Ælfmær, who had helped the Vikings into the city, was released. Most of his fellow clerics would face slavery, but for one captive in particular there would be a grimmer and more grisly fate. Ælfheah, the Archbishop of Canterbury, was in the city when it fell. Wounded, he was seized and dragged through the streets in chains, before being held to ransom.

There was something very special about Ælfheah. He had, apparently, saved Ælfmær's life before his betrayal, though frustratingly none of the authorities who report this fact add any detail to it. He had reached the pinnacle of the English Church late in life, after a long and distinguished career: he had been a prior, an abbot and Bishop of Winchester, but he had also, as a young man, lived for some time as a hermit. As Archbishop of Canterbury he had participated in the drawing up of the Eanham Code. Now, an old man, he was held by the Danes for seven months, during which time he continued to practice the faith to which he had adhered all his life, and even converted the odd Dane to Christianity. On Easter Saturday 1012, he was given an ultimatum: he was to raise a ransom of £3,000, or he would be executed.

Ælfheah insisted that he not be ransomed. The people of Canterbury, and Kent, and indeed England, had paid quite enough: he would not be complicit in demanding even more. This enraged his captors, and a week later he was hauled out of his dungeon to be executed. The Danes had been feasting, and drinking, and this exacerbated their displeasure: they hurled their leftover bones and anything else they could lay their hands on at the archbishop, before he was finished off with an axe to the head. Even some Danes thought this had been gruesomely excessive. It might be going a little far to suggest that Ælfheah had impressed them, but certainly he had given a better account of his nation than its king or many of its leading magnates. His body, perhaps a little shamefacedly, was handed over to his people for a Christian burial.

The tribute was paid, and the Danes finally withdrew. Most boarded their ships and dispersed, but forty-five ships' worth of warriors did not: they remained in the country, now paid mercenaries in the service of King Æthelræd, still led, extraordinarily, by Thurkill, who was now transformed overnight into a cornerstone of England's defences.

* * * *

The anonymous author of the *Encomium Emmae Reginae* is notoriously untrustworthy, but the encomiast's account of discussions at Sweyn's court in the first half of 1013 is our best explanation for what happened next. He explains that although Sweyn had authorised Thurkill's activities in England up until Easter 1012, these recent developments caused serious consternation in Denmark. He reports courtiers reminding their king that Thurkill had been responsible for 'leading away a large part of your army', and grumbling that 'having become an ally of the English, whom he has conquered through your power, he prefers the enjoyment of his glory to leading his army back'. This might not have been wholly fair, but whether Thurkill was enjoying his own personal glory or not, it would certainly be understandable if some Danes did indeed consider themselves to have been 'cheated of our companions and forty ships, which he led with him, manned from among the best Danish warriors'. That, after all, was exactly what Æthelræd was paying Thurkill for. Sweyn agreed that it was an intolerable situation, and gave the order for an invasion fleet to be gathered. He was going to put an end to the situation: he was going to conquer England for himself.

In the early summer of 1013, the longships swept up the River Humber to Gainsborough. There Sweyn set up a base camp and waited. It didn't take long for Uhtred, the ealdorman of Northumbria, to come and submit to him. Uhtred was followed by the leading thegns of Lincolnshire, the Five Boroughs, and then the whole of the Danelaw.[7] This wasn't a military surrender involving the payment of tribute: it was a recognition of Sweyn as King of England. Straight away, he started acting like one, and called out the fyrd to fight for him, before marching to Oxford, and then on to Winchester. Across the country, prominent Englishmen hurried to make their submissions and hand over hostages to their new lord. 'The whole people,' reported the *Anglo-Saxon Chronicle*, 'had him for full king', with only London defiantly refusing to accept the reality of their new situation. Sweyn, enjoying his new position, demanded a full *geld* be raised, and that the country supply his men with provisions. And straight away he started planning for the future: he had his teenage son, Cnut, married to Ælfhelm's daughter, establishing ties with a family which had every reason to prefer any alternative to Æthelræd's régime.

Æthelræd, holed up in London, sent Queen Emma, accompanied by their children, back to Normandy. On discovering that they had

---

7 The 'Five Boroughs' – Lincoln, Nottingham, Derby, Leicester and Stamford – were the major towns of 'Danish Mercia': that is, the eastern part of Mercia which was part of the Danelaw.

safely made it, he decided against an heroic last stand. Instead, abandoning London, he took refuge with Thurkill's fleet, which was still in his service, and under their protection he sailed out to the Isle of Wight. Perhaps he stayed in the same lodgings which had recently accommodated the Danes. Then, after Christmas, he too crossed the English Channel to Normandy, the first King of England to be exiled from his country and to have to take refuge at a foreign court.

London no longer had anyone to hold out for. For twenty years its citizens had resolutely resisted the Danes: now it opened its gates to King Sweyn. The country had fallen.

3

EDMUND IRONSIDE

Nations that went down fighting rose again,
but those who surrendered tamely were finished.

Winston Churchill

Sweyn Forkbeard had managed what none of his predecessors had done: he had received the submission of the entirety of the English people. His movements through England in 1013 had been more of a triumphal procession than a campaign. But he did not have long to enjoy it. In February 1014, just a few weeks after Æthelræd's departure, he died.

What happened then is rather interesting. The Danes, still based at Gainsborough, acclaimed Sweyn's son, Cnut, as his successor. But the English had other ideas. According to the *Anglo-Saxon Chronicle*, 'all the witan who were in England, ecclesiastical and lay', agreed 'that they should send for King Æthelræd; and they declared that no lord was dearer to them than their own natural lord, if he would rule them better than he did before'.

Æthelræd did not come straight back. Instead he sent his eldest son by Queen Emma, Edward, to convey his reply to the witan's offer. He 'said he would be to them a gracious lord and amend each of those things which they all hated, and each of those things should be forgiven which had been done or said to him on condition that they all unanimously without treachery turned back to him'. This answer was acceptable to the witan. And so 'in the spring King Æthelræd came home to his own people, and he was gladly received by them all'.

Perhaps he was, at least in some quarters. There was still residual respect or affection for the Crown, and perhaps for its rightful wearer, for all his personal inadequacy. And his restoration certainly seems to have inspired a renewal of the nation's fighting spirit. He marched against Cnut and, remarkably, the Danes decided not to fight, instead taking to their ships and sailing back to Denmark. The encomiast's justification for Cnut's behaviour is entertaining: he withdrew 'not because he was fleeing afraid of the harsh outcome of war, but in order to consult his brother Harald, King of the Danes, about so weighty a matter'. Æthelræd was triumphant, and in these circumstances even his payment of £21,000 to Thurkill's mercenaries might have seemed less onerous: perhaps it was a price worth paying for victory. With no enemy to face, Æthelræd's army contented itself with harrying Lincolnshire, warning the other shires that there would be consequences for inaction so serious that it might as well be treason.

Sweyn's death had left three empty thrones. In Norway, he was succeeded by Olaf, a native chief, who took advantage of the situation to seize control of that country for himself. In Denmark and England he was succeeded by the men on the spot, Harald and Cnut respectively. The encomiast states that this was in accordance with Sweyn's designation, and perhaps it was; certainly it made sense for him to leave Harald in Denmark and take Cnut with him to England if that was his intention.

Cnut did indeed consult his brother. If the encomiast is to be believed, and there is no reason to disbelieve him on this, he behaved respectfully, almost deferentially, towards Harald. They shared 'tears shed partly for love and partly for their father's death'. Cnut then proposed that they divide Denmark between them, then invade England together, and that afterwards Harald could choose which of the kingdoms he would take for himself, with Cnut taking the other. Harald, unsurprisingly, declined, but agreed to help his brother to invade England. Of course he did: the alternative was to have a frustrated and resentful rival at his own court. The interests of both brothers would be served by a successful invasion of England, and over the forthcoming winter that is what they prepared for and planned.

* * * *

Meanwhile, back in England, Æthelræd was trying to make good on his promise to deliver better government. Within a few months of his return he had a new law code drawn up, this too focussing very much on improving the country's religious life.

It begins with a defence of the principle of sanctuary, which allowed anyone to take refuge in an ecclesiastical building and be safe from the secular authorities. The king, so the law code explained, was required to uphold this law and to punish anyone who violated it. 'A Christian king is Christ's deputy in a Christian people, and he must avenge very zealously offences against Christ.'

This was a royal document issued in the king's name, but no one reading it can have failed to notice that it contained an only slightly implicit indictment of Æthelræd's part in the events of St Brice's Day 1002, when the sanctuary of St Frideswide's Priory had been completely ignored, during the commission of a grievous sin, which had most certainly not been zealously avenged.

The law code goes on to deal with offences by ministers of religion, and how they would be handled. In doing so it gives some insight into the kind of thing which Æthelræd, or rather Wulfstan, the Archbishop of York who drafted the code, wished to see tackled. A clergyman, so the code reiterated, 'has no concern with a wife or with worldly warfare'. Furthermore, it went on, 'we desire that abbots and monks live more in accordance with the rule than they have been in the habit of doing up until now'.

This concern with the moral standards of the clergy might seem somewhat disingenuous from the Archbishop of York, who was, after all, one of the very few people who actually had the power to do anything about these failings; and who was, after all, himself a pluralist.[1] Still, while his hypocrisy might be criticised, his most famous disquisition on this matter, the 'Sermon of the

---

[1] Pluralism was the practice of clergymen holding more than one benefice. It was a convention that the Archbishop of York should also hold the position of Bishop of Worcester. The see of Worcester was significantly wealthier than the see of York, and its revenues could maintain the incumbent in a suitable fashion. Rome was finding this an increasinly indefensible state of affairs, though: Wulfstan surrendered the see of Worcester around 1016, and thereafter the practice ceased.

Wolf to the English', which was delivered in 1014, was also rather dramatic.[2] It begins apocalyptically:

> Beloved men, know that which is true: this world is in haste and it nears the end. And therefore things in this world go ever the longer the worse, and so it must needs be that things quickly worsen, on account of people's sinning from day to day, before the coming of Antichrist. And indeed it will then be awful and grim widely throughout the world. Understand also well that the Devil has now led this nation astray for very many years, and that little loyalty has remained among men, though they spoke well.

He went on:

> Nothing has prospered now for a long time either at home or abroad, but there has been military devastation and hunger, burning and bloodshed in nearly every district time and again. And stealing and slaying, plague and pestilence, murrain and disease, malice and hate, and robbery by robbers have injured us very terribly. And excessive taxes have afflicted us, and storms have very often caused failure of crops; therefore in this land there have been, as it may appear, many years now of injustices and unstable loyalties everywhere among men.

Wulfstan was unimpressed by everyone. He was appalled by the Vikings, but did not really expect anything better from them. They were the manifestation of divine displeasure, and it made no sense to rage against them and their crimes. What concerned

---

2 When writing in Latin, Wulfstan often identified himself as 'Lupus', or 'the Wolf'.

him more was the degeneracy of his own society, the habit of disloyalty which had permeated it, and indeed the incompetence of Æthelræd's government. The English, he said, had brought all this on themselves. But he did share the national mood when it came to tribute. 'We pay them continually,' he grumbled, 'and they humiliate us daily.'

The exact circumstances in which Wulfstan delivered his homily is not known for sure, but its survival strongly suggests that he gave it more than once. The witan probably heard it; so, almost certainly, did anyone who listened to the Archbishop of York preaching from the pulpit. He was scathing about men who failed to defend the female members of their family:

And often ten or twelve, each after the other, insult the thegn's wife disgracefully, and sometimes his daughter or close kinswomen, while he looks on, he that considered himself brave and strong and good enough before that happened.

He also thundered against one of the grimmer elements of eleventh-century English society:

It is terrible to know what too many do often, those who for a while carry out a miserable deed, who contribute together and buy a woman as a joint purchase between them and practice foul sin with that one woman, one after another, and each after the other like dogs that care not about filth.

English society had a very dark side. A century later, William of Malmesbury was similarly appalled by the treatment of female slaves, and told his readers what could happen to them next.

'There was one custom,' he wrote, 'repugnant to nature, which they adopted: namely, to sell their female slaves, when pregnant by them and after they had satisfied their lust, either to public prostitution, or to foreign slavery.'

In the eleventh century slaves probably made up about a tenth of the population. England was a slave society. But it was not necessary to actually be a slave in order to be treated like one. Wulfstan denounced a society in which 'poor men are sorely betrayed and cruelly defrauded ... infants are enslaved by means of cruel injustices ... the rights of freemen are taken away'. William of Malmesbury was later to echo his disgust. 'The common people,' he wrote, 'left unprotected, became a prey to the most powerful, who amassed fortunes by either seizing their property or selling their persons.'

All slave societies have had their defenders. Their justifications often centre around the indulgent attitude which Scripture takes to the institution, or to the notion that for whatever reason slavery was generally thought to be unavoidable or the natural order of things. At the beginning of the eleventh century Archbishop Wulfstan disapproved, not so much of slavery, as to the maltreatment of slaves. In the Sermon of the Wolf he criticises slave owners for depriving their slaves of 'that property which, on their own time, they have obtained by means of difficult labour, or that which good men, in God's favour, have granted them, and given to them in charity for the love of God'. This reveals that slaves, at least in theory, were legally permitted to own personal possessions, though it also reveals that this right was often disregarded by slaveholders.

By the end of the eleventh century, though, the English Church clearly disapproved of the entire practice. Slavery was associated with barbarism: it was common in Scandinavia, but in most of

Western Europe, including in Normandy, it was dying out or dead. Nonetheless, it persisted, well beyond the Norman Conquest.

It is probably fair to say that there was a spectrum of freedom rather than a sharp distinction between the free and the unfree. There was a legal difference between a slave and the poorer ceorls, but in practice their lives were similar. Neither owned property; both were dependent on their lords for their livelihoods, and spent much of their lives working for those lords, but both could also, outside of that time, work for themselves as well, and keep some of the proceeds.

These social distinctions were hereditary, but they were not eternal. Slaveholders could free their slaves, and often did so in their wills. And free people could become slaves as a result of being captured in war, or as the punishment for a crime; and handing oneself into slavery was sometimes the last resort of the destitute.

How was all this received by the assembled grandees of the realm? Perhaps Wulfstan was considered a pompous egotist. The likes of Eadric Streona were almost certainly not hanging their heads in shame as he admonished them for their sins, and no doubt some of them told themselves that it was easy for Wulfstan to criticise those who had to lead men into battle. He would not be expected to fight to the death in defence of the realm himself, though the death of Ælfheah had graphically illustrated that even archbishops were not always safe from the Danes.

At the very least, Wulfstan was a pious, vain, and perhaps somewhat brave man. Æthelræd had form when it came to ruthlessly punishing subjects who displeased him (including leading clergymen, as the inhabitants of the diocese of Rochester could testify). He had fairly recently arranged the assassination of the ealdorman of Northumbria, and the same hatchet man who had carried out that murder for him was now England's foremost ealdorman as well as one of Æthelræd's most trusted servants. Wulfstan was careful to denounce all those who had shown disloyalty to their sovereign, but he was also explicitly critical of the tribute payments, and the failure to defend the country, and someone who wanted to interpret the Sermon of the Wolf as an attack on Æthelræd's kingship would have little difficulty in doing so.

That probably wasn't the dynamic between Æthelræd and Wulfstan. The Archbishop of York was very much part of the Establishment of the first quarter of the eleventh century; he had been the king's choice for the bishopric of London in 996 before being translated to York (and Worcester) six years later. It is most likely that his fulminations represent the 'official' position, and that they constitute an exculpation of royal policy. The failure to repel the Danes was a national failure, and the underlying cause was not royal incompetence but national degeneracy and the consequent wrath of God. In theory at least an archbishop urging his flock to behave in a more Christian manner was not controversial. Even so, the apocalyptic tone of the Sermon of the Wolf is that of someone who was well aware that Æthelræd's England was on the brink of a final collapse, and didn't care who he offended.

Some people, inevitably, were irreconcilable. It had been eight years since Æthelræd had ordered the assassination of his ealdorman of Northumbria. Since then, two of Ælfhelm's cousins, Sigeferth and Morcar, had risen to prominence in the Five Boroughs. Their position was a delicate one. They could not trust their king, nor could they be fully trusted in return; nonetheless, they were thegns of considerable wealth and sufficient influence to attend the witenagemot which was held at Oxford in 1015. Eadric Streona, who as ealdorman of Mercia had his own chambers in the town, invited them to visit him. They must, after what had happened to their cousin, have been suspicious, but they attended nonetheless; Eadric plied them with alcohol and then murdered them. That this was done by royal command, or at the very least with royal approval, is clear from Æthelræd's response to the assassination, which was to confiscate the dead men's property and order Sigeferth's widow to be arrested and incarcerated at Malmesbury Abbey.

No account of what Morcar or Sigeferth are supposed to have done has survived. They probably didn't need to have done anything. According to the ancient principle of the blood feud it was their duty to avenge their kinsman's death, and so Eadric in particular had good reason to want them out of the way: it is quite possible, therefore, that the killings were his initiative, and that Æthelræd's part was no more than giving the nod of approval. However, it is also quite possible that Æthelræd himself was the instigator; they may well have earned their punishment. As east midland thegns, it had been their duty to fight for their lord the king when the Danes landed. Instead, at best they capitulated to Sweyn without a fight; at worst they supported or even served in the fyrd which he raised from that region and fought for Sweyn against Æthelræd.

If that is what happened, it is difficult to summon up much sympathy for them. It would certainly explain why Æthelræd made an exception to the promise he made to forgive those who had trespassed against him, a promise which he otherwise kept. (It would also explain why he had Eadric punish the thegns rather than go through the process of a trial: strictly speaking they had been pardoned for anything they had done, which might make for some awkwardness before the assembled witan.)

And yet it appears that someone very important thought that Æthelræd's conduct here was unacceptable: his oldest surviving son, Edmund.

* * * *

In the absence of systems for recording births and deaths, estimating life expectancy in early medieval England is extremely difficult. What can tentatively be said is that childhood was a particularly dangerous time; that war, famine, and disease were all common and ended many adult lives early; that it was not particularly rare to live to sixty years of age; but that few people made it to seventy. There were exceptions: Emma of Normandy lived until her late sixties at least, Dunstan into his late seventies, and if Eilmar of Malmesbury really did remember seeing Halley's Comet in 989, then by 1066 he must have been in his eighties. Interestingly, the men of the House of Wessex, England's ruling dynasty, were not particularly long-lived: now aged around fifty, Æthelræd was already within a couple of years of being the oldest man to have worn the crown. Four of his six sons by Ælfgifu of York had already predeceased him. Edmund, their third son, was in his twenties; so, probably, was his fifth son, Eadwig. His sons by Emma of Normandy, Edward and Alfred, were not yet in their teens, and so Edmund was, for now at least, the obvious successor.

And Edmund was mightily unimpressed by what had just happened. He may have thought his father's actions were indefensible; he may have calculated that enough people would agree with such an assessment that it would be a convenient position to take. Or he may have been motivated by more primal instincts. He certainly took a shine to the damsel in distress: disregarding his father's orders, he turned up at Malmesbury, released her from her imprisonment, married her, and then demanded that Æthelræd allow him to take possession of the family estates in the Five Boroughs and Northumbria for himself. The king refused, and Edmund defied him, seizing the lands anyway.

This was open rebellion, and it was about time too. Not just because Æthelræd had forfeited any moral right to the loyalty of his people, though he had: it was quite clear from his treatment of Lincolnshire, as well as his pursuing his vendetta against Ælfhelm's kin, that he had no intention of sticking to the agreement he had made with the witan before his return to England. But there was more at stake now. Æthelræd was not just a murderous tyrant. He was King of England, at a time of enormous danger, and while Cnut was in Denmark preparing his invasion force he had concentrated on purging his political enemies. They might not have defended the country with particular vigour or enthusiasm, but then no one had shown less of those qualities on the battlefield than Æthelræd's favourite Eadric Streona. England was about to face the army of Cnut. Everyone knew it. A responsible king would have identified his best generals and given them what they needed. Instead, he played divide-and-rule. Ulfcytel was never given the recognition he should have been; and here, because he was worried about Edmund forcing the issue of the succession, he did not give him command of the royal armies.

The Danes were bound to return, and there was no prospect of Æthelræd leading any English armed forces to victory. England had suffered enough. Eadric Streona and Æthelræd had brought the country to the brink of disaster. Now, in the late summer of 1015, when the dreaded longships were once again spotted off the Kentish coast, it was too late.

Cnut was back. He sailed into the port of Sandwich, then along the south coast. The Danes carried out their usual harrying, and the West Saxons surrendered without a fight. Æthelræd, who was at Corsham in Wiltshire, was too ill to respond himself; he was probably already suffering from the disease which would soon take his life, though he managed, as Wessex fell to the Danes, to escape to London. He ordered Edmund to raise the north and the Five Boroughs, and Eadric to raise the rest of Mercia, and told them to join forces to fight the Danes. They did, but when they rendezvoused they were unable to agree on a plan of action, and they went their separate ways without engaging the enemy.

The chronicles are united in blaming Eadric. 'The ealdorman intended to betray the ætheling,' reported the *Anglo-Saxon Chronicle*, and John of Worcester elaborates by explaining that he 'laid all manner of snares' for Edmund, and 'plotted his death'. William of Malmesbury explains that Edmund had attempted to prepare for battle, but that Eadric had thwarted him. This is all rather plausible, and probably a reasonably accurate reflection of what happened, though it is worth considering these accounts with a little caution. It is quite possible that the principle difference between the two men was that Edmund wanted a showdown with Cnut, while Eadric wanted to avoid one. Perhaps Edmund was keen to prove himself in the field and considered Eadric at best a coward and at worst a traitor; perhaps Eadric, who had seen this situation on several occasions already, preferred not to be too hasty, and despaired at the inexperienced Edmund's recklessness.

This isn't to say that Eadric was right. Eadric had plenty of experience, but he hadn't had many military successes to boast about. Even so, there's a difference between being wrong and being treacherous; and up until this time, only Edmund had disobeyed his sovereign.

However, it is not surprising that Eadric should have been denied the benefit of any doubt by his contemporaries. Having fallen out with Edmund, he approached Cnut: not to offer battle, but to offer his submission, and that of the army he had just raised on behalf of King Æthelræd, and that of the forty ships whose crews he had persuaded to defect alongside him.

If the men of those forty ships constituted Thurkill's fleet, which is the obvious conclusion to which to jump, Eadric might well have persuaded the Danish mercenary to join him in transferring his allegiance to Cnut. The English sources are remarkably quiet about Thurkill's activities in this period and do not record him fighting on either side. He had clearly helped Æthelræd escape to Normandy, but thereafter he disappears from the English record. This itself is a little suspicious. Neutrality, or avoiding battle, was not (or should not have been) an option: he was paid large sums to defend the country, and if he wasn't defending the country he wasn't doing his job. According to the encomiast, who for all his deficiencies as a source is the best authority we have, Sweyn was displeased with Thurkill's remaining in Æthelræd's service. When Sweyn died, Thurkill was keen not to displease Cnut in a similar way; and so, leaving the bulk of the fleet in England, he sailed with a handful of ships back to Denmark, where he stayed for a month, and helped to persuade Cnut to invade England again, before fighting alongside his countrymen in the last campaign of the long war.

Eadric's defection, and the capitulation of Wessex, plunged England into yet another existential crisis. Edmund's first attempt to summon the fyrd failed: he might have been the king's son, but he was not the king, and the thegns refused to fight for him.

Perhaps any excuse not to take up arms yet again was welcome: any optimism which Æthelræd's campaign against Cnut had engendered had dissipated, and the best possible outcome seemed to be a quick defeat rather than months of harrying followed by yet another capitulation. Perhaps the English thegns were tired of fighting for a king who gave every impression of expecting everyone else to do his fighting for him.

Edmund tried again, this time threatening 'full penalties' to any thegns who refused to join the fyrd; he managed to cobble an army together out of the remaining fighting strength of the country, from Mercians who had not been led over to the enemy by Eadric, from East Anglians, including Ulfcytel, and from Northumbrians. Together, they moved into Cheshire, Staffordshire and Shropshire, and harried: presumably these were areas which, being under Eadric's thumb, were owned by men who had followed their ealdorman into treason. Cnut, meanwhile, harried Buckinghamshire and Bedfordshire, but when he heard that Edmund's army was in the west midlands, he spotted an opportunity and marched north to York. Uhtred hurried back to Northumbria, but rather than defend his ealdormanry he submitted to Cnut instead, presumably hoping that doing so would save his neck.

It didn't. According to the *Anglo-Saxon Chronicle*, Cnut initially accepted Uhtred's submission, but shortly afterwards, 'on the counsel of ealdorman Eadric', he had the ealdorman of Northumbria executed instead, and replaced him with his own man, Erik, who had been Sweyn's viceroy in Norway. With English resistance collapsing all around him, Edmund made for London, where Æthelræd had already taken refuge, and prepared for a last stand. Cnut gathered his forces, which rendezvoused with their ships, and then sailed to Greenwich, within sight of London.

By the time they arrived, Æthelræd had succumbed to his illness. He died on St George's Day 1016, having reigned England for thirty-eight years.

Since the great Victorian historian E. A. Freeman, in the first volume of his comprehensive *History of the Norman Conquest of England*, famously described Æthelræd as 'a bad man and a bad king', it has become fashionable for historians to attempt to rehabilitate Æthelræd from his dismal reputation. In the preface to her biography of him, Ann Williams, writing at the beginning of the twenty-first century, even went so far as to confess that she

ENGLAND IN APRIL 1016

Northumbria, East Anglia, Edmund's territories in the Five Boroughs & London supported Edmund

London

Wessex & Eadric Streona's territories in Western Mercia supported Cnut 'developed a certain fondness, even a certain admiration, for him'. The *Anglo-Saxon Chronicle*, so the argument goes, was unfair to him: written shortly after his death and the collapse of the kingdom it seemed natural to the author to tell a tale of unremitting gloom, a lament in which all the failures of the régime were magnified and all its successes diminished, dismissed, or ignored. By the twelfth century, his reputation had been shattered, and the likes of William of Malmesbury could enjoy themselves with exaggerated accounts of his ineptitude. Real life is usually more nuanced, and it is easy to see why historians have tried to find that nuance.

And it is certainly fair to say that Æthelræd had more than his fair share of bad luck. In Sweyn Forkbeard he faced an exceptionally strong adversary. He inherited a country which, despite a functioning system of military organisation, had not needed to fight for its survival, and in which too few leaders had an appetite for war. The secular élite was appallingly selfish and routinely undermined his rule. And yet for thirty years he managed to hold the country together. The machinery of government continued to work. He pre-empted an attempted coup in 1002; he decisively crushed resistance and rebellion in the Danelaw; he projected power into the rest of Britain and the Irish Sea; and he was able to do what it took to keep the Danes away for most of his reign. He did so through inglorious means, and yet the alternative quite clearly wasn't standing and fighting, and driving them away duly chastened: it was to summon armies which wouldn't appear, fight battles which would be lost, and allow the country to be stripped of all its wealth at the point of a sword. The great landowners of the realm had to pay. They were dissatisfied, but they recognised that their king was making the best of a bad situation; perhaps they even recognised that as a collective they only had themselves to blame. It is easy to hail great victories: it's much harder to recognise the work of an embattled king, surrounded on all sides by people who preferred to protect their own position than to defend their country, and whose service to his people was to mitigate the effects of a disastrous war, and try to bring it to an end, on several occasions. Æthelræd did not want to spend his reign fighting the Danes. He did not choose to be a warrior king. He was not suited to it, and he knew it: he would have much preferred not to have been one. But kings don't get to choose the circumstances in which they reign. They have a situation thrust upon them, and the situation thrust upon Æthelræd was an impossible one.

It is a seductive argument, and there's something to be said for it. Æthelræd was no warrior, and that wasn't his fault. But nor was he a gentle, civilised man with whom either contemporaries or posterity can sympathise. He was a vindictive coward. He grovelled before the powerful and, in turn, he was cruel to his subjects. He did not just allow the churches to be ravaged: he participated in it himself. He allowed sanctuary to be violated in the service of mass slaughter. He murdered his own ealdormen and harried his own people. His failure to lead an army into battle against the Danes was inexcusable. His preference for the likes of Eadric Streona is all too explicable: Æthelræd was not just inept, he was unable to put the national interest above his own.

He was indeed a bad man and a bad king.

****

The clinching argument for the importance of Æthelræd's personal deficiencies being of such great importance is what happened after he died. The city of London, the only part of the country definitively still under English control, chose Edmund as his successor; the witan, meanwhile, met at Southampton, and elected Cnut.

No doubt the election took place under Cnut's beady eye, perhaps literally. Had Edmund been concerned with constitutional principles he might well have cited the impossibility of the witan making a real choice under these circumstances to support his case. It would, of course, have been as ill-advised as the recently dead king to have openly voiced the opinion that Edmund ought to succeed his father in that forum. Equally, though, it is easy to understand why an Englishman would prefer Cnut to Edmund. Once the land was Cnut's, the harrying might finally stop. The country could hold its breath and brace itself for what the new king would do, but after a while life might even improve. As for Edmund, well, those who had endured nearly four decades of his father's rule might prefer to avoid finding out what sort of king the son would turn out to be.

Edmund was well aware that holding London would not be enough. He could deny the city to Cnut, but not indefinitely, and the longer he confined himself there the more Cnut would be able to tighten his grip on the rest of the country. And so, leaving London properly defended, Edmund slipped out and headed for the heart of Wessex. The West Saxons might have accepted Cnut as their king, but Edmund was betting on this having been through desperation and hopelessness, and that they would prefer to have one of their own, if only one of their own could offer a fighting chance.

He was right. On arrival in his ancestral homeland, the king received a warm welcome. The West Saxons had only recently submitted to Cnut, but now they repudiated him and embraced Edmund as their king.

It is tempting to raise an eyebrow, and perhaps that was the immediate reaction of many at the time, but it turned out that the thegns of Wessex were serious when they pledged their allegiance to Edmund. The new king called out the fyrd, and this time he was met with an enthusiastic response; he led his new followers against the Danes at Penselwood in Somerset, and defeated them. 'There was great slaughter,' records the *Anglo-Saxon Chronicle*, 'on both sides', while according to John of Worcester Edmund 'put them to flight'. William of Malmesbury agrees that the Danes were 'routed', while the encomiast, always reluctant to acknowledge Cnut's defeats, is silent about the matter.

Perhaps, though, this silence was less because of a desire to hide a military failure and more because of the limited scale of the engagement. It was an English victory, but it was probably little more than a skirmish. This was at most a month or two after Æthelræd's death. Cnut did not have a significant force in Somerset: the bulk of the Danish army was besieging London. So the battle was between Edmund and whichever unlucky Danes happened to have been mustered from the surrounding areas in a hurry. Still, it was a victory, and as such it could be celebrated: the English had not had many of those.

Cnut, on learning what had happened at Penselwood, sent a larger force under the command of Thurkill and Eadric Streona westwards; Edmund, knowing this would be a far greater test, marched eastwards towards it. The two armies met at Sherston, in Wiltshire, in June 1016.

Both English and Danish tradition regarded the battle as a pivotal one. Before it began, according to John of Worcester, Edmund reminded his followers that they were fighting for 'their country, their children, their wives, and their homes'. Thurkill, meanwhile,

reminded the Danes that this really was do or die. The encomiast
has him warn them that 'there was no place to which they might
flee, that they were, of course, foes in the land, and that their ships
were far from the shore, and that accordingly, if they should not
conquer, they would necessarily fall together'.

Edmund now showed what he was made of. Having drawn up
his battle plan, he took his place in the front rank of the English
shield wall, leading his men by example.

A shield wall was, as the name implies, a defensive structure,
formed by each man holding his shield out in front of him with one
hand and interlocking it with the shields of the men on either side
of him. He would hold a spear, or a seax, in the other hand, and
use it against the enemy.[3] This was the conventional formation in
northern Europe, where battles would often begin with the clash of
two shield walls. There was little room for military genius in these
encounters: they were tests of strength, endurance, and armour.

A battle would last for as long as both shield walls held. At
Sherston, the armies fought each other to a standstill. Although
both took heavy losses, neither line was broken, and it wasn't until
nightfall (around the time of the summer solstice) that they finally
separated from each other. Neither army had defeated the other, and
in the morning, both formed up again and resumed the battle. Once
more, there was no breakthrough. The fighting lasted throughout a
second day, and when night fell again, the warriors fell back again.

The encomiast attempts to award the victory to the Danes,
but the attempt is entertainingly unconvincing. 'After they had
seized the spoils from their foes,' he wrote, 'they returned and
made themselves ready for an invasion of the adjacent country.'

---

3 A seax was a bladed weapon, bigger than a knife but smaller than a sword,
   and therefore ideal for use by a warrior in a shield wall.

In other words, they withdrew, leaving Edmund in possession not just of the field of battle, but of Wessex.

Suddenly, it seemed as though England might be saved after all. Edmund had shown that a king who fought with vigour and intensity could turn an impossible position into an encouraging one, and the men of Wessex, allowing themselves to think that there was now a chance of success in the war against the Danes, joined his army as it marched eastward towards London. They arrived at the city and raised the siege, chasing the Danes and their ships away. Edmund then led his followers up the Thames to Brentford, crossed the river there, and smashed another Danish force to pieces. Just a few weeks previously Cnut had been on the point of victory: now he was on the verge of defeat.

As the news of Edmund's successes reached Wessex, there was a surge of enthusiasm for him. The battles in the West Country had not been flukes. England had a king who could take on the Danes and win. Eager to share the honour and the glory, more West Saxons leapt up from their benches, donned their armour and answered their country's call. Edmund carried out a lightning tour of his ancestral homeland, gathering new recruits and leading them back towards the enemy. And as he approached, Eadric Streona, a man who knew how to assess which way the wind was blowing and how to adapt accordingly, appeared to have been making calculations. Apparently deciding that he had been wrong to quarrel with Edmund after all, he brought his men over from Cnut's command and rejoined the English army. This time the English were unopposed until they reached Otford, in Kent, where once again they scattered the Danes.

Edmund prepared to deliver the knockout blow. It had been an extremely successful campaigning season, perhaps the most successful in the whole history of his dynasty. Cnut, on the other hand, had suffered setback after setback since Æthelræd's death. The temptation to press home the advantage was difficult to resist. The Danes were in disarray, and there might never be a better chance to crush them. Maybe they could destroy the Danish army so conclusively that it would not return for a generation. Edmund might even have smiled at the thought that when the chroniclers came to write the history of his time, they would record that two deaths just over two years apart were crucial in England's survival: that of Sweyn, who was succeeded by his inexperienced and less talented second son, and that of Æthelræd, who was succeeded by his energetic and steelier third son.

At this critical moment Edmund hesitated. The Danes were still the Danes, and as such were worthy of being taken seriously. The numerical advantage which the English enjoyed would increase as more men from Wessex, and indeed from Mercia, now that Eadric Streona was fighting on his side, joined them. Men had already been needlessly lost through carelessness, drowning in the Thames while attempting to ford the river. It might be wiser and safer to gather a larger force before fighting the battle which could dispatch Cnut for good. Furthermore, the ealdorman of Mercia advised the king that forcing such a showdown was probably unnecessary. Summer was already over, and the Danes had suffered heavy losses: better to let them sail back to Denmark.

And so the survivors were allowed to retreat further, and to finally take refuge on the Isle of Sheppey. Edmund headed westwards, and raised the fyrd for one last time.

It was a mistake.

The Danes did indeed board their ships. Their destination, though, was not continental Europe. Instead, they crossed the

Thames estuary, and rumbled into southern Mercia, where their harrying was even more savage than usual.

When the news reached Edmund, he summoned England's leading loyalists to join him. Eadric Streona, Ulfcytel of East Anglia, and Ælfric of Hampshire all gathered to fight one last decisive battle. On these men rested the nation's hopes of salvation, as even the encomiast, a hopeless partisan of Cnut, acknowledged: when, on 18 October, they formed up to face the Danes at Assandun in Essex, he has Edmund call on everyone in his army to 'fight for your liberty and your country'.[4] For the past six months the Danes had struggled against Edmund, but this time they were thoroughly prepared.

The battle was a close one, but it hinged on the pinnacle of Eadric Streona's whole treacherous career. With the armies evenly matched, and the fate of the entire country as well as the participants in the balance, he carried out the manoeuvre for which he had been preparing since he left Cnut's camp and approached Edmund's. In the midst of the fighting, with neither side yet having the upper hand, he ordered his men to turn and flee.

His change of heart had not been a change of heart after all. It had been a ruse, devised by Eadric and Cnut, and implemented at the perfect moment to do maximum damage, not just to Edmund's strategic position, but also to his men's morale. The fyrdsmen had bad memories of battlefield betrayal, of comrades fleeing before the enemy, and of the routs which could happen when the warrior code was discarded. The habit, or so they had thought, had died with Æthelræd. They had been wrong.

But if nervous eyes turned to Ælfric, who had a less than perfect record when it came to standing and fighting, they needn't have. This

---

4 Assandun is probably the village of Ashingdon, a few miles north of Southend, but no one knows for sure.

time the ealdorman of Hampshire was going to win, or he was going to go down fighting. The men of East Anglia, rallied by the presence of Ulfcytel, were not giving up either. They fought stubbornly well into the evening, but this time nightfall did not signal the end of the battle: the Danes continued to attack in the moonlight, sensing that this was their opportunity to destroy a weakened enemy.

They were right. Ulfcytel and Ælfric were killed; so were several ealdormen. Even a bishop and an abbot who had come to minister to the English army's souls were killed by Cnut's men. Edmund was not. When defeat became inevitable, he abandoned the field, incurring the disdain of the encomiast. 'Edmund,' he wrote contemptuously, 'the fugitive prince, was disgraced'.

This was an exaggeration, but there was no doubt that the Battle of Assandun had destroyed Edmund's chances of ridding the country of Cnut. He retreated westward, and considered his options.

Perhaps surprisingly, the sources agree that Eadric Streona was with Edmund in the days after the battle. Quite why Edmund tolerated his presence is incomprehensible. The encomiast's best guess is that he was 'an able counsellor', but the best exculpation of Eadric's conduct at Assandun is that his defection from Cnut had been real, and that his flight had been motivated only by selfishness or cowardice rather than by treachery. That, presumably, was what Eadric told Edmund, and presumably it was just about plausible enough to persuade a desperate king that he could indeed count the ealdorman of Mercia, and the men who would follow him into battle, among his supporters.

Might the accounts of Eadric's perfidy be exaggerated? It is sometimes suggested that they might be, but finding excuses for his actions in 1016 is even more difficult than defending his record in the preceding years. A creative advocate might enjoy the challenge of arguing that his abandonment of the dying Æthelræd can be

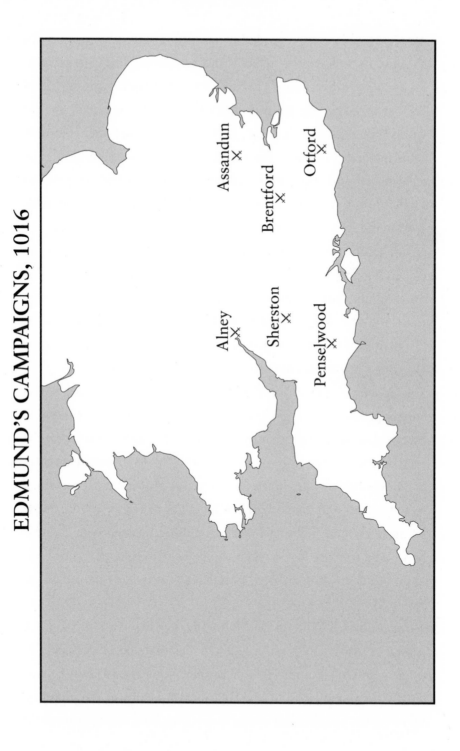

EDMUND'S CAMPAIGNS, 1016

Assandun
X

Brentford
X

Otford
X

Alney
X

Sherston
X

Penselwood
X

explained away on the grounds that, having served him loyally for so long, he was entitled to look out for the national interest. But even the most committed contrarian would avoid trying to justify his behaviour in the latter stages of Edmund's campaign against Cnut. Either he betrayed one, or he betrayed the other: the only other possibility is that he never actually acted as a double agent, and instead betrayed them both, making him perhaps the only man in English history to commit treason against three monarchs in one year.

Edmund now summoned the witan. Eadric, now again the senior ealdorman of the realm, recommended that the possibilities of making peace be investigated. Edmund put the case for carrying on the fight, but the overwhelming feeling was against him, and reluctantly the king agreed to heed the advice of his counsellors. He invited Cnut to a summit, to be held at Alney Island, near Deerhurst in Gloucestershire, 140 miles west of Assandun.

Ever since Æthelræd's exile in 1014, the witenagemot had been a very important institution in the government of England. Following Sweyn's death, it had conducted a remarkable negotiation with the man whom it had already once elected king. In making his re-election conditional, it was straying way outside its proper functions, which were to select and then advise the king, not to dictate to him. Now its members told Edmund that he could not proceed with the war he wanted to fight. It was too risky: he was to make peace instead.

Edmund did not dissolve or dismiss the witan: he did as he was told.

According to William of Malmesbury, when they met on the island of Alney, Edmund suggested deciding the succession by single combat; Cnut rejected the proposal on the basis that he was significantly smaller than the Englishman. Henry of Huntingdon, allowing his imagination to run away with him, went further, and included an account of a duel between the two men, which ended only when both were exhausted and acknowledged each other as equals. As a metaphor for the events of 1016 this may have some merit: as history, it's very unlikely.[5] Edmund may have made such an offer, but if he did he must have known it would be rejected, and so he made another, one which he knew Cnut would have to at least seriously consider. The kingdom would be divided: he would take Wessex, while Cnut would take Mercia and the Danelaw. This was essentially the deal which Alfred had made with Guthrum in 878: Edmund could consider it peace with honour.

Cnut was ready to accept. The Danes had taken heavy casualties, and although the act of making the offer had emphasised the weakness of Edmund's position, there was little doubt that if it was rejected he would rather resume hostilities than submit. It was also clear that Edmund was an exceptional leader, a decent commander, and able to muster significant numbers. The division of England was therefore probably unsustainable: neither man was likely to accept being king of half a country for very long, and so a resumption of hostilities sooner or later was inevitable. But for the time being at least, agreeing a truce was the best course of action. Cnut responded with a counter-offer. He demanded tribute, and that the city of London, which had held out against him and his father for so long, be part of his kingdom. Through gritted teeth, Edmund acquiesced.

---

5 Challenging an enemy to single combat could, of course, be entirely rational: the challenger just had to believe that he had a greater chance of prevailing through single combat than through conventional warfare. However, anyone issuing such a challenge was admitting that he thought his overall military position was weaker than that of his opponent, so the logical response was to refuse. Usually, therefore, these challenges were rhetorical flourishes, either by the individuals themselves, or by chroniclers. Norman chronicler William of Poitiers has William the Conqueror challenge Harold to single combat on the morning of the Battle of Hastings: there is no corroboration, because the tale was almost certainly made up.

The division of the country only lasted for a few weeks. On the last day of November, Edmund died. There is no contemporary suggestion of foul play, but later chroniclers claimed that he had been assassinated. Henry of Huntingdon has the most entertaining account of the alleged murder:

> When the king, fearful and most formidable to his enemies, was prospering in his kingdom, he went one night to the lavatory to answer a call of nature. Then the son of Ealdorman Eadric, who by his father's plan was concealed in the pit of the privy, struck the king twice with a sharp knife in the private parts, and leaving the weapon in his bowels, fled away.

William of Malmesbury tells a similar tale, though he has Eadric bribing royal servants to do away with the king rather than entrusting the job to a son.

Edmund's death was certainly very convenient for Cnut, and plotting his murder was entirely consistent with Eadric Streona's career. Still, it is quite possible that the ealdorman of Mercia had nothing to do with the death of the king. Edmund might have died of wounds he'd received in battle; or he might, like his grandfather and several of his brothers, have died of natural causes at a relatively young age.

His death, naturally, was mourned. Even the encomiast conceded that the English 'wept long and sorely'. If anyone could have saved them from Cnut, it was Edmund. But they were now at the mercy of the Danes, and they had learned from bitter experience just how little of it they could expect.

Cnut summoned the witan. He noted that many of those present had witnessed the treaty he had made with Edmund.

Did any remember, he asked innocently, what arrangements had been made in the event of the early death of one of the parties? Was there, for instance, a clause in which it was agreed that the throne would pass to a brother or a son? The assembled nobility of England assured him that there wasn't. Indeed, Cnut should not only assume the throne, he should also become the guardian of Edmund's two infant sons, Edmund and Edward.[6] Neither boy was more than a year old when their father died. For as long as they lived they would be a potential threat; which is presumably why, at least according to John of Worcester, Eadric Streona advised Cnut to have them killed.

But Cnut could not quite bring himself to give that order. Perhaps he feared the potential consequences, for his regime or for his reputation. He might even have worried about his immortal soul. So instead of having the boys murdered, he denounced Eadric's proposal as a 'foul disgrace' and had them sent to his kinsman the King of Sweden, Olof, an ally in a faraway country where their deaths could be more easily concealed. But Olof was reluctant to help, and before they could be slaughtered they were spirited out of Sweden and, eventually, found refuge in Hungary.

There is no other source to confirm that Eadric suggested murdering the æthelings. But if that is indeed what happened, and there's no reason to suggest that John of Worcester was making it up, the story is quite remarkable for another reason: not as evidence for the ealdorman's moral fibre, but because it shows the king outwitting him. Eadric had been one of the greatest men of

---

6 Baby Edmund may well have been born posthumously: Old English kings didn't usually name their sons after themselves. Or the two boys may have been twins, in which case they were the first, and possibly the only, twins ever to be born to an English monarch.

the realm for a decade. His new lord was still a teenager. And yet the wily old fox was cornered by a sharp-witted young hound.

Cnut knew how to manipulate advisors. For Eadric's advice, and Cnut's rejection of it, to have been recorded for posterity, the exchange must have taken place in public, perhaps at a meeting of the witan. Cnut had no doubt already decided on his preferred course of action before asking Eadric for his opinion. The infants could not stay, and they could not be killed, so they had to be exiled, even if that exile was presented as their being placed with their guardian's trustworthy relatives for their upbringing. If they survived long enough, then they might have to be quietly done away with, but that was far in the future. There was no need to consult anyone. So why ask?

Quite possibly because it was impossible to answer. What were the options? To suggest that the æthelings be allowed to grow up in England would have been to advise the king to nurture his own rivals, and any counsellor who recommended such a course of action might raise questions about his own loyalty as well as his political nous. (As for the 'right' answer, in the sense of the course of action which Cnut himself eventually took, that was easier done than said.) Cnut gave Eadric the opportunity to discredit himself, and Eadric, possibly because he was trying too hard to convince Cnut of his loyalty, badly misjudged the situation and took it.

Why, then, did Eadric, the consummate politician, get it so wrong? Presumably he reckoned that if Cnut wanted to use him then he would want to use him as Æthelræd had done. Eadric had been an enforcer and, in a way, the archetypal 'wicked counsellor': a man who would do with relish what the king might be too squeamish to do himself, and a man whose reputation could shield the king from the worst opprobrium of the victims of royal policy. It's not completely inconceivable that Eadric considered himself to be playing a self-sacrificial role: in advocating the murder of two babies he was allowing himself, rather than the king, to be blamed for a crime which, were it ever to actually be committed, would only ever be carried out at Cnut's command.

Cnut did not see it this way. It wasn't just that he didn't want infant civilian royal blood on his hands, though clearly he didn't. It wasn't just that he was unimpressed with Eadric's lack of judgment, though clearly he was. And it wasn't just that he was appalled by Eadric's moral deficiencies, though it certainly suited him to be able to angrily distance himself from an unpopular ealdorman and his reprehensible record.

Indeed, if that were his objective all along, might Cnut have set Eadric up? Could he have privately hinted that he needed the highest-ranking English ealdorman to call for a political assassination to provide cover for him when he decided to authorise it? Could he even have explicitly primed him, implying or promising that he would sadly nod and accept that the safety of his kingdom depended on it?

Of course he could. And if that's what happened, well, there would be some poetic justice in Eadric Streona having been so effectively double-crossed.

In any case, the boys were not harmed. One of them, Edmund, died in Eastern Europe without leaving any children. But his brother, known to history as Edward 'the Exile', was still alive forty years later, when he briefly reappears in our story.

Cnut now set about reorganising the government. Whereas Æthelræd had preferred not to allow his ealdormen too much authority, Cnut's approach was different. England, he reasoned, was too large for one man to govern, and so he adapted the system with which he was most familiar. His ancestors had ruled Denmark, as his brother did, themselves. But they did not try to do the same in Norway, when that country was under Danish control, or in Orkney. Instead they installed jarls, men who could be trusted to exercise royal authority on their behalf.

Erik, whom Cnut had just put in charge of the north after having Uhtred executed, had previously been Sweyn's jarl in Norway. (He had lost the position when Sweyn died, and the Norwegians had chosen Olaf to succeed him, and chased the Danes out.) Cnut essentially restored his old status to him, appointing him not ealdorman but *jarl* – or, in English, Earl – of Northumbria. Eadric was similarly transformed from ealdorman to Earl of Mercia, and Thurkill was appointed Earl of East Anglia. Wessex did not yet need an earl: Cnut was going to govern it himself.

Then the new king decided to wield his seax. One of the first to go was the Earl of Mercia. Cnut had been content to exploit his duplicity for as long as it was useful to him, but it was the last quality he wanted at the heart of his government. There was a bloody purge, with several prominent Englishmen among its victims: three ealdormen's sons were executed along with Eadric Streona in 1017, followed by another ealdorman less than three years later. Some of these executions, including that of Eadric himself, were intended to punish the betrayal of Æthelræd and Edmund, or at least that was the official version. Certainly Cnut had been thoroughly unimpressed by those who had betrayed their kings, despite having personally benefitted. By punishing them anyway, he was upholding the majesty of the Crown: these men had broken their oaths of allegience and deserved their fate. But there was a pragmatic reason to eliminate such men too. The encomiast has Cnut ask a simple rhetorical question of the likes of Eadric: 'shall you, who have deceived your lord with guile, be capable of being true to me?'

Dealing with Eadwig, Edmund's younger brother and the last surviving son of Æthelræd's marriage to Ælfgifu of York, was trickier. There was no crime of which to accuse him, and similar considerations applied to him as had applied to Edmund's infant sons: evidently Cnut did not think he could publicly execute him for the crime of having a rival claim to the throne, so instead he banished him, and then later gave the order for him to be assassinated.

There is an intriguing reference in the *Anglo-Saxon Chronicle* entry for 1017 to 'Eadwig, King of the Ceorls', whom Cnut banished but with whom, at least according to John of Worcester, he was eventually reconciled. Frustratingly, there is no further information about this individual. Quite possibly he never existed, and it was a title which was briefly attached to the ætheling of that name. The *Anglo-Saxon Chronicle* entries for Cnut's reign appear to have been written some time after the events which they describe: information is rather scanty and occasionally it is known to be inaccurate.[7] Maybe, after his brother's death, Eadwig attempted to challenge for the throne himself, called out the fyrd, and received some support. Such a bid would have been quite obviously doomed, and is unlikely to have been supported by many members of the witan, who had plenty to lose from opposing the man whom they had just elected; those whom it did attract could be dismissed as mere ceorls, even if a few of them were from thegnly families. It is tempting to start joining up too many dots here, and to suggest that perhaps those ealdormen's sons who were executed in 1017 had been part of an abortive plot in which their fathers were too sensible to participate.

---

7 The *Chronicle* dates Cnut's pilgrimage to Rome, for example, to 1031, but it actually happened four years earlier: he attended the coronation of Conrad II, the Holy Roman Emperor, which took place in 1027.

But it's also tempting to speculate about the tantalising hint of an eleventh-century peasants' revolt. In the Sermon of the Wolf, the Archbishop of York had lamented that 'there are in the land many who betray their lords in various ways', and perhaps this wasn't just a reference to events on the battlefield. The ruling orders had failed miserably, and the ceorls had suffered for it. Thegns who consistently failed to tackle the Danes, but who never failed to demand yet another contribution to the *geld* or the *gafol*, must have been hated. It is not at all difficult to see why an English ceorl might conclude that those above him in the social hierarchy had not kept their part of the ancient bargain: they had taken his service, but they had done nothing to protect him from their enemies. And whereas such murmurings would, in ordinary times, be promptly crushed, the upper echelons of society had themselves been shattered by the battles of 1016. Perhaps Eadwig, the King of the Ceorls, claimed to speak for the ordinary man of early eleventh-century England.

* * *

The Encomium was written to glorify Queen Emma, and so it is perhaps not a surprise that it should include passages such as this one, describing Cnut's search for a spouse:

> The king lacked nothing, except a most noble wife. Such a one he ordered to be sought everywhere for him, in order to obtain her hand lawfully when she was found, and to make her the partner of his rule, when she was won. Therefore journeys were undertaken through realms and cities and a royal bride was sought, but it was with difficulty that a worthy one was ultimately found, after being sought far and wide. This imperial bride was, in fact, found within

the bounds of Gaul, and to be precise in the Norman area, a lady of the greatest nobility and wealth, but yet the most distinguished of the women of her time for delightful beauty and wisdom, inasmuch as she was a famous queen. In view of her distinguished qualities of this kind, she was very much desired by the king...

She refused ever to become the bride of Cnut unless he would affirm to her by oath that he would never set up the son of any wife other than herself to rule after him, if it happened that God should give her a son by him. For she had information that the king had sons by some other woman, so she, wisely providing for her offspring, knew in her wisdom how to make arrangements in advance, which were to be to their advantage. Accordingly the king found what the lady said acceptable, and when the oath had been taken, the lady found the will of the king acceptable, and so, thanks be to God, Emma, noblest of women, became the wife of the very mighty King Cnut.

The *Anglo-Saxon Chronicle* was pithier and altogether more honest. 'The king,' it reads, 'commanded Richard's daughter, the widow of the other king, Æthelræd, to be fetched for his queen.'

Almost every element of the encomiast's account is misleading. One thing Cnut did not lack was a noble wife. He had one, Ælfgifu of Northampton, the daughter of Ælfhelm, whom he had married several years before. The encomiast refers to her as 'some other woman', but she had already borne him two sons, Sweyn (after his grandfather) and Harold (after his uncle). There was no need for a search to be carried out: for Cnut to marry Emma suited both England and Normandy.

It wasn't, of course, just Cnut who already had children. Emma did too. The encomiast's attempts not to embarrass his patron are entertaining: he decided that he had better acknowledge the existence of Edward and Alfred, as they were going to become far too prominent to ignore, but he preferred not to give Æthelræd the same courtesy, and so his account heavily implies that the boys were Cnut's. When, soon after their marriage, Emma gave birth to another son, Harthacnut, the royal couple 'sent their other legitimate sons to Normandy to be brought up'.

This is sometimes dismissed as improbable, but it doesn't seem all that unlikely. Edward and Alfred were sent to Normandy ahead of their father at the end of 1013. That they might have returned to England once their father was restored is certainly possible: Edward was sent back in the spring of 1014 to convey Æthelræd's message (agreeing to reform, and offering a general amnesty in return for being allowed to return) to the witan, but what happened next is not mentioned: Edward might have stayed in England, or he might have reported back to Normandy and then remained there, or he might have reported back to Normandy and then returned alongside his father in the spring of 1014. Alfred's movements are even less clear, but he might well have accompanied either his brother or his father on one of their voyages to England, and certainly if either or both were in England when Edmund Ironside took power, they were exiled shortly thereafter.

The reference to 'legitimate sons', though, is deliberately misleading. Of course Edward and Alfred were legitimate; so, though, were Sweyn and Harold. Cnut's bigamy is sometimes explained by suggesting that his first wedding had been *more danico*, a 'handfasting' ceremony 'in the Danish custom'. It's a tidy explanation, because it gives an answer as to why he found setting Ælfgifu aside straightforward; it may also have been that a traditional Scandinavian ceremony was rather different to a formal Christian one, and suggesting that he had never been 'properly' married might have been a way for clergymen who ought to have disapproved of a king having two wives to justify Cnut doing so. Even so, Ælfgifu was quite clearly more than a concubine, and her sons were quite clearly considered potential successors to their father.

As for the oath guaranteeing the English succession to a son, such a promise was easy for Cnut to make. He would, after all, never have to make good on it. The royal couple could, of course, try to ensure that any son they might have would become England's next king, but there could be no promises, or at least none that could be relied on: the witan would make their decision when the time came.

In 1018, Cnut levied a massive tax, raising £72,000 from the native population, plus an extra £10,500 from the city of London. There can be no doubt that this was a heavy burden for the country to bear. Even the archbishopric of Canterbury, and the famous abbeys of Glastonbury and Malmesbury, had to sell off some of their lands in order to pay their share of the bill. Thereafter, the *geld* became a routine annual payment to fund the armed forces, though not on that scale.

The new king appointed men whom he trusted to key positions. Many of these, such as Earls Erik and Thurkill, were fellow Danes. Cnut had Danish courtiers in his household and Danish commanders of his armed forces. But he did not try to govern England without the English, and after the initial reshuffle there was no further assault on the natives' positions. Indeed, once the taxes of 1018 had been collected, most of the Scandinavian mercenaries were paid off, and the king's next expedition saw several Englishmen serving in his army.

That expedition was prompted by the death of Cnut's brother, Harald, the King of Denmark. The circumstances of his death are unknown, but it left a vacancy, and Cnut was the only credible candidate to fill it. Even so, he would have to fight for it, or at the very least demonstrate to the rest of Scandinavia that fighting him for it would be unwise. He set sail for Denmark, leaving Thurkill as his regent in England, and subdued the land of his birth without much difficulty.

England remained quiet while he was gone. Cnut had made enough of an impression. Taxation aside, there was no particular reason to rebel against him, and even the *geld* may not have seemed quite so onerous as it had in the past: yes, it was significantly larger, but it was extracted from a country which had not been plundered for two years. Cnut's accession in Denmark was, in this respect, particularly good news for England. The new king would use his authority to extract financial resources from the country. But this was far better than having a foreign warlord extract the country's resources by force. Cnut was a foreigner, but he was determined to rule the English in the manner to which they had become accustomed, only better; in the light of the disastrous thirty-eight-year reign from which the country was just recovering, this would not be difficult.

While in Denmark, Cnut wrote to the English people. The letter was clearly intended for a fairly wide audience, and was perhaps read out at public meetings. He began by defending the amount of taxation which he had just extracted, and explaining how it had helped the very people who might complain about it:

> I have not spared my money as long as hostility was threatening you. I have with God's help put an end to it with my money. Then I was informed that greater danger was approaching us than we liked at all; and then I went myself with the men who accompanied me to Denmark, from where the greatest injury had come to you, and with God's help I have taken measures so that

never henceforth shall hostility reach you from there as long as you support me rightly and my life lasts.

He also ordered his reeves and his ealdormen, plus the bishops and the archbishops, and Thurkill personally, to govern the country justly in his absence, and demanded that the people obey the laws which had just been promulgated at Oxford.

This law code, drawn up by Wulfstan, whom Cnut had inherited from Æthelræd, was more detailed than its predecessors, and covered a wide range of laws, both ecclesiastical and secular. Rather interestingly, one of its earliest items is a rejection of what the framers of the Constitution of the United States would have called cruel and unusual punishment: 'The decree of the councillors is that although a person sins and commits a serious offence, the punishment be prescribed as is appropriate before God and acceptable to men.'

It goes on to emphasise the importance of forgiveness, citing the Lord's Prayer, and then echoes Wulfstan's earlier code, requiring that 'Christian men be not condemned to death, at least for very trivial offences'. Cnut himself, well before he was King of England, had exemplified this mercy: his mutilation of the hostages in 1014 is often interpreted as a barbaric act, intended to punish and to intimidate, but it was more merciful than the alternative, which was having them killed.

This theme runs through the code. Punishments for criminals were mitigated by the phrase 'unless they cease'. There was emphasis on the obedience and loyalty due to one's social superiors; there was a reminder that those in holy orders were expected to be celibate; there was, also, an injunction against bigamy, which may have raised the odd eyebrow at the witenagemot where the document was formally approved. The ecclesiastical dues which the laity were expected to pay to the Church were reiterated, as was the requirement to observe the Sabbath and to observe fast days (which included every Friday). The laws around the coinage were restated, and those around inheritances; so too was the responsibility to contribute to the maintenance of bridges and fortifications, and the duty to do military service.

Wulfstan, who had been at the top of English politics for a quarter of a century, was now an old man, and this was his last great contribution to the country. Perhaps Cnut allowed himself a satisfied smile as the aged archbishop, who had once seen him as a scourge sent by the Almighty to punish the English for their sins, now produced a statement of intent on his behalf. Cnut was not just a Scandinavian barbarian: he was King of England, and he was going to do it properly.

Indeed, the men with whom Cnut most clashed appear to have been his fellow Danes, while he was prepared to give Englishmen, including those whose kinsmen he had executed, a chance. Shortly after his return from Denmark he banished Thurkill; they were reconciled a couple of years later, and the Earl of East Anglia was sent to exercise the authority of a *jarl* in Denmark. Cnut sent Harthacnut to Denmark, and made Thurkill his guardian; and that is the last posterity hears of him. Erik, meanwhile, also disappears from the historical record after 1023. William of Malmesbury and Henry of Huntingdon say that he too was banished, but there is no record in the contemporary chronicles, nor indeed in any Scandinavian source.

It has been suggested that Thurkill may have been replaced as Earl of East Anglia by one of Cnut's Danish courtiers, Osgod Clapa, though there isn't any real evidence for this. It is just that his presence fills a gap: there is no record of an Earl of East Anglia between Thurkill's return to Denmark and the early to mid-1040s, when Osgod Clapa was exiled. This is immensely unsatisfactory, but it's the best we can do: the historical record for England in the 1020s is extremely patchy. These were not interesting times, a blessing for which the native inhabitants could heave a sigh of relief.

In Mercia, though, Eadric was not replaced by a Dane. Instead, Cnut appointed Leofric, whose brother had been among those executed in 1017. Leofric was the son of a Mercian ealdorman who had served Æthelræd; his wife was the (in)famous Lady Godiva (or, in the original Old English, Godgifu), who almost certainly did not ride naked through the streets of Coventry.[8] He was an excellent choice: Leofric, a devout Christian, provided stability as Earl of Mercia for the next thirty years. In Northumbria, Erik was replaced by another Scandinavian, or at least another man with Scandinavian origins. Siward (who makes an appearance in Shakespeare's *Macbeth*) was nicknamed 'the Strong': his origins are obscure, but he did what Kings of England needed doing in that earldom, which was to prevent events there from becoming a national problem.

While on campaign in Denmark, Cnut had noticed the ability of a South Saxon thegn. Godwin was the son of Wulfnoth, whose hijacking of twenty ships had led to the destruction of the English fleet a decade previously. When Æthelræd's eldest son, Æthelstan, had died in 1014, he bequeathed lands in Sussex to Godwin. These may have been lands which had originally been his father's: Wulfnoth was no doubt outlawed after his escapade, and in those circumstances his property would normally have reverted to the Crown. In restoring them to Wulfnoth's son, Æthelstan may have been recognising that his father's infamously bad judgement had been especially unfair on this particular family; it may even have been that by the late 1010s having been an antagonist of Eadric Streona's was better than having been

---

8 The tale was invented later, possibly as people sought to explain how so distinguished and dignified a man as Leofric could have had such utterly unimpressive sons and grandsons.

an ally of his. Still, Godwin was the son of a convicted traitor when he accompanied the new king on his Danish campaign.

In battle, Godwin distinguished himself. Henry of Huntingdon suggests that he carried out a night attack on Cnut's enemies, without consulting the king first, which was a rather audacious thing for him to have done, and is probably invented. Henry was probably trying to explain why someone of Godwin's relatively unimpressive lineage should have risen as high as he did. For Godwin rose very high indeed. With Denmark now added to England, Cnut had two realms to rule, and he could not be in two places at once. His priority, for much of the rest of his reign, would have to be Scandinavia: not so much because it was his ancestral homeland as because that is where his position was most open to challenge. (He was to spend rather more of his reign defending his position in Denmark than he did in England, and more English warriors saw action in his service in Scandinavia than in defence of their own country.) He would be spending plenty of time outside the country, and could not do without a deputy in Wessex. The southern earldom, which the king had originally intended to keep for himself, was the wealthiest and the most populous, and therefore the most prestigious. Cnut quite clearly rated Godwin, and trusted him too: he allowed him to marry his wife's sister-in-law, Gytha, and he also appointed him to the vacant earldom.

As it turned out three of Cnut's earls remained in their positions for more than a quarter of a century. Siward, Earl of Northumbria; Leofric, Earl of Mercia; and Godwin, Earl of Wessex; all of whom were appointed by Cnut, served both of his sons and held their earldoms (with one brief but dramatic interlude in 1051/2) until their deaths in the 1050s.

* * * *

In the Sermon of the Wolf, the Archbishop of York lamented that English Christians did not treat the Church as respectfully as the inhabitants of 'heathen lands' treated 'the servants of false gods'. He did not name those heathen lands, though it isn't much of a stretch to assume that he meant his audience to understand that he was talking about Denmark. Yet Denmark had been part of Christendom, at least nominally, since the conversion of Harald Bluetooth, Sweyn Forkbeard's father, in the second half of the tenth century.

It is easy to sneer at or dismiss Cnut's Christianity. In several obvious ways he was very far from a perfect Christian prince, and this is sometimes explained by noting that Christianity's roots in Denmark were still somewhat shallow, and certainly shallower than they were in England: converting a king was one thing, but winning the souls of his people was quite another. (There is a hint in the Sermon of the Wolf that this may have been true in England too: his demand that 'heathen practice' be cast out' may be a reference to the ongoing survival of some elements of Germanic pagan traditions among the English.) However, it's worth remembering that Cnut's failure, and indeed that of his fellow Danes, to conform to all the precepts of the Christian faith was far from unique. If the murder of an archbishop should have been unthinkable to a Christian, so should the burning of a church and the slaughter of those inside it. If plundering ecclesiastical property was wrong, it was wrong when Æthelræd ordered his men to ravage Rochester. And if Viking raiding was inconsistent with the Sermon on the Mount, then so was the Old English warrior code. Cnut's Christianity was authentic.

In 1027 he want on a pilgrimage to Rome, and attended the coronation of the new Holy Roman Emperor. He went, so he told the English in another letter, 'to pray for the forgiveness of my sins', but also 'for the welfare of my dominions and the people under my rule'. On his way, he was generous with his gifts to the religious establishments he visited. The encomiast was particularly impressed with Cnut's contribution to his own abbey, where he presented his offering: 'not a mean one, nor such as might be shut in any bag, but a man brought it, huge as it was, in an ample fold of his cloak'. While in the Eternal City, he tackled the great and the good of European royalty on behalf of English pilgrims and merchants, persuading them to lift the barriers and tolls which were routinely levied on travellers. He also convinced the Pope to stop charging extortionate fees to archbishops when, on being consecrated, they went to Rome to receive their pallium. His return to a grateful people was via Denmark, where there were some minor disturbances to deal with; there were no such problems in England, where everything was calm.

Henry of Huntingdon's famous tale about Cnut should be seen in this context. Disappointingly it is almost certainly apocryphal. (Cnut was a shrewd political operator, and even had such a stunt appealed to him, he would probably have been far more aware than the twelfth-century historian how it would be misinterpreted.) Even so, it gives an insight into popular memory of the king:

When he was at the height of his ascendancy, he ordered his chair to be placed on the sea shore as the tide was coming in. Then he said to the rising tide, 'You are subject to me, as the land on which I am sitting is mine, and no one has resisted my overlordship with impunity. I command you, therefore, not to rise on my land, nor to presume to wet the clothing or limbs of your master.' But the sea came up as usual, and disrespectfully drenched the king's feet and shins. So jumping back, the king cried, 'Let all the world know that the power of kings is empty and worthless, and there is no king worthy of the name except for Him by whose will heaven, earth and sea obey eternal laws.' Thereafter King Cnut never wore the golden crown, but placed it on the image of the crucified Lord, in eternal praise of God the great king.

* * * *

Being King of Denmark and England had not been enough for Cnut. In 1028 he had taken advantage of commotions in Norway to assert his claim there too. Norway's king, Olaf, had seized control of the country after Sweyn Forkbeard's death, and had been reigning ever since. However, in that year there had been a rising against Olaf, who had found himself chased out of the country. Cnut, seeing an opportunity, had invaded and seized the kingdom for himself. He had appointed Hakon, the son of Erik, Earl of Northumbria, as its governor, but Hakon had died in a shipwreck little more than a year after taking office. Olaf had tried to return, but had been killed by the people whom he sought to rule. It was at this point that Cnut's first wife, Ælfgifu of Northampton, reappeared: evidently she was rather more important than the encomiast allows, as she had been sent, with her elder son Sweyn, to govern Norway on Cnut's behalf.

It was not a great success. Ælfgifu and Sweyn were not helped by a series of bad harvests, but their rule was particularly unpopular, and by the mid-1030s they too found themselves at the wrong end of a Norwegian uprising, one in which they were expelled from the country in favour of Olaf's eleven-year-old son, Magnus.

Cnut had lost one of his territories, but it was too late to do anything about it. In November 1035 he died, aged only about forty.

THE HOUSE OF WESSEX

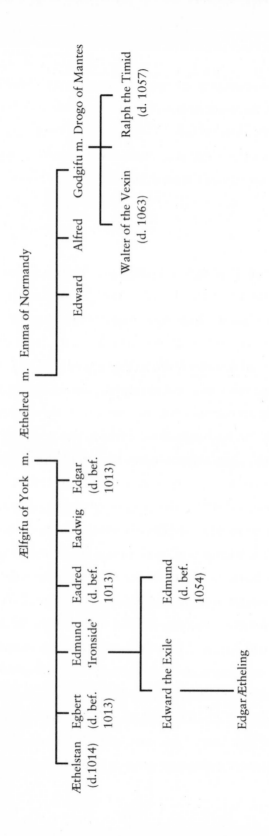

4

GOOD KING EDWARD

To be a king, and wear a crown, is a thing more glorious to them
that see it, than it is pleasing to them that bear it.

Queen Elizabeth I

Cnut's bigamy, however convenient it might have been for
him, created problems after his death. He left two surviving
sons: Harthacnut, the son of Emma of Normandy, and Harold
'Harefoot', the son of Ælfgifu. Sweyn would have been another
potential candidate for the English crown, but he died shortly after
his father in 1036.

The witan's preferred successor was Harthacnut. But Harthacnut
was in Scandinavia, securing the throne of Denmark; he was also
preparing for war with Norway, though eventually he and Cnut's
successor in that country, Magnus 'the Good', concluded a peace
treaty rather than resort to war, agreeing that, should either of
them die childless, the other would inherit their throne.

To begin with the witan tolerated his Scandinavian commitments.
The *Anglo-Saxon Chronicle* records that Harold Harefoot was

appointed 'governor' of England, 'for himself and for his brother'. However, by 1037 their patience had evidently run out. Harthacnut had 'stayed too long in Denmark', and it was decided that Harold should become king after all. One of his first actions was to have his stepmother, Emma, banished.

It was in these circumstances, with the succession to the Crown uncertain, that one of the exiled æthelings made a trip back to England. In 1036 Alfred, the younger son of Æthelræd and Emma of Normandy, arrived on the south coast. This was not an attempt at (re)conquering the country: Alfred didn't come alone, but his entourage consisted of a few hundred followers, not an invasion force. Even so, his presence was unwanted. He had been prompted, so it seems, by his mother, and although he did not come with an army he was doubtless hoping to receive a warm welcome.[1]

If so he was to be sorely disappointed. He was apprehended by Godwin, Earl of Wessex, and handed over to the royal authorities. It seems that their intention, at first at least, was to blind him rather than kill him (which itself shows how insignificant a threat he posed, even in the unstable circumstances of the time), but they did it so brutally that he died of his wounds.

In years to come Edward was to blame Godwin for his brother's death. Yet it's difficult to see what else Godwin should have done. As Earl of Wessex he owed his allegiance to the king. There was, of course, some ambiguity about the identity of the king in 1036,

---

1 According to the Norman chronicler William of Jumièges, Edward was also invited by his mother to make a trip to England, did so, found that there was no support for him, and prudently returned to Normandy. There is no corroborating evidence for this, but nor was there any reason (that we can discern) for William of Jumièges to have fabricated the story, and if Emma was trying to organise a rebellion against Harold Harefoot then it would have made sense for Edward, the elder son, to have been in England as well as Alfred.

but it was either Harold Harefoot or it was Harthacnut, and if it was Harthacnut then Harold was at the very least his officially designated regent. There was quite clearly no real support in 1036 for the idea that Emma's eldest son by Æthelræd was somehow the 'rightful' king.[2]

Harold Harefoot's reign only lasted another three years. He died in 1040, aged just twenty-four, apparently of natural causes, and was succeeded by Harthacnut, whose reign was also brief and ignominious. According to the *Anglo-Saxon Chronicle*, he 'did nothing worthy of a king', and it's not easy to find evidence to contradict this view. On arrival in England he had his half-brother's body dug up from its grave and thrown into a pit; he then levied a heavy tax to pay for the army which had accompanied him to England. He doubled the size of the navy, which incurred further taxation, and when the people of Worcester resisted his demands he had the town harried. He also had Eadwulf, Earl of Bernicia, murdered.[3]

But Harthacnut was dying, and it seems that he knew it. Like his predecessor he was a young man with no son to succeed him. Life expectancy in the Danish royal house had collapsed: Sweyn had lived well into his fifties; Cnut lived until his early forties at most. Cnut's brother, and two of his sons, had already died in their beds in very early adulthood. Perhaps they were suffering from a genetic disease. After Harthacnut, there was only one possible successor: Edward, who had been exiled to Normandy as a boy and had been

---

2 Indeed, when Harthacnut became King, Godwin was put on trial for Alfred's murder and exonerated.

3 As Earl of Bernicia, the northern part of Northumbria, Eadwulf was subordinate to Siward, the Earl of Northumbria. Nonetheless he was an earl, and having him murdered without a trial was perhaps a little too reminiscent of Æthelræd. (What Eadwulf had done to anger Harthacnut is not known.)

there for nearly thirty years. In 1041, presumably at his mother's instigation, he was invited to return to England.⁴ He was then 'sworn in' as king.⁵

Emma was not delighted at this turn of events. Harthacnut was without doubt her favourite son, and her relationship with Edward was a difficult one. She had, after all, left him in Normandy and married his father's nemesis, and according to the *Anglo-Saxon Chronicle* she 'did less for him than he would have liked before he became king'. He was, nonetheless, now her best option: when Harthacnut died Edward would be her last surviving son, and although they were far from close, she presumably hoped for slightly better treatment than she had received from Harold Harefoot.

Harthacnut died in the summer of 1042 after less than two years on the throne. His death is unlikely to have been unexpected, but it does appear to have been sudden: he was drinking at a wedding when he collapsed. He was unable to speak, and six days later he was dead. At this point, the *Chronicle* records that 'all the people chose Edward for their king', and he was consecrated on Easter Day 1043, nearly a year later.

It seems that the accession of Edward was a cause for celebration. According to the *Vita Ædwardi Regis*, the 'Life of King Edward', which was written around 1066, 'the English, who had suffered so long under the yoke of the barbarians', were delighted. 'Now

---

4 From what we know of Harthacnut it is unlikely that he was particularly exercised by what would happen to England after his death: the country was never his priority, nor does he appear to have felt much affection towards its people.

5 Crowning a king while his predecessor was still alive did not usually happen in England, which is another reason to suppose that Harthacnut knew he was dying: it would have made no sense for a healthy king in his early twenties to have settled the succession on his significantly older half-brother.

that the kingdom was settled under its native rule,' the anonymous author reported, 'there was rejoicing by all.'[6]

If Emma rejoiced, it was precipitate of her. Shortly after his coronation, Edward had her treasury seized, and she lived out the rest of her life in quiet retirement, away from her son's court, where she was not welcome.

So who was Edward? The same source describes him as:

a very proper figure of a man – of outstanding height, and distinguished by his milky white hair and beard, full face and rosy cheeks, thin white hands and long translucent fingers; in all the rest of his body he was an unblemished royal person. Pleasant, but always dignified, he walked with eyes downcast, most graciously affable to one and all. If some cause aroused his temper, he seemed as terrible as a lion, but he never revealed his anger by railing. To all petitioners he would either grant graciously, or graciously deny, so that his gracious denial seemed like the highest generosity. In public he carried himself as a true king and lord; in private with his courtiers as one of them, but with royal dignity unimpaired.

Physically, this does resemble the Edward of the Bayeux Tapestry. The famous embroidery was commissioned by Odo, Bishop of Bayeux, Earl of Kent, and William of Normandy's half-brother, around 1070, and produced by English seamstresses in the vicinity of Canterbury. There have been attempts to ascribe political opinions to the Tapestry's makers, but none of them are particularly convincing, and certainly when it comes to this question by far the

---

6 The anonymous author was probably a monk of St Bertin's Abbey in St Omer: that is, the same monastery which produced the encomiast.

most likely reason for the consistency between the biography and the textile is because that's what Edward looked like.

His appearance might not have been wholly without meaning though. William of Malmesbury tells us that Englishmen tended to be clean-shaven; the Bayeux Tapestry depicts them as having been moustachioed but beardless. Perhaps, in indulging himself with a long white beard, Edward was also making a statement about his identity. He might be King of England, but that didn't make him wholly English.

The English, after all, were remarkable for their lack of decorum. 'Drinking in parties,' the monastic historian wrote, about a time that was well within living memory, 'was a universal practice, in which occupation they passed entire nights as well as days.' He disapprovingly added that 'they were accustomed to eat until they became surfeited, and to drink until they became sick'.

That was not who Edward was.

* * * *

All things considered, the new king was not in a bad position. He had attained the position because there was no realistic alternative, but this meant that – unlike his immediate predecessors – there was also no obvious rival. Fortunately for Edward, and for England, the kings of Norway (Magnus the Good until 1047 and Harald Sigurdsson, or 'Hardrada' – 'the hard ruler' – thereafter) were preoccupied with trying to seize the throne of Denmark (which was precariously occupied by Sweyn Estrithsson, Cnut's nephew), which meant that neither Norway nor Denmark could present much of a threat to England. Indeed, by 1050 the Scandinavian danger had diminished so much that Edward could dismiss most of his fleet and rescind the *geld*, which his predecessors had been levying since Æthelræd's days.

However, although Edward's throne was safe, he was not in a position to do exactly as he pleased. In particular, his power was constrained by the three great earls who had been appointed by Cnut: Siward in Northumbria, Leofric in Mercia, and, most importantly, Godwin, the man whom Edward held responsible for his brother's death, and the man whose personal wealth and power, as Earl of Wessex, rivalled Edward's wealth as king.[7]

Edward and Godwin were stuck with each other. There was no alternative king, and there was no alternative Earl of Wessex: neither was strong enough to unseat the other. And in the early days of Edward's reign, it appears that Godwin had the upper hand. By 1045, Edward had elevated both Godwin's eldest son, Sweyn, to a minor earldom in the west, and his second son, Harold, to the earldom of East Anglia; he had also married Godwin's daughter, Edith, who towards the end of his reign was to commission the aforementioned *Vita*.

These were almost certainly not freely made choices. Sweyn seems to have been somewhat unhinged. He is alleged to have claimed to be the son, not of Godwin, but of Cnut,[8] and it wasn't long after

---

7 There were other, smaller earldoms (such as the aforementioned Eadwulf's territory of Bernicia) but these were created on an ad-hoc basis and usually disappeared when their holders died (or lost favour). But from Cnut's reign until the Conquest these four great earldoms always existed, and their holders were always among the most powerful and important men in the realm. (Of the four, though, East Anglia was significantly smaller than the others, and Edward the Confessor seems to have used it as a 'starter' earldom, giving it first to Harold, son of Godwin, and then to Ælfgar, son of Leofric, while their fathers were still alive. Both were eventually 'promoted' to succeed their fathers, in Wessex and Mercia respectively, so clearly being Earl of East Anglia was somewhat less prestigious.)

8 There is only one authority for this, John of Worcester, who was writing several decades later. However, geographically Worcester was close to Sweyn's earldom, so perhaps the author knew something that others didn't; in the light of the rest of Sweyn's career, it doesn't seem wholly out of character.

his appointment that he abducted the Abbess of Leominster and, in the words of the *Chronicle*, 'had her as long as he liked'. For this he was banished: he went to Denmark, and 'ruined himself', but was later allowed to return to England; he then disgraced himself again by murdering his cousin, Beorn. Extraordinarily, Edward appears then to have forgiven him again, though soon afterwards Sweyn seems to have repented of his sins, and underwent a barefoot pilgrimage to Jerusalem, dying at Constantinople on the way back.

The indulgence of Sweyn is usually seen as indicative of the untouchability of Godwin and his sons: Sweyn was obviously a troublemaker. But there is an alternative interpretation. Maybe Edward's willingness to overlook Sweyn's behaviour was rather more cynical. Sweyn was, after all, an embarrassment. Godwin already had a distinguished record of service to several kings; so too would his younger sons, Harold and Tostig, who were no doubt already showing their potential in the 1040s. But for as long as Sweyn was around, he served as a reminder, to Leofric and Siward and indeed the other English magnates, of the dangers of Godwin becoming too powerful.

And if it *did* come to a confrontation between the king and the Earl of Wessex, and if the latter *were* to overthrow the former, Sweyn would be the obvious successor when Godwin, who was already at least fifty years old at the beginning of Edward's reign, died. The prospect of Sweyn as the most powerful man in the kingdom might serve as a warning to anyone who might consider supporting Godwin in such a confrontation. Did Edward smirk as he told a disappointed Godwin that he would indeed be welcoming Sweyn back to court and restoring him to his earldom? It's certainly possible.

* * * *

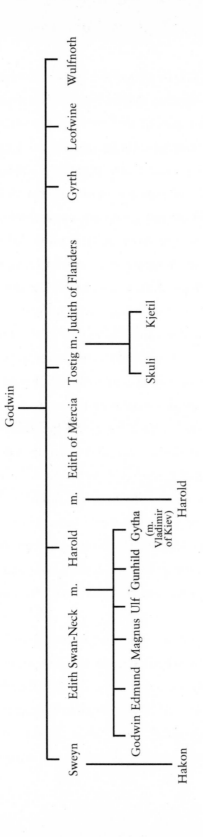

If Edward didn't have everything his own way, nor did Godwin. The Earl of Wessex had married well: his wife, Gytha, was Sweyn Estrithsson's aunt as well as Cnut's sister-in-law. In the 1040s he urged Edward to send military and naval support to his wife's nephew. This wasn't just Godwin looking out for his own family's interests. Magnus was on the point of total victory when he died in 1047: had he seized complete control of Denmark as well as Norway he would have been a powerful ruler indeed, and powerful rulers in that part of Northern Europe were not always good news for England. But Edward did not take Godwin's advice, preferring to stay out of Scandinavian affairs.

Edward's marriage to Edith was altogether less dramatic. No source hints at any scandal, and so far as we can tell the king and the queen had a happy marriage. But it was a childless one, and the reasons for this have been the subject of much speculation.

It could, of course, have been bad luck: one or other of them might have been infertile. An alternative interpretation, advanced by the *Vita*, is that Edward's piety inspired him to embrace a life of celibacy. Now this is theologically dubious, as the anonymous monk who wrote the book well knew: a married man was not expected to remain celibate. (Though perhaps, having only agreed to marry Edith for political reasons, and under pressure from Godwin, Edward did not really consider himself to be 'properly' married to her.)

There's no evidence for his having had any other sexual relationship: he reached the age of forty without marrying, and there is no trace either of any illegitimate children or of any suggestion that he might have been homosexual.

Edward's relationship with Edith is often described as being like that of a father and a daughter. He was significantly older than her, perhaps as much as a quarter of a century: as the couple didn't choose each other for romantic reasons, it's not impossible to imagine him having no sexual interest in her.[9]

And one more possibility has been suggested. Did Edward refuse to consummate his marriage to deny Godwin a victory? The birth of an ætheling might cement his family's position for ever: Godwin might not live to see all of it, but his sons, already becoming powerful men in their own right, would ensure that his grandson inherited the Crown from his son-in-law. Maybe Edward didn't like that idea. And why should he care about the succession? That, when the time came, would be someone else's problem.

It's all speculation; nobody knows for sure. But Edward, let's not forget, held grudges. Perhaps those grudges were unreasonable: no doubt his mother thought so. But if, fifteen years after Alfred's death, Godwin thought that Edward had forgiven him, he was about to be enlightened.

* * * *

The Church was very important to Edward. That, after all, is why he was called 'the Confessor'.[10]

The anonymous author of the *Vita*, who emphasised how pious Edward was, might have gone a little over the top in doing so. But there's no question that he took his faith seriously. Contemporary accounts might distort the truth. They might even do so deliberately. But to assert shortly after his death that Edward

---

9 Or maybe in anyone. We don't know anywhere near enough about Edward to speculate about his sexuality, but (to use the terminology of our own age) it seems that he might have been asexual.

10 To 'confess' a faith is to openly affirm one's belief in it.

had been a profoundly religious man, when everyone knew that not to be the truth, would have destroyed the author's credibility.

Edward was of Norman as well as English descent, and before being recalled to England he had spent over a quarter of a century, and his whole adult life, in Normandy. It was not, therefore, surprising that he would bring with him a coterie of Norman advisors. Nor was it unexpected or controversial that his nephew, Ralph of Mantes, should have been made Earl of Hereford. However, in 1051, Edward made a particularly provocative appointment. On the death of the Archbishop of Canterbury, he appointed a Norman, Robert of Jumièges, to replace him.

Theoretically the Archbishop of Canterbury was elected by the monks of Canterbury Cathedral. In reality it never worked like that: the archbishopric was of great national importance, and the king was usually free to make his own choice. For Edward to overrule the monks was neither unprecedented nor unreasonable. But on this occasion they had chosen Æthelric, who was a member of Godwin's extended family; for Edward to appoint Robert instead was confrontational.

English clerics who were irked by Robert's appointment were immediately given another reason to resent it. Edward nominated an Englishman, Spearhavoc, the Abbot of Abingdon, as the new Bishop of London, but Robert refused to consecrate him. The Pope, he said, had forbidden him to do so. (If this was true, it can only have been on Robert's own advice.) Now this appears to have been Robert's initiative, not Edward's, but Edward then nominated another Norman, by the name of William, to the vacancy.

It may well be that Edward considered his Norman appointees to be better churchmen. It would be a little excessive to describe the English Church as having been riddled with nepotism (the appointment and promotion of men to ecclesiastical offices based on family connections rather than ability) and simony (the buying and selling of those offices) as well as pluralism and clerical marriage, but these criticisms were often made at the time, sometimes by English reformers as well as by Norman critics. -, for instance, had been frequently appalled by his fellow clergy. The English Church was far from uniquely corrupt: pluralism, for instance, was common in other European countries too. And among the lower levels of the clergy some of this was understandable and unavoidable: priests just could not live on one benefice (that is, the income which they would receive in return for carrying out their duties in a parish) and so had to take on more than one to survive.

However, it would certainly be fair to say that overall the situation was far from perfect. William of Malmesbury was not a contemporary, but he was a clergyman; and his description of the pre-Conquest Church is a memorable one:

> The clergy, contented with a very slight degree of learning, could scarcely stammer out the words of the sacraments; and a person who understood grammar was an object of wonder and astonishment. The monks mocked the rule of their order by fine vestments and the use of every kind of food. The nobility, given up to luxury and wantonness, went not to Church in the mornings in the manner of Christians, but merely, in a careless manner, heard matins from a hurrying priest in their chambers, amid the blandishments of their wives.

If Edward was inclined to agree with these criticisms, then the English candidates for the archbishopric of Canterbury and the bishopric of London might have confirmed his opinion.[11] Æthelric was not obviously unfit for office, but neither was he a particularly distinguished cleric. Spearhavoc, who had already paid for his new position, was outraged. As the royal goldsmith he had been entrusted with the making of a new crown, but on learning that he was not actually going to get his promotion, he disappeared, taking the gold with which he was supposed to be making the new crown with him. What became of him, nobody knows.

It is probably fair to say that Spearhavoc wasn't a shining example of the priesthood. Still, Robert is described by the *Vita* as 'always the most powerful confidential adviser of the king', and it presumably looked to many as though this, and not any ecclesiastical merit, had been his principal qualification for the archbishopric. Anyway, even if they were made for purely religious reasons, these two appointments were unavoidably political. The advancement of Normans was at the expense of Englishmen in general, and Godwin in particular.

Edward was playing a dangerous game.

✳ ✳ ✳

In the late summer of 1051 Eustace of Boulogne, who was Edward's brother-in-law and ally, was returning home after visiting the King of England. His journey took him through the port of Dover, where he and his entourage got themselves involved in a deadly brawl.[12]

---

11 According to the *Vita*, Edward often welcomed foreign clerics to England, and 'exhibited such men as models to the abbots and monks of his own kingdom'. It is difficult to imagine that this was positively received among the native clergy.

12 He had been married to Edward's sister, Godgifu, though by 1051 she was dead.

According to the *Anglo-Saxon Chronicle*, this was a fracas for which Eustace was to blame. He might even have deliberately provoked it.[13] He and his men, allegedly, demanded that Dover's citizens provide them with accommodation, and presumably they did not do so politely: there were altercations, and several men were killed on both sides. Eustace managed to escape, and reported back to Edward that 'the guilt of the townsman was greater than his', to which the *Chronicler* could not resist adding, 'But it was not so.'

Edward's reaction was to order Godwin to harry the town. This put the Earl of Wessex in a tricky situation: he could either disobey a royal order, or he could carry out a punitive military action against the people of his own earldom.

Godwin chose to refuse the order, and was summoned to appear before Edward to account for his actions. This was bad enough, but it became quite clear that Edward was not interested in investigating the incident when he sent a messenger to Godwin, informing him that all he needed to do to have everything restored to him was to bring back Edward's brother Alfred. Godwin, knowing which way this was going, did not appear before the king. Instead, he and his sons got on board ships and left the country.

Edith, meanwhile, was sent away to a convent. This was, of course, a political decision. The House of Godwin was in disgrace, and the queen was part of the House of Godwin. But she was also the king's wife, and had been for years. Perhaps the harmonious relationship described in the *Vita* was not an entirely accurate reflection of the nature of their marriage; perhaps Edward was as indifferent to her as the absence of children may imply.

---

13 The *Anglo-Saxon Chronicle* records that Eustace and his men put on their armour when they were approaching the port, suggesting that they were preparing for military action.

With the House of Godwin out of the way, Edward started making changes. The earldom of East Anglia, which had been held by Godwin's second son, Harold, was given to Leofric's son Ælfgar. But he seems not to have replaced the Earl of Wessex, instead preferring to keep most of that earldom for himself. Wessex was the traditional heartland of the Old English ruling house, from which Edward was descended, but by assuming control over it he was not only claiming what he might have seen as his patrimony. It was large enough and rich enough that its holder, whoever it was, would be a powerful man. So although the western part of the earldom was handed over to a loyal supporter, Odda of Deerhurst, the rest became royal territory.

But Godwin was not finished just yet. He and his family might have been exiled, but they had friends abroad: indeed Tostig, Godwin's third son, was married to Judith of Flanders, and most of the family made their way to that country after their expulsion. (Harold, and his younger brother Leofwin, took refuge in Ireland instead.) They had plenty of support back in England too. Godwin had been Earl of Wessex for thirty years. Few men of fighting age could remember a time before he had been their lord. As events were to show, he had a personal following which even the king could not match.

A year after his departure, Godwin returned. He and his family sailed along the coast of Wessex, harrying, raiding and picking up supporters as they went. As they approached London, they docked at Southwark, on the other side of the River Thames. Rather than try to meet the royal army which Edward had summoned in battle, they waited.

It was a wise move. The *Vita* testifies that 'the whole city went out to help and protect the earl'. And the royal army was not keen on battle. According to the *Anglo-Saxon Chronicle*, 'they were most of them loth to fight'. Leofric and Siward were cautious. They were 'united in opinion with the king that they would have sought out Godwin's forces if the king had so willed'. But at the same time, they thought 'it would be a great folly that they should join battle, because there was nearly all that was most noble in England in the two armies, and they thought that they should expose the land to our foes, and cause great destruction among ourselves'.

What had changed?

Maybe nothing, or nothing much. In 1051 Godwin had gone into exile rather than stand and fight: perhaps, if he'd decided not to go quietly, he'd have found that neither then men of Wessex nor the Earls of Mercia and Northumbria would have been willing to support the king instead of him. Edward had caught him unawares, and events had moved quickly. Godwin didn't know whether, if civil war broke out, the country would support him, and so he decided not to risk it. That doesn't, though, mean that the country wouldn't have supported him; maybe it would have.

Or maybe it wouldn't. Maybe it was Edward's actions that made people wonder whether a more powerful king might be just as bad as a more powerful Earl of Wessex. Maybe the high-profile ecclesiastical appointments – and quite possibly the changes at court, with Edith being sent away and Normans seemingly in control – worried Leofric and Siward. A king who could destroy Godwin and his family was, after all, a king who could destroy them and their families too.

But there was nothing they could gain through war. A victory for Edward would preserve the status quo. And that was the best outcome they could hope for, because if Godwin won he might well destroy everyone who had fought against him. Persuading the king to come to terms with Godwin, and restore him to his earldom, was probably their least risky option.

Edward had been defeated. Godwin was once more Earl of Wessex; Harold was once more Earl of East Anglia. Edith returned to the royal court. A few Norman advisors – and, most prominently, the Archbishop of Canterbury, Robert of Jumièges – were exiled.[14] It was almost as though Godwin's exile had never happened.

Almost. But not quite.

During Godwin's absence, at least according to the Norman chroniclers, Edward had offered the succession to William the Bastard, Duke of Normandy.[15] In theory the Duke of Normandy was still a vassal of the King of France, who did homage to him and acknowledged his overlordship, but in reality William governed the duchy himself, and it was increasingly becoming a significant military power in its own right.

William had become Duke of Normandy in the summer of 1035, at just eight years of age, when his father died returning from a pilgrimage to Jerusalem. As a child he had, of course, been unable to exert his authority; he had spent the first years of his adult rule establishing it. By the time he was (allegedly) offered the English crown he was in the prime of life and had proved himself a soldier to be reckoned with as well as an effective ruler.

---

14 Officially, though, at least in Rome, Robert was still recognised as Archbishop of Canterbury: a monarch cannot sack a bishop. In England, a replacement was found: Stigand, Bishop of Winchester, a former chaplain to Cnut. But since, as far as the Papacy was concerned, there was already an Archbishop of Canterbury, Stigand's position was never recognised outside England.

15 The word 'bastard' carried the same double meaning in the eleventh century as it does today, of unpleasant character as well as illegitimate birth. William was the son of Robert, Duke of Normandy, but his mother, Herlève, was not Robert's wife. Even so, in the absence of an alternative, William was accepted as his father's heir.

Even so, this was not sufficient to make him a credible candidate to succeed Edward.

Why would Edward have made such a promise?

One of those chroniclers, William of Poitiers, attributes it to Edward's gratitude for his treatment in Normandy. There might be something in this: Edward was as much Norman as he was English, and clearly felt affectionately towards the duchy. Unfortunately for his own credibility, William of Poitiers did not stop there.[16]

After the death of Harthacnut, the English determined upon the most advantageous course, agreeing to accede to the just demands of Norman envoys rather than to contend with Norman power. They eagerly arranged Edward's return to them with only a small Norman escort to avoid Norman conquest if the Norman count should come himself, for they well knew his reputation in war. Edward, on the other hand, gratefully remembering with what generous munificence, what singular honour, what affectionate intimacy, William had treated him in Normandy, by all of which he was even more closely bound to the duke than by ties of kinship; remembering also with what zeal the duke had helped to restore him from exile to his kingdom, determined as a matter of honour to repay him in equal measure – and as an appropriate gift resolved to make him the heir of the crown obtained by his efforts. To this end, with the assent of his magnates, and by the agency of Robert, Archbishop of Canterbury as his ambassador in this manner, he sent him, as hostages of the most powerful family in the kingdom, the son and the grandson of Earl Godwin.

---

16 William of Poitiers served as William of Normandy's personal chaplain. His book, *The Deeds of William, Duke of Normandy and King of England*, was written in the 1070s.

This is, in several ways, indisputably inaccurate. Edward was invited to England by Harthacnut. At fifteen years of age, the Duke of Normandy could have had no 'reputation in war'. And the idea that the witan was terrified of the prospect of a Norman invasion in 1042, and accepted Edward as king to avoid it, is not credible. That he had the 'assent of his magnates' for such a promise can only possibly be true if we pretend that neither Godwin nor his sons were magnates, which was for this brief period strictly speaking true, but which is nonetheless rather misleading.

It is rather more likely that Edward had good political reasons for making the offer. Either he was simply trying to deny Godwin (or rather his sons) the succession, or he made the offer to William in return for something.[17] From Edward's perspective, this would have been the ideal treaty: he would never have to make good on it, since his side of the bargain would only be activated when he died.

There is no contemporary English source to corroborate this account, just as there is no corroboration for the story, told in only one version of the *Anglo-Saxon Chronicle*, that the Duke of Normandy visited England during Godwin's exile. But what does seems to be almost beyond dispute is that in the 1060s there were two hostages living in the court of the Duke of Normandy: Godwin's youngest son, Wulfnoth, and his grandson, Hakon (the son of Sweyn). This supports William of Poitiers' account, because if his account isn't true, the question of how they came to be there is rather difficult to answer.

The *exchange* of hostages was a fairly common way to seal an agreement which depended on both sides' good faith: if one party

---

17 What might that something have been? There is no record, but it might have been similar to the agreement which was sealed by the marriage of Edward's parents back in 1002, that Normandy would not assist England's enemies.

to a deal reneged on it, the lives of his family members would be in danger. But there is no record of William sending any hostage to Edward, or to Godwin, or indeed to anyone else. A vassal might be required to give hostages to his lord without the lord reciprocating, if the lord suspected the vassal of potential disloyalty, but Edward was not William's vassal. Indeed, if the Norman accounts are true, and Edward did make William his heir, then it doesn't seem to make sense that Edward would give William hostages. For what? It was his own freely made decision, after all.

There is, though, a reference in the *Anglo-Saxon Chronicle* to Godwin giving Edward hostages, during the initial stages of the crisis in the summer of 1051. This would make sense: it would have been reasonable for Edward to have demanded hostages from Godwin to demonstrate his loyalty.

Why, then, were these hostages not returned when Godwin came back?

Well. Had they been in England, Edward would have found a demand for their release irresistible. It may therefore have been that they were a better guarantor of Godwin's good behaviour in Normandy than they would have been in England. Perhaps, even in his brief moment of triumph, Edward had envisaged Godwin's possible return; and perhaps he appreciated that in such a scenario Godwin would have been able to demand the release of the hostages. If, though, Hakon and Wulfnoth were in Normandy, Godwin would not be able to get at them; and the threat to their lives might possibly discourage him from doing his worst.

If Edward did designate William as his successor, then maybe the hostages, who had first been given to Edward as surety for Godwin's loyalty to him, were now put to another use. In handing them over to William, it is possible that Edward was trying to secure the loyalty of Godwin and his family to the Duke of Normandy as his successor.

There is no evidence for this. It's pure speculation. If that's what happened, it strongly suggests that Edward suspected Godwin and his family of harbouring the ambition of founding their own royal dynasty many years before 1066. But if that's *not* what happened, there's a question which can't be answered: how did these two close relatives of Godwin find themselves in Normandy on the eve of the Norman Conquest?

After his triumph, Godwin barely lasted another six months. In the spring of 1053 he died, probably of a stroke, though it can't have been a huge surprise. The date of Godwin's birth is unknown, but having been appointed Earl of Wessex thirty years previously he must have lived a long life. His eldest surviving son, Harold, succeeded to the earldom of Wessex.

* * * *

His contemporaries were ageing too. Siward died soon afterwards, in 1055. But the earldom of Northumbria was not as easy to reassign. Siward had had two sons, but one of them had predeceased him, while the other, Waltheof, was too young to assume the office and responsibilities of an earl. Edward would have to replace Siward with someone from another family.

There were two candidates. One was Harold's younger brother, Tostig, the third son of Godwin; the other was Leofric's son Ælfgar. Either choice would make an already powerful family even stronger.

Ælfgar was once again Earl of East Anglia, the earldom which he had held since Harold's promotion to his father's earldom two years previously; he had also held it, briefly, during the crisis of 1051–2. He might therefore have appeared the obvious successor: he had experience, which Tostig didn't. On the other hand, Leofric was bound to die soon, and then Ælfgar would be his natural successor as Earl of Mercia. Better, Edward may have thought, to have kept Ælfgar in East Anglia than to send him to Northumbria, only to recall him when his father died.

For whatever reason, Edward decided to appoint Tostig. Perhaps he simply thought Tostig was the better man for the job: Ælfgar certainly seems to have lacked both judgment and loyalty.

The different versions of the *Anglo-Saxon Chronicle* take intriguingly different perspectives on what happened when this was announced. All agree that Ælfgar was outlawed. The Worcester and Abingdon versions broadly concur, saying that he was 'almost without any guilt', and that any offence was 'unintentional', but the Peterborough version says that 'he made a confession of it … though the word escaped him unintentionally'.[18]

This is sometimes treated as a mystery, though it's easy to understand how such differing accounts might have arisen. One possible explanation is that on hearing Edward's decision, Ælfgar questioned it; maybe he did so more vigorously than was prudent. Perhaps he expressed his disapproval of the decision-making process; perhaps his immediate reaction was excessive. This could be interpreted as treason, or it could be interpreted as fair comment, though it's clear what the man whose opinion mattered thought.

---

18 While the Peterborough chronicler was a partisan of the House of Godwin, the Abingdon chronicler was usually more critical, and this may help to explain why they put a different gloss on the behaviour of one of Harold's principal rivals.

Ælfgar's reaction to being outlawed was to take refuge in Wales, at the court of Gruffydd, the Welsh king, and to join forces with him to raid Herefordshire.[19] The Earl of Hereford, Edward's nephew Ralph, was defeated in battle, and Edward had to send Harold with the royal army to repel the invaders.[20]

Ælfgar's actions, though, had got him what he wanted. He was restored to his position as Earl of East Anglia and, when his father died in 1057, he succeeded him as Earl of Mercia. Extraordinarily, Ælfgar then appears to have rebelled again. 'This year,' states the *Anglo-Saxon Chronicle*, in a very concise entry for 1058, 'Ælfgar was banished, but he soon came in again by force, through Gryffydd's assistance; and a naval fleet came from Norway. It is tedious to tell the whole story.'

(What were the Norwegians doing getting involved in this affair? It has been suggested, but not very persuasively, that this was an attempt at conquest, but were this the case it would surely have received rather more attention at the time than it did: no contemporary authority even hints at it. Perhaps the *Anglo-Saxon Chronicle* was mistaken, and the fleet was not from Norway but from one of the Norse kingdoms in the British Isles, the leaders of which Ælfgar is rather more likely to have had connections to.)

It may well have been tedious for the Chronicler to have to report yet again on an earl's banishment and armed return. It is nonetheless frustrating not to have further details. The reasons

---

19 For most of the medieval period Wales was divided. The country's hills and mountains provided natural frontiers separating Gwynedd (in the north), Powys (in the east), Dyfed (in the west) and Glamorgan (in the south) from each other. Gruffydd, unlike anyone else in the Middle Ages, managed to unite these territories under his rule, and was briefly recognised as King of Wales.

20 Ralph had tried to get his (mostly English) soldiers to fight in the Norman way, on horseback. It did not go well, and the debacle earned Ralph the moniker 'the Timid' for his unimpressive performance in the field.

for Ælfgar's rebellion just a year after being granted his father's earldom are now unknown. It's possible that the allocation of earldoms provoked him this time too. Ralph died in 1057, and he was not replaced. Instead Herefordshire was transferred to Wessex: maybe Ælfgar thought it should have been added to Mercia.[21] What does seem clear, though, is that the Earl of Mercia, perhaps feeling threatened by being surrounded by the sons of Godwin, forged an alliance with Gruffydd, an alliance that was sealed by Gruffydd's marriage to Ælfgar's daughter, Edith.

So why did Edward tolerate this behaviour? Was it because by now Ælfgar, for all his flaws, was the only earl not to be a son of Godwin, and so the only man left who might act as some kind of counterbalance against that family? It is plausible. Edward could probably have crushed Ælfgar, but had he done so, he'd have needed a new Earl of Mercia. The only realistic option would have been one of Harold's brothers: Ælfgar had two sons, but neither were old enough to assume the duties of an earl in 1058 or 1059.[22]

Maybe that was it. But clearly Edward was not *that* opposed to the dominance of the House of Godwin. All the trouble with Ælfgar had started when Edward made Tostig Earl of Northumbria; and when Ælfgar was appointed Earl of Mercia to replace Leofric, the earldom of East Anglia was given to Godwin's fourth son, Gyrth.

---

21 This would be entirely consistent with Ælfgar's usual unreasonableness. Obviously Edward needed a proven warrior in Herefordshire to protect it from the Welsh, not someone who was in cahoots with the King of Wales. Perhaps Ælfgar just refused to see it, as he had refused to see the obvious logic of not sending the only son of an earl who was about to die to a different earldom.

22 They would be ready within a decade, though. Were Edward to have had their father done away with, they would have become implacable enemies, and Mercia might well have backed them; better, he may have reasoned, to put up with Ælfgar and hope that his sons would turn out to be better earls than their father.

(At the same time an earldom was also created for Leofwin, Godwin's fifth son, in the south-eastern corner of the country.) These were not the actions of a king who was determined to keep his brothers-in-law out of positions of power.[23]

It's tempting to suggest that Edward, like his father, was just a man who preferred peace to war. If he could avoid a battle, he would. Edward was no more of a warrior king than Æthelræd had been, and like him, when he decided that he had to go to war, as he did against the Scots in the 1050s, he put his earls in command of the royal forces rather than take control himself.[24] For a man of Edward's disposition, the case against a military showdown with Ælfgar was probably that it was just too risky considering the limited potential benefits which a victory would yield: so if the situation could be resolved without fighting, better, he may well have reasoned, to take the path of diplomacy.

This is the last significant event in which Ælfgar was involved. Historians can get rather sniffy about the use of the term 'Dark Ages' to describe the early medieval period, especially the eleventh

---

23 Yes, they could be interpreted as the actions of a king who was in the pocket of his Earl of Wessex. But that, as we shall see, would be an inaccurate reading of the situation. (And anyway, if Harold *was* able to dictate to Edward, that raises another question: what reason did *he* have for leaving Ælfgar in place? The policy is even more difficult to make sense of if it was Harold's rather than Edward's.)

24 In 1054 Siward invaded Scotland, defeating Macbeth (memorably described by the author of the *Vita* as 'the King of Scots with an outlandish name', as 'Macbeth' is an Anglicisation of the Gaelic 'Mac Bethad mac Findlaich') in battle and installing Malcolm on the Scottish throne. (It was on this campaign that Siward's elder son, Osbeorn, died.) Malcolm had spent his childhood in exile at Edward's court, and Edward might have hoped or expected that he would therefore be a grateful and amenable ally on England's northern border. Or he might have just been stirring up trouble in Scotland. This would explain why Siward left Malcolm to 'finish off' Macbeth: it took three years before Macbeth was finally killed, in 1057, and in that time the Scots were fighting each other, not raiding England.

century, but there's no denying that, in England at least, the years between 1057 and 1064 (like the 1020s) have been sparsely recorded, and even the fact of the death of the Earl of Mercia does not get a mention in the chronicles. The tidy answer to the question of when it happened is 1062, as there is no surviving entry for any version of the *Anglo-Saxon Chronicle* for that year. Certainly by 1065 he had been replaced as Earl of Mercia by his son, Edwin.

Another reason to prefer 1062 as the date of Ælfgar's death is that in December of that year Edward dealt decisively with Gruffydd. Harold launched a daring attack from Gloucester on Rhuddlan, in Gwynedd, 100 miles away, and the capital of the King of Wales.[25] Gruffydd was tipped off at the last minute and managed to escape by ship, but everything he left behind was either plundered or burned. Then, a few months later, in the spring of 1063, Harold and Tostig were dispatched to Wales for a longer campaign. Harold sailed from Bristol, while Tostig invaded from the north, and together their forces crushed the Welsh. There was no set-piece battle: that wasn't how the Welsh fought. They were guerrillas, used to launching raids across the border and then dispersing; a 'proper' battle would have enabled the English, with their far superior resources, to annihilate them.

So Harold and Tostig embarked on a campaign of harrying Wales, the interior as well as the coastline. As they marched,

---

25 Kings didn't really have 'capitals', in the sense of a seat of government, in the eleventh century, or for some time thereafter. Instead courts were 'itinerant', with kings and their entourages moving from place to place. However, some cities did have particular significance. Winchester is sometimes described as the 'capital' of Anglo-Saxon England, because that's where the royal treasury was. London had always been a place of strategic importance, situated as it is on the River Thames, the main 'gateway' into southern England (and the traditional boundary between Wessex and Mercia). As a settlement Rhuddlan wasn't comparable to Winchester or London, but as a base with a royal palace it was perhaps of similar importance to Gruffydd.

rode and sailed unopposed through the country, Gruffydd's prestige melted away along with his followers. The King of Wales had no answer to the invasion, and the demonstration of military force was sufficiently overwhelming that the brothers did not need to hunt him down themselves. He had utterly failed his people, who suffered the ravaging of their land, and so he forfeited their loyalty: he was killed by his own followers and his head delivered to Harold, who sent it on to Edward.[26]

There was no successor to Gruffydd's title. Nor was there any attempt to annex Wales: instead, it was once more divided between rival warring chieftains, who acknowledged Edward as their overlord and pledged their allegiance to him, a pledge which was supported by the handing over of hostages. It was a comprehensive victory, and that was all Edward needed. It kept Wales quiet: actually governing that country would be far more trouble than it was worth.[27]

* * * *

There is a clearly discernible air of fatalism about Edward in the later years of his reign. It may have been that, having lost his great confrontation with Godwin, he was essentially a puppet who withdrew from active politics and allowed others to govern. The *Vita* hints at this:

---

26 The people of southern Wales may well not have considered themselves as Gruffydd's 'people' anyway: he was a northerner who had only conquered those territories a few years previously.

27 With clear military and naval superiority an English force could always return to Wales and subdue it again. However, to annexe Wales or impose a more permanent English settlement there would have required a far greater commitment and an indefinite war footing.

With the kingdom made safe on all sides, [Edward] spent much of his time ... in the glades and woods in the pleasures of hunting. After divine service, which he gladly and devoutly attended every day, he took much pleasure in hawks and birds of that kind which were brought before him, and was really delighted by the baying and scrambling of the hounds. In these and suchlike activities he sometimes spent the day, and it was in these alone that he seemed naturally inclined to worldly pleasure.

This makes Edward sound like nothing more than a stereotypical English country gentleman. But, as its author goes on to explain, 'otherwise this man, of his free will devoted to God, lived in the squalor of the world like an angel'. He only reluctantly wore 'the pomp of royal finery' at the prompting of the queen, and 'he would not have cared at all if it had been provided at far less cost'. As a couple they were charitable, though 'while he would give now and then, she was prodigal'. And both funded the rebuilding of a religious house. Edith sponsored the convent at Wilton, while Edward's grand project was at Westminster Abbey, where his tomb and shrine can still be visited. The author of the *Vita* approvingly described their efforts as 'a contest which was pleasing to God', and takes care to record the result: 'The prudent queen's building, because it was more modestly planned, was completed more quickly.'

He also explains why Edward was able to spend his days so congenially. 'No age and no province,' he wrote, 'has reared two mortals of such worth at the same time. The king appreciated this, and with them thus stationed in his kingdom, he lived all his life free from care.' These two mortals, Harold and Tostig, were undoubtedly remarkable men. 'Both had the advantage of distinctly handsome and graceful persons … and both were equally brave. But the elder, Harold, was the taller, well practised in endless fatigues and doing without sleep and food, and endowed with mildness of temper and a more ready understanding. He could bear contradiction well … Tostig was endowed with very great and prudent restraint, although occasionally he was a little over-zealous in attacking evil … he renounced desire for all women except his wife … Both persevered with what they had begun, but Tostig vigorously, and Harold prudently.' They were, in that monastic writer's poetic words, 'the kingdom's sacred oaks'.

Now, this description must be treated cautiously, and not only because it was commissioned by their sister. It goes on, for instance, to say of Harold that 'the fault of rashness or levity is not one that anyone could charge against him, or Tostig, or any son born of Godwin'. The record of Sweyn Godwinson would suggest otherwise, as would some of Harold's actions at the end of Edward's reign and during his own. Still, in so far as the portrayals can be tested against other evidence they can mostly be accepted as reasonable interpretations, even if some might consider them excessively generous.[28]

And it is clear that Harold in particular was very influential indeed. He inherited all his father's authority as Earl of Wessex shortly after his family's triumph; he also inherited his position as the wealthiest man in England, both through the private wealth of the House of Godwin and through the land he acquired as the chief of England's richest earldom. As befitted a man of his status,

---

28 Tostig is described as 'over-zealous in attacking evil', for instance, while Harold is described as 'rather too generous with oaths'. These acknowledge character flaws, but critics of the brothers might use rather stronger or more direct language.

he was married to one of the medieval age's most famous women.[29] He met Edith 'Swan-Neck', a wealthy landowner, when he was Earl of East Anglia, and together they had at least five children, three of them boys.[30] She was famous for her fortune as well as for her aesthetic appeal and was also nicknamed 'the Fair' and 'the Rich'.

Harold and Edith used their wealth to generously, or extravagantly, rebuild the Church of the Holy Cross at Waltham. A marble altar was supported by twelve golden statues of the Apostles; there were sixty holy relics, mostly imported from abroad; everything was decorated with gold, silver, and pearls. And, of course, it was richly endowed: its twelve canons lived very comfortably indeed.[31]

Unlike his father, Harold did not have to contend with two other great earls. Godwin had been the greatest of the three, but Leofric and Siward had been heavyweights and therefore potential counterbalances to his power. As we have seen, though, those two did not produce successors of a similar calibre. Godwin did. He had several sons who, by the time he died, were well into their adulthood and ready to become earls. Harold, as the eldest surviving son, replaced his father as the head of the dynasty. Tostig's appointment as Earl of Northumbria might not have been ideal (nor was Ælfgar's as Earl of Mercia) but there was no

---

29 Their marriage, like Cnut's to Ælfgifu of Northampton, is also sometimes described as 'more danico', but only by historians writing centuries later. Did Harold avoid the sacrament of Christian marriage because he wanted to have the option of setting his bride aside at some point in the future? Almost certainly not: Edith Swan-Neck was quite a catch, and Harold cannot have expected, when they married in the 1040s, that he would one day be in a position to succeed Edward as King.

30 The sons were, in birth order, Godwin, Edmund, and Magnus; the daughters were Gunhild and Gytha.

31 At the end of the twelfth century it was refounded as a monastery, and became known as Waltham Abbey.

practical alternative. Edward could not elevate men of lower status to those earldoms and disregard the adult sons of their previous earls. Even if the law theoretically allowed him to (which it did: these were not hereditary entitlements) there was no practical way to do it. England in 1057 only had five credible earls: Harold, Tostig, Ælfgar, Gyrth, and Leofwin.

From 1053 onwards Harold was Edward's chief advisor and the power behind the throne. And it appears that both were content with this arrangement. There is no hint of any discord between the king and the Earl of Wessex and no trace of a power struggle between them. There is no suggestion that either ever even contemplated trying to replace the other. All the evidence indicates that the relationship was as it is described in the *Vita* – an ageing king happy for his trusted brothers-in-law to carry out the government of his kingdom and to command his armies. If only, he might have thought to himself, men like them had been around to serve his father. Edward was entirely unsuited to war, but thanks to the Earls of Wessex and Northumbria, it didn't matter.

It is probably fair to say that Edward would not have entrusted his housecarls or his fleet to Godwin.[32] But then Edward neither liked nor trusted Godwin, and although Edward bore grudges, this particular grudge appears to have expired with Godwin's death. Perhaps this was because while Godwin was alive, his offspring's loyalties were inevitably unreliable, whereas once he was gone, Edward could judge them according to their own qualities. Yes, he was stuck with Godwin's family, just as he was stuck with Ælfgar, and so the wisest course of action was indeed to try to make

---

32 The royal housecarls were the king's personal bodyguard of élite soldiers. (There were also 'butsecarles', who were the naval equivalent: full-time professional sailors in the king's service.)

the best of it. Even so, it is remarkable how little tension can be detected between Edward and the men he had exiled and tried, along with their father, to destroy. This may be partly explained by the paucity of records later in Edward's reign, but the absence of any flashpoints between Edward and his brothers-in-law in any surviving document is striking.

The simplest explanation may well be the best. An older and mellower Edward, perhaps to his own surprise, found that he really rather liked his new Earl of Wessex.

5

TWILIGHT

Things fall apart; the centre cannot hold;
mere anarchy is loosed upon the world.

W. B. Yeats

As far as England was concerned, the sons of Edmund Ironside
had disappeared when Cnut became king. But Edward the Exile
had been a lucky baby. He grew up in Eastern Europe; married
a princess by the name of Agatha; had three children, including a
young son, Edgar; and he was living in Hungary when, in 1054,
Ealdred, then the Bishop of Worcester, was dispatched to find him
and persuade him to return to England.

The only possible reason for bringing him back to England
was to address the question of the succession. It was by now
clear that Edward the Confessor, who was in his mid-fifties,
and therefore already older than any previous King of England,
would die childless. Edward the Exile was in his early forties; and,
crucially, he was not a dynastic dead end. It took three years to
arrange, perhaps because he was reluctant to abandon the life of

a Hungarian aristocrat for the throne of a country he had never known and the language of which he (probably) could not speak, but in the spring of 1057, just over forty years after his departure, he returned.

He might have been escorted 'home' by Harold. We know that Harold was in continental Europe in 1056, but we don't know why: his involvement in the mission to give England an heir to the throne would be a tidy explanation, and not just because this was the sort of important, challenging, long-distance mission which the king would have entrusted to the Earl of Wessex. Harold was not just a loyal and reliable earl: he would have vastly preferred Edward the Exile to William of Normandy.[1]

Why? Well, principally because Edward the Exile had no Norman connections. Indeed, as a new king he might well have been rather like Edward the Confessor: lacking personal lands and a personal following, and probably dependent on an Earl of Wessex who had plenty of both. William of Normandy was a wholly different proposition. At the very least Harold could expect to lose his position as the undisputed chief counsellor in the kingdom and to see his father's decisive victory of 1052 reversed. And because he was already the ruler of the duchy of Normandy William would be in a far stronger position than Edward the

---

1 How can we know that Harold was in continental Europe, but not know anything else about the trip? Because he witnessed a charter (a formal written record of a transaction) and that charter has survived. Charters can be made to be rather useful pieces of evidence, even when they don't reveal events like that at St Frideswide's during the St Brice's Day massacres. Not only do they reveal who was with the king at a particular time in a particular place, they also reveal something of the hierarchy of the country: that Eadric Streona was an influential man is asserted not just because the chroniclers like to denounce him, but because his name appears towards the top of many surviving charters from the last decade of Æthelræd's reign.

Confessor had been, because he wouldn't just bring courtiers and clerics with him: he'd bring soldiers too.

But shortly after arriving in England, and before he even met the king, Edward the Exile was dead. That he had been considered a credible successor is clear from the *Anglo-Saxon Chronicle*'s commentary on his death. 'Alas,' it laments, 'that was a rueful time, and injurious to all this nation – that he ended his life so soon after he came to England, to the misfortune of this miserable people.' Interestingly, though, the Chronicler adds another comment, which has occasioned some speculation. 'We don't know why,' he writes, 'he was not allowed to see his kinsman, King Edward.'

Evidently the Chronicler was suspicious, though this is only a very oblique hint that something was amiss. Perhaps Edward the Exile was not allowed to see the king because he was suffering from the disease which was shortly to kill him, and was either too ill to attend or was potentially contagious. Perhaps the Chronicler was mistaken, and a meeting had been planned, but what was obviously a sudden death intervened before it could take place. These are less dramatic possibilities than an assassination, but on the balance of probabilities rather more likely. Who, after all, would have had Edward the Exile murdered? A long-distance, short-notice assassination carried out by an agent of the Duke of Normandy, the King of Norway or the King of Denmark is just too far-fetched to be realistic. The only other suspect is Harold, but nowhere is Harold accused of the crime: it's not just that such an accusation is missing from the English sources, but there's nothing in the Norman chronicles, nor in the Norse sagas, nor even in any post-Conquest accounts. So for an historian to start making such accusations centuries later is a little unreasonable.

If Edward the Exile really was murdered, the assassin made the sort of mistake which, given the supposed victim's own history, seems remarkable: he left the Exile's son, Edgar, alive. Edgar spent the next nine years at the royal court, and by the 1060s was being referred to as an ætheling. Alfred the Great's old royal line was not yet quite extinguished.

This affair demonstrates several things. One is that either Edward was concerned about the succession, or at the very least that he was prepared to allow others around him who were concerned about the succession to try to solve the problem while he was still alive. The English succession did not depend on primogeniture, but royal blood mattered, and a son of Edmund Ironside was an ideal candidate. Another king might have preferred such a potential successor to remain safely in Hungary, but clearly by 1054 Edward was sufficiently secure in his position not to fear the presence of an alternative.

Another is that clearly he was not set on offering the Crown to William of Normandy. The Crown was not, of course, private property, for its current owner to pass on to whichever heir he chose. Ultimately the witan would decide. But while he was alive Edward could advance the interests of his preferred candidate for the succession, and this episode is utterly inconsistent with the narrative that Edward always intended William to succeed him.

This doesn't mean that Edward *never* wanted William to succeed him. He might just have changed his mind between the offer of the succession and the decision to recall the Exile. This isn't as unlikely as it sounds. There were two major events between those dates: Godwin's return, and Godwin's death. As we've already seen, Edward's approach to government was rather different in 1054 to what it had been in 1051. He accepted the dominance of

Godwin's sons; he abandoned his policy of appointing Normans to prominent positions; perhaps he also dropped his support for a Norman succession.

But what it also shows fairly conclusively is that at least one of two fairly common misconceptions about this period must be wrong. It cannot both be true that Edward was under Harold's thumb and that Harold had a long-term plan to succeed Edward himself. Were both true, Harold would not have allowed Edward to invite an alternative successor, and his son, to the royal court.

That isn't to suggest that Harold wasn't thinking about the future. He might well have been. At no point in Edward's twenty-four-year reign was there a satisfactory answer to the question of who would succeed him: Harold's wouldn't have been the only mind to have considered it. But it is difficult to detect any evidence of his taking any steps to attempt to secure the succession for himself until 1065.

He may well, of course, have had informal and hypothetical discussions with some of the leading men in the kingdom about whether, in the event that something unforeseen and unfortunate should happen to the king, and there was no other alternative, they would support a proven military leader with plenty of experience at the heart of government but without any royal ancestry. No one would expect to find records of such conversations, and no one has.

When might such conversations have happened? When might Harold have asked his brothers (a category which, after all, included quite a few of the leading men in the kingdom) if, were the king to die, they would back him to take over? So far as we know, despite his relatively advanced age, Edward gave no impression of having an impending meeting with his Maker until the last few months of his life. Meanwhile there was an ætheling at court. If Harold was hoping to succeed Edward, he might well have calculated that he needed the old man to die sooner rather than later: the older Edgar was, the less inclined the witan might be to elect a man with no royal blood.

If Harold was plotting, he was doing it subtly, without leaving any record, and without even leaving any discernible trace of suspicious activity.

Until, one day, he wasn't.

* * * *

As the eldest brother, and the head of the family, Harold held the most glamorous and prestigious earldom; and as Wessex was the heartland of the royal dynasty, the House of Godwin, and the kingdom, he was physically close to the king much of the time. Harold's younger brother, Tostig, had a tougher assignment. As Earl of Northumbria he was responsible for law and order in the most lawless and disorderly of England's earldoms; he was also responsible for protecting the northern border.

History has not been kind to Tostig, and history ought to be ashamed of itself. For ten years, Tostig grappled with the difficulties of ruling the earldom of Northumbria. The path of least resistance would have been to have indulged the local thegns. That, after all, was what Siward had done. The man nicknamed 'the Strong', who on his dying day insisted on putting his armour on and mounting his horse because it was only fitting for such a man to die arrayed as for battle, was significantly softer than Tostig; or, alternatively, he preferred not to deal with Northumbria's problems.

During Siward's tenure, reports the *Vita*, 'even parties of twenty or thirty men could scarcely travel without being either killed or robbed by the multitude of robbers in wait'. Now this state of affairs was partly a consequence of the geography of Northumbria, which was ideal for bandits: the terrain was far less fertile than the more southern regions, which made it harder to earn an honest living from the soil, which made it more sparsely populated, which meant that travellers would often find themselves a long way from anyone who might have the power and inclination to prevent such banditry.

But it was also partly the doing of the Northumbrian thegns themselves. They couldn't, even if they'd wanted to, have eliminated all the criminality from that earldom. But they could have done more to repress the lawless violence. The 'multitude of robbers' was not an unavoidable natural disaster but the consequence of indolence at best, and corruption at worst. As the king's servants, it was the responsibility of Northumbria's royal officials to impose law and order. They were not doing so.

Tostig, by contrast, took the job of upholding law and order seriously. It didn't make him popular with the Northumbrian aristocracy. But it wasn't his responsibility to please the Northumbrian aristocracy. It was his responsibility to serve the king, and that meant doing his best to ensure that the law was obeyed. His predecessor had not discharged this part of his duty very well. But that was no reason for Tostig to disregard its importance. He had a job to do, and he intended to do it properly.

He also had the problem of dealing with the Scots. Like the Welsh, 'this irresolute and fickle race of men', as the author of *Vita* describes them, 'were better in woods than on the plain; trusting more to flight than manly boldness in battle'. At first the Scots

1. Corfe Castle, where Edward the Martyr was killed. (Courtesy of Peter Trimming under Creative Commons)

2. Æthelræd 'the Unready'. (Courtesy of the York Museums Trust)

3. The likely site of the Battle of Maldon, where Byrhtnoth, Ealdorman of Essex, was defeated by a Viking force. It is likely that the Viking force had to cross from Northey Island (on the left of the picture) to confront Byrhtnoth's men on the shore (top right). (Courtesy of Terry Joyce under Creative Commons)

4. Cuckamsley Hill, where an invading Danish force paused in a show of bravado, having penetrated all the way to this spot a few miles south of Oxford. (Courtesy of Andrew Bowden under Creative Commons)

5. The fifteenth-century Gainsborough Old Hall, on the site of Sweyn Forkbeard's camp. (Courtesy of Gary/Happymillerman under Creative Commons)

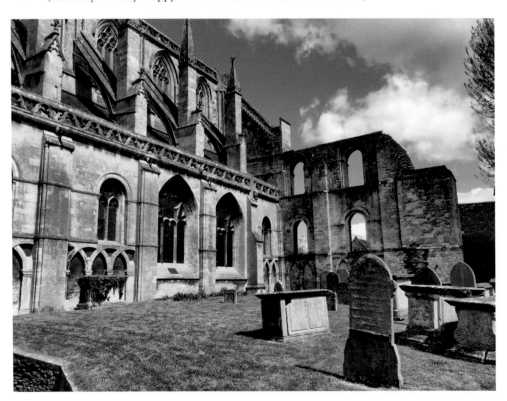

6. Malmesbury Abbey, home of chronicler William of Malmesbury and the site of incarceration for the wife of Æthelræd's enemy Sigeferth, who was subsequently freed, and married, by his son Edmund Ironside. (Courtesy of Timo Newton-Syms under Creative Commons)

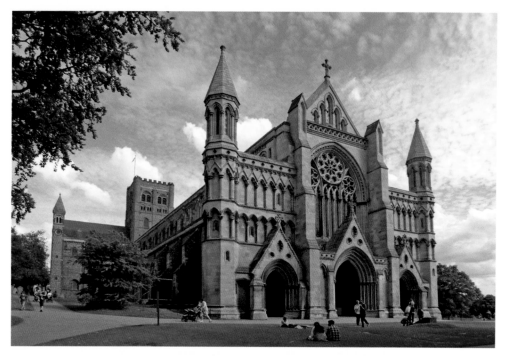

7. The post-Conquest Winchester Cathedral, where the remains of both Cnut and his son Harthacnut remain today. (Courtesy of Polyrus under Creative Commons)

8. Harold Godwinson is given permission for his sea voyage by Edward the Confessor. (By kind permission of the city of Bayeux)

9. Harold embarks upon his ill-fated trip, which led him to the court of William the Bastard, Duke of Normandy. (By kind permission of the city of Bayeux)

10. Here the Tapestry purports to depict Harold swearing an oath, supposedly to support William's claim to the English throne. (By kind permission of the city of Bayeux)

11. A submissive Harold appears to inform King Edward of his promise to William. (By kind permission of the city of Bayeux)

12. The deceased Edward is carried into his abbey at Westminster. (By kind permission of the city of Bayeux)

13. A newly enthroned Harold is told of the 'hairy star' of ill omen, looked upon with awe by citizens. (By kind permission of the city of Bayeux)

14. An action shot of the Battle of Hastings, with Odo of Bayeux chief among the combatants, wielding a club so as not to 'shed blood'. (By kind permission of the city of Bayeux)

15. A wounded Harold is slain, handing the kingdom to William. (By kind permission of the city of Bayeux)

Left: 16. A page from the Domesday Book, William's last great project as king, which attempted to determine what taxes had been owed in the reign of Edward the Confessor. Much of what we know of the period is thanks to this great survey.

Below: 17. The Abbey of Saint-Étienne in Caen, where William was laid to rest. (Courtesy of Patrick Morio under Creative Commons)

may have wondered whether Tostig might have been weak, or at least weaker than his predecessor. 'Since they had not yet tested him and consequently held him more cheaply,' reports the same authority, they 'harassed him often', though this was 'with raids rather than war'. If so, they learned their lesson. Tostig kept the northern border quiet. And this wasn't just coincidence. Malcolm's only brief incursion during Tostig's decade as Earl of Northumbria was in 1061, when Tostig was on a pilgrimage to Rome.[2]

Tostig is not usually remembered as a man of God, and it's fair to say that he wasn't religious in the way that Edward was. Still, he respected the demands of Christianity. He was faithful to his wife. And he was generous to religious houses, including Durham Cathedral, for which he was remembered fondly half a century later.[3]

In a way, he was a model earl.

****

In the summer of 1064 Harold set out on a boat and ended up in Normandy.[4] While there, he took an oath pledging to support William's claim to the English throne. The trip isn't recorded in

---

2 This journey was not just a pilgrimage. Tostig was accompanied by Ealdred, who had been chosen as the new Archbishop of York, and who was on his way to recieve his pallium. The Pope refused to ordain Ealdred as Archbishop until he promised that he would not follow the traditional custom of holding the see of Worcester in plurality with the see of York, a condition to which Ealdred eventually and reluctantly agreed.

3 Symeon of Durham, a monk who wrote a history of that community, gratefully recorded several gifts given by Tostig and Judith.

4 There is some debate about when, but the consensus is that 1064 is more likely than 1065 (the possible alternative date). Whether it was 1064 or 1065 the chances are that Edward was aging visibly and becoming more frail but that his death was not expected imminently.

any contemporary English source, but there's no doubt that it happened: the Norman chronicles describe it and the Bayeux Tapestry depicts it. It's particularly irksome that the author of the *Vita* chose not to mention the voyage explicitly, because Harold's reasons for going are difficult to understand. The Bayeux Tapestry shows Harold with Edward before his departure, but it does not reveal what was said; Queen Edith presumably knew, but no explanation found its way into the *Vita*.

No interpretation is altogether convincing. The standard Norman version is that Edward sent Harold to confirm to William of Normandy that the succession was still his. William of Poitiers claimed that Edward got 'the consent of his magnates' for the offer of the succession, but the magnates of 1052 (including the archbishops) were all dead, so sending Harold as a representative of the next generation would make sense. But if this is an accurate version of events, it was extraordinary. It would imply that Edward was still, at the end of his life, able to order Harold to set aside his own ambitions and acquiesce in the reversal of his father's victory in 1052. It would imply that the relationship between the king and the Earl of Wessex was far less friendly than the sources suggest. It also suggests that the king was far more powerful than is usually thought, and the Earl of Wessex far less powerful.

Now this can't be wholly discounted. Maybe Edward had never really wanted to give Godwin's family so much power. Maybe he only did it because he had no alternative. Maybe, knowing he was beaten, he had seen no point in bringing the temple crashing down by forcing a confrontation; maybe he had consoled himself that a life of prayer and country sports was not, after all, so bad a way to spend his days. But maybe he had never been fully reconciled to his situation. Maybe, with death in sight, he still resented his wife's family. Maybe he still felt the loss of his brother. Maybe he wanted to inflict one last, posthumous, defeat on his old adversary.

It's not inconceivable, at least not from Edward's perspective. He was dying: if it all ended in a civil war, what did he care?

But if that's what happened, Harold's obedience to Edward is utterly inexplicable. He had been a loyal earl, but his loyalty was not inexhaustible, and the Crown was a prize which he was willing to put before his loyalty to people even closer to him than the king. Why would Harold obey such an order? By now he must have been planning to seize the throne himself. And Edward must have known that he was. If he really did order Harold to deliver the news to William, he was taking quite some risk: it would have been a tremendous test.

Fortunately there is an alternative explanation. Perhaps Harold wanted to get the members of his family who had been sent to Normandy as hostages, and who were still there, back. Wulfnoth, Harold's youngest brother, and Hakon, the son of Harold's oldest brother, Sweyn, were being held as hostages in William's court, where they had been living since 1052. They had (probably) been sent to guarantee that the House of Godwin would abide by Edward's designation of William as his successor. Harold attempting to seize the Crown for himself was precisely the scenario their presence in Normandy was supposed to discourage: in that event their lives would be in danger. It would therefore make sense for him to bring them safely back to England before Edward died.

This is the story preferred by later English chroniclers. But it has its own problems. Harold was an impulsive man, but trying to imagine just how he thought he would manage to secure the release of the hostages is rather difficult. Was he hoping to charm

William into letting them go home? Harold was not lacking in confidence, but such a bet would have been phenomenally risky.

Perhaps he was planning the sort of raid he had carried out against Gruffydd at Christmas 1062: maybe the idea was to sail across the English Channel to Bayeux, or up the River Seine to Rouen, or to wherever the hostages were, pick them up, and bolt straight back to England. He'd need to know exactly where the hostages were, but that might not have been too difficult: they were after all established residents of Normandy and had been for well over a decade. They were unlikely to have been kept in a fortress under a heavily armed guard: it was neither necessary nor conventional to treat hostages in such a way.[5]

If this all seems rather fanciful, then you might prefer William of Malmesbury's interpretation. Unable to find a convincing explanation for Harold's actions, he claimed that the Earl of Wessex was on a fishing trip when the weather intervened.[6]

Whatever Harold's plan, it went wrong straight away. On the voyage across the Channel, he was blown off course and shipwrecked on the coast of Ponthieu, to the north of Normandy. Harold was apprehended and taken to Guy, the count of that territory. This was rather bad luck. As William of Poitiers explained, 'certain peoples of Gaul', including the inhabitants of Ponthieu and its count, had 'an appalling practice, barbarous and

---

5 If that was the plan, then the discussion between the King and the Earl of Wessex as portrayed in the Bayeux Tapestry cannot have happened – or, if it did, Harold must have fibbed to Edward about his plans. Edward would presumably have forbidden such an adventure: if it had actually succeeded, William would have been furious, and would no doubt have demanded that action be taken against Harold.

6 Doubt is sometimes expressed as to whether this was the sort of thing which eleventh-century aristocrats would do, but clearly a twelfth-century historian thought it might be.

far removed from all Christian justice. They seize the powerful and the rich, throw them into prison and inflict violence and torture upon them. Then, weakened by every sort of ill-treatment and close to death, they are released, most often for a large ransom.'[7]

William of Normandy was to receive several strokes of good luck on his way to conquering England, and the news that Harold had been captured by Guy of Ponthieu was the first. William demanded that the Earl of Wessex be handed over, a demand to which Guy, who was William's vassal, had reluctantly to accede. Harold was handed over and became simultaneously William's honoured guest and his prisoner: if gratitude for being rescued from captivity did not induce him to give his host the undertakings he wanted, the prospect of being held at the duke's court indefinitely might be more persuasive.

Harold's visit was eventful, and some of the details have doubtless been embellished. But what can be ascertained is as follows: William took him on campaign, against the Bretons; Harold and William made promises to each other, one of which was Harold's promise to support William's claim to the English throne when the time came; and Hakon was allowed to return to England.[8]

---

7 It was, though, breathtakingly cheeky of William of Poitiers, the great Norman propagandist, to shake his head disapprovingly at Guy of Ponthieu for his treatment of prisoners. Just a year before Harold's visit, William of Normandy had conquered the county of Maine and captured Walter, Count of the Vexin (son of Drogo of Mantes and, therefore, nephew of Edward and grandson of Æthelræd) and his wife. Both were to die in prison, suspiciously, soon thereafter. Falling into Norman custody was dangerous too.

8 Hakon is a particularly anonymous figure, and it's possible that he might not even have existed. Being a hostage in Normandy is his only appearance in history. Sweyn is not known to have married, though given his reputation it wouldn't be surprising were he to have fathered a son. But not only is there no record of Hakon before 1051, there is no record of him after 1064 either. If he participated in the campaigns of 1066 or the events of the following years, clearly no one thought it worthy of mention; nor did his death strike any chronicler as worth recording.

It isn't wholly clear whether the Brittany campaign or the oath happened first. William of Jumièges, who wrote the earliest surviving account of the Norman Conquest, puts the oath first; the Bayeux Tapestry puts the campaign first. Nor is it obvious why William would entertain Harold in such a way. Was he showing off his military prowess? (If so, perhaps Harold felt the need to reciprocate: the Tapestry shows him rescuing two soldiers from quicksand.) Perhaps the campaign had already been planned and William was reluctant to postpone or abandon it. Or perhaps William of Jumièges was right, and the oath had come first, and Harold had made his promises so convincingly that William genuinely believed that he had meant them: had William been reassured that Harold would advance his case when Edward died, there would be no reason to think of him as anything other than a new ally.

The location of Harold's oath to William is also unclear. The Bayeux Tapestry puts it in Bayeux; William of Poitiers puts it in Bonneville-sur-Touques. (Orderic Vitalis, an Anglo-Norman historian who, like William of Malmesbury, had an English mother and a Norman father, and who was writing in the early twelfth century, put it in Rouen. Fortunately it doesn't really matter.) But if we believe everything else – everything that isn't mutually incompatible – that the Tapestry and William of Poitiers tell us, this is what happened.

While still on campaign, William knighted Harold. Back in Bonneville, Harold swore on holy relics that he would do all he could to support William's claim to the throne, including funding a Norman garrison at Dover, and others elsewhere in Wessex, at his own expense. Harold also did homage to William, and was enfeoffed with all his lands.[9]

---

9 Enfeoffment was the granting of land in return for military service.

Much of this may have been exaggeration. William of Jumièges, writing before William of Poitiers, condenses these events into one line: 'Harold remained with the duke for some time, and swore fealty concerning the kingdom with many oaths.' Maybe William of Poitiers was trying to embellish the story, either to make it more memorable or to enhance the Norman case; though equally he might have been adding important detail to an otherwise rather cursory statement. (If, after all, what William of Poitiers wrote was true, it was well worth including.)

By the early twelfth century the story had been embroidered a little more. Harold had promised to marry William's daughter, or William had promised to marry Harold's sister, or both. There's nothing implausible about this: a marriage was a traditional way of sealing an alliance, but because the references to such an arrangement only emerge decades later they are usually treated as unreliable.

There's another twist on another element of the story for which there is no surviving documentary evidence before the twelfth century. According to Eadmer, a Canterbury monk who wrote *The History of Recent Events* in the early 1110s, Harold did not know he was swearing an oath on holy relics: instead, he believed that he was just taking an ordinary oath, only for the cloth on which he had placed his hand to do so was whipped away, revealing the sacred nature of the promise he had just made. It's rather melodramatic, and yet the Bayeux Tapestry's image of Harold taking the oath might possibly depict a table covering which is concealing something underneath it. Was that a deliberate reference to a rumour which was already being whispered? Or did a myth arise out of the way the embroiderers of the Bayeux Tapestry had inadvertently depicted a table?

Does it make any difference if the story is true? Clearly it made a difference to Eadmer, for whom it was a dirty trick enabling William to conscript a saint into his service. But it's tempting to see it as the beginning of 900 years of people trying to make excuses for Harold taking and then breaking an oath. It is difficult to find a modern account of the affair which doesn't observe that the oath was taken under duress and that Harold was therefore justified in disregarding it. But oaths were taken under duress all the time. Just a year previously Edward had demanded oaths of homage and fealty as well as hostages from Gruffydd's successors in Wales. After an ignominious defeat the Welsh were in no position to resist, and they had seen what had happened both to Gruffydd and to the country: with the threat of Harold and Tostig being unleashed again hanging over them, they made promises to Edward. Harold probably did not consider those promises to be meaningless.

The most dubious elements of the story are those which involve the knighting and the homage. A ceremony of knighthood, in which a lord would bestow arms on his vassal, was perhaps rather an odd thing for a Duke of Normandy and an Earl of Wessex to participate in: Harold was, of course, a man of considerably higher status than a knight. As for the homage, neither man was in much of a position to make the pledge which William of Poitiers says they made. Doing homage and fealty to a designated successor before the death of a lord was acceptable, though it tended to be done at the instigation of an incumbent who worried that his preferred heir might otherwise be rejected by his vassals: William's own father had done this before leaving for Jerusalem.

But unless Edward *did* send Harold to Normandy with an explicit instruction not only to confirm the offer of the succession but also to go ahead with such a ceremony, which he probably didn't, Harold's conduct was somewhat questionable. (Assuming he didn't send him, Edward might reasonably have been perturbed that his greatest magnate had just pledged allegiance to another prince.) While it is somewhat too simplistic to dismiss the oath as having been taken under duress and therefore invalid, it is certainly also worth recognising that in the circumstances in which it was taken it could only ever be provisional and conditional. For William to enfeoff Harold with his lands in England, he would have to be king; until that day, Harold might reasonably argue that William had not yet fulfilled his side of the agreement, and was not therefore owed anything.

There was, moreover, a crucial difference between Robert demanding that his vassals do homage to his son, and Edward demanding that Harold do homage to William. Neither Edward nor Robert had a free hand to dispose of his title to whomsoever he wished: in France the inheritance of the duchy of Normandy was subject to the approval of the king, while in England the king was elected by the witan. But whereas Robert had checked with his overlord that he would accept his son as Duke of Normandy, Edward, so far as we know, never put a similar question about the succession to the witan.

Harold was, of course, in a sticky situation, even if it was one of his own making. As William of Jumièges says, he was there 'for some time', and as that time went by he must have become increasingly nervous about what might happen. If he decided to give in to the pressure and give William of Normandy the promises he wanted in return for his release then that's understandable. But perhaps it was an unfortunate decision. William had the upper hand, yes. But if Harold had refused to take an oath to him, what could he have done?

He could have refused to release him. He could have had him killed, as he (probably) did with Walter of the Vexin, or he could have had him tortured and ransomed, which might well have been Harold's fate had William not rescued him from Guy.

None of that would have helped his claim to the English throne though. At best it would have removed a potential rival. What would Edward have thought? It's just about possible, though pretty unlikely, that if his intention had always been to ensure William's succession then Harold's indefinite captivity or death might have suited him. (It's rather more likely that he would have resented the Duke of Normandy's temerity in depriving him of his Earl of Wessex.) But trying to persuade the witan that this would make William a suitable successor would have been difficult. It is quite clear that William had no support in England: even after the Battle of Hastings, when there was no credible alternative, the witan were reluctant to accept him.

The House of Godwin would certainly have been damaged, and it's probably fair to say that it wouldn't have become England's ruling dynasty in 1066. But Harold still had three younger brothers and several sons, and transferring the earldom of Wessex out of the family would have been unthinkable. They would have inherited, or controlled, the family's wealth. The only way William could possibly have secured their support for his claim would have been for the head of the family to have led them in that support, and he wouldn't have done that as a prisoner or a corpse.

Harold knew all this. He probably had good reasons to take the oath and get back to England. He could be rash, but he could also be a calculating politician, and it seems that he had time to mull his options. But what would have happened had he demurred?

William would not have been able to portray Harold as a perjurer when asking the Pope, as he went on to do, to support his invasion of England. Whether that would have made a difference in Rome, or indeed whether the absence of Papal support would have made any difference to the outcome of the campaign, is unknown and now unknowable.

What we can say is that it wouldn't have turned out any worse for Harold, or for England, than what actually happened.

* * * *

In the autumn of 1065, the Northumbrian thegns rebelled against their earl.

Tostig was at the royal court when it happened. 'All the thegns in Yorkshire and Northumberland,' reported the *Anglo-Saxon Chronicle*, 'gathered themselves together and outlawed Earl Tostig.'[10] They broke into his residence at York, killing any soldiers in his service or members of his household they could find, and stripped the treasury. 'Then,' continues the Chronicler, 'they sent for Morcar, the son of Ælfgar, and chose him for their earl.' The rebels then marched south to Northampton, 'where his brother Edwin came to meet him with the men that were in his earldom. Many Welshmen also came with him.' This was clearly quite some force. 'The northern men did much harm around Northampton.' They 'slew men ... burned houses and corn ... took all the cattle' and took 'many hundreds of men' back to Northumbria.

---

10 In other words, they convened some sort of kangaroo court – which, as it was constituted in defiance of the Earl and the King, rather than by their authority, had no legal standing – and pronounced their verdict and sentence there.

The *Vita*, while not endorsing them, reports the Northumbrians' grievances. It refers to 'the heavy yoke of his rule', and implicitly accepts this by explaining it as having been necessary 'because of their misdeeds'. He was 'too cruel', and his zeal for justice was motivated not by the desire to see law and order in the earldom, but because he wanted to personally profit from punishing malefactors. John of Worcester, writing in the first half of the twelfth century, went further. He accused Tostig of levying a 'tribute' on the people of Northumbria, and of having three Northumbrian thegns murdered, one of whom was slain while attending Edward's court.

Edward's immediate reaction was to try to be reasonable, but the insurgents were not interested in negotiating. They wanted Tostig to be replaced by Morcar, and they would remain in rebellion until the king agreed. They also demanded that the Laws of Cnut be renewed.

This response infuriated Edward, whose reaction to being told that the rebels would not listen to his attempts at conciliation was to raise an army to put down their uprising. But winter was approaching: it was getting rather late to call out the army, and Northumbria was not the sort of region suited to winter campaigns. More ominously, while Edward might have wanted to crush the rebels, not everyone around him agreed. 'In that race,' explained the author of the *Vita*, 'horror was felt at what seemed civil war.' It was 1052 all over again, and the *Vita*'s hints at treason are not very subtle. 'Some strove to calm the raging spirit of the king and urged that the attack should not be mounted', while others intended to 'not so much divert the king from his desire as wrongfully and against his will desert him'.

Edward may have been furious, but he was also impotent. His kingdom was collapsing around him and he could do nothing about it. Northumbria was in rebellion, backed by the Earl of

Mercia, and the people who should have been helping him to put it down were advising him not to, and indicating that they thought he should back down. With no other option, that was what he did. At a meeting of the witan in Oxford, Morcar was installed as the new Earl of Northumbria; Tostig was exiled, and made his way to his wife's family's homeland of Flanders.

The conventional wisdom is that Tostig brought the rebellion on himself. He was too inflexible, and his rule was too harsh: in trying to impose customs on Northumbria he alienated its thegns. Even the *Vita*, usually regarded as being sympathetic to Tostig, conceded his faults as a ruler.

Historians have tended to treat the rebels as, if not in the right, then at least as men whose grievances were understandable. This interpretation is not wholly consistent with the usual account of the rebellion, in which the protagonists deserve rather less sympathy than they are usually given.

First of all, this was outright defiance of the king. That the mutineers were not just protesting about Tostig's rule is transparently obvious. Sometimes their defiance of Edward was naked: their refusal even to negotiate with the man to whom they owed loyalty and obedience shows how dismissive they were of their lord and sovereign. They did not, of course, have the right to outlaw an earl, and in doing so they were infringing the royal prerogative. More seriously, demanding the reinstatement of King Cnut's law code was effectively announcing that they did not intend to obey their actual king.[11]

---

11 In centuries to come Englishmen would demand the restoration of King Edward's laws. It was just as meaningless: so far as we know he never published a law code. The point was to compare the current régime unfavourably with a legendary past.

Why did they want King Cnut's laws restored? Probably not because of anything specific in Wulfstan's last code. If they were thinking of something in particular, it's likely to have been the item which decreed that 'he who violates just law in the Danelaw shall pay the fine prescribed there'. This could perhaps have been interpreted as a recognition by the Crown that the Danelaw, and its different customs and practices, should and would be respected. If that were so, then the demand might well have been a demand for less law altogether, or it might have been a demand that Northumbrians be left to their own devices, rather than have a West Saxon earl impose West Saxon law in the name of a West Saxon king. Or perhaps it was a purely symbolic demand, and that all that the rebels really meant was 'the good old laws of the good old days when we had better rulers'. In any case, however it be interpreted, this was essentially a demand that Northumbrian thegns be allowed to ignore the actual law. And when they complained about 'tribute', what they were really saying was that they did not recognise the right of the King of England to levy taxes on them: what the Earl of Northumbria was levying was not 'tribute' (which was money paid by the inhabitants of a conquered territory to the occupying power) but taxation.

As for the comments about Tostig's motivations in enforcing the law, the disingenuousness is obvious. Yes, they concede, they were breaking the law … but Tostig only went after them because he wanted to raise money? These weren't men pushed beyond breaking point by a tyrannical earl. They were the eleventh-century equivalent of motorists grumbling about parking fines and speeding tickets.

Were they on stronger grounds when complaining about Tostig's orchestrating the killing of three of their number?

No. Such behaviour was a fact of political life. Let's not forget that the rebels spent the autumn of 1065 ravaging the county of Northamptonshire, killing people, and stealing crops and livestock, never mind the lawless behaviour which had inspired Tostig's crackdown in the first place. These were not men who were appalled by the prospect of using violence.

Historians usually regard the criticisms of Tostig reported in the *Vita* as likely to be true. It is strange, therefore, that something which appears in the same document just a few lines away is not given the same respect.

'It was also said,' wrote the anonymous author, 'if it be worthy of credence, that they had undertaken this madness against their earl at the artful persuasion of his brother, Earl Harold (which heaven forbid!).' The author went on to distance himself from the accusation. 'I dare not and would not believe that such a prince was guilty of this detestable wickedness against his brother.' But 'Earl Tostig himself, however, publicly testifying before the king and his assembled courtiers, charged him with this.' It is at this point in the story where the author drops in his famous line about Harold being 'too generous with oaths', explaining that the Earl of Wessex swore that he had not done what he was accused of.

Why did the Northumbrian thegns demand Morcar as their leader? Why not Siward's son Waltheof, who was by now nearly old enough to be given an earldom? (As indeed he was: Northamptonshire and Huntingdonshire were allocated to him when Morcar was made Earl of Northumbria.) Why did Edwin join the rebels? As Earl of Mercia it was his responsibility to support the king, not rebels in arms. Why, indeed, were any Welsh present?

The answer is that this wasn't a spontaneous uprising, and it wasn't about Tostig's alleged misrule. It was a carefully orchestrated and successful coup d'état, intended to enhance and protect the position of Ælfgar's sons. No doubt the Northumbrian thegns were angry about Tostig. They probably didn't need much persuasion to rebel against him. It's possible that many were unaware of the demands being made in their name: only the highest-ranked, who would have been expected to speak for them, might have needed bribing to demand Morcar rather than Waltheof. Or maybe making that particular demand was the price required by the Earl of Mercia for lending his support to their treason. In a pitched battle, after all, the forces of the rest of the country would have had little difficulty in defeating the Northumbrians: if they were to get any of what they wanted, they needed support.

That some of this support should have come from Wales is perhaps surprising. What did the Welsh care about Northumbrian grievances? Nothing, of course. Presumably Edwin had reactivated his father's alliance with at least some of the Welsh, perhaps Gruffydd's kinsmen, whose instinctive reaction must have been to support the son of Ælfgar against Tostig.

Meanwhile, what was Harold up to? Other than swearing an oath that he had had no part in causing the uprising, he is suspiciously absent from contemporary accounts of these momentous events. Presumably Harold's was one of those voices urging Edward to avoid civil war by conceding the rebels' demands. But why would he support Ælfgar's sons against his own brother?

The most charitable explanation would be that he genuinely thought that Tostig was in the wrong, and that it was his responsibility to act in the interests of the country rather than his own family. Edward was dying. (The *Vita* suggests that Edward's decline was caused by the crisis, and it can't have helped, but by the autumn of 1065 Edward was an old man who had lived for at least a decade longer than any of his predecessors. It's more likely that his increasing decrepitude and the prospect of his imminent demise had prompted the uprising.) England was facing a succession crisis and an invasion: it was obvious to Harold, after his trip to Normandy, that William was determined to press his claim and, if the country appeared vulnerable, there might well be interest in Scandinavia too. So unity was essential. This meant trying to accommodate Ælfgar's sons, however young and inexperienced they might be. (This was a further problem. The wise old heads had gone. The sons of Ælfgar were probably in their teens, as was Waltheof. Almost all the governing experience in the country was held by Harold and Tostig.) But the House of Godwin was not the House of Wessex: it could not automatically command the support of the country. Tostig might be able to justify his record in Northumbria, but ultimately that didn't matter: the Northumbrians had made up their minds. And so Harold had to sacrifice his brother for the good of the country.

It is just about plausible.

It was around this time that Harold appears to have set aside his wife Edith Swan-Neck and remarried. His new spouse was the widow of Gruffydd, the sister of Edwin and Morcar, and the daughter of Ælfgar: her name was Edith.[12] This might also be seen as the action of a man seeking to unite the country, to put England in a position whereby it might be able to resist the invasion which, once the witan did not elect William of Normandy as its new king, was almost inevitable.

---

12 Edith was a popular name in eleventh-century England, at least among high-born women. Old English spellings were not standardised and the name could be spelt in a variety of ways: Eadgifu and Ealdgyth are the most common renderings, but sometimes the same Edith's name would be spelt in different ways.

That's how it might have seemed, but the real story is somewhat more sinister. With Edward dying, it was time for Harold to address the question of the succession. Not just to consider it, but to do something about it. It is impossible to know how long he had been pondering, but it is clear that by the autumn of 1065 Harold had convinced himself that he should be the next King of England.

There were obvious obstacles to this. Edgar was by now probably in his early teens. His hereditary credentials were impeccable: he was not just the last representative of the House of Wessex but the eldest surviving son of the eldest surviving son of Edmund Ironside, and therefore the descendant, through the male line, of both Æthelræd the Unready and Alfred the Great.

He was young. But he was not an infant. England had had boy kings before: indeed, the last four tenth-century kings had all been elected while in their teens. Æthelræd was probably around the same age as Edgar when he became king in 978. It wasn't ideal perhaps, but the circumstances of 1065 would actually have been fairly benign for a young king: had Edgar succeeded he would have been advised by a very experienced Earl of Wessex and a loyal and vigorous Earl of Northumbria, both in the prime of life.

Clearly Edgar wasn't considered utterly unsuitable: in the aftermath of the Battle of Hastings the witan elected him rather than William of Normandy as the new King of England. If he could be a contender then, he could presumably have been a contender a year before.

But that, evidently, was unacceptable to Harold. He was not willing to be Edgar's subject. He wanted the Crown for himself. To get it, Edwin and Morcar would need to be squared. They could not impose their will on the country, but they could defy Harold's will. They had allies in Wales; and if they were given no reason to support Harold's bid, they might as well support someone else: indeed, they might fancy their chances more under a foreign king than under Harold.

So Harold either gave them what they demanded, or he made them an offer they couldn't refuse. Edwin would remain Earl of Mercia. Morcar would become Earl of Northumbria. And their sister would marry Harold and become queen. The House of Leofric would become as influential in the Midlands and the North as the House of Godwin had been in Wessex; it would be a formidable bloc in the witenagemot and at court. Harold would be king, but he would be constrained by an aristocratic family with extensive tentacles throughout the realm, including in the royal household.

Harold probably didn't worry too much about parallels with his predecessor. He was richer and far more experienced, both politically and militarily, than Edward had been in 1042; Edwin, by contrast, was poorer and far less experienced, both politically and militarily, than Godwin had been. As for the price to be paid for his coronation, Harold was clearly prepared to pay it – or rather, to have Tostig and Edith Swan-Neck pay it for him.

Perhaps Harold thought that an alliance with the House of Leofric would compensate for loss of those he betrayed.

If so, he was making a colossal mistake.

6

BROTHERS IN ARMS

But these were merciful men, whose righteousness hath
   not been forgotten.
Their glory shall not be blotted out.
Their bodies are buried in peace.
But their name liveth for evermore.

The Book of Ecclesiasticus

Edward spent his last Christmas at Westminster. The Abbey into which he had poured so much of his energy in the last years of his reign was finished, but he was too ill to attend its consecration. The witan had gathered for the ceremony, and when it became clear that Edward was unlikely to survive the Christmas season they remained, waiting for the inevitable. The king deteriorated after Christmas Eve and by January was on the point of death, so weak that he could barely speak, and tended to by those closest to him: Edith, Harold, and Stigand, the Archbishop of Canterbury.

On his deathbed Edward began to see visions. He told those gathered around him that 'God has delivered all this kingdom, cursed by Him, into the arms of the enemy, and devils shall come through all this land with fire and sword and the havoc of war'. Stigand tried to reassure Harold that these were the words of a man 'broken with age and disease', for which he earned a rebuke from the author of the *Vita*.[1] Edward had kinder words for the queen. 'May God be gracious to this my wife for the zealous solicitude of her service,' he said, 'for she has served me devotedly and has always stood close by my side as a beloved daughter.'

Then he reached out to Harold. 'I commend this woman,' he said, 'and all the kingdom, to your protection.'

His last words were to comfort Edith. 'I shall not die now,' he told her, 'but by God's mercy regain my strength.'

****

In some ways, Edward had undoubtedly been fortunate. While he lived there were no credible pretenders to challenge his position: the men who fancied themselves as his successors were prepared to wait. Nor was there a serious threat from Scandinavia to test him. He had inherited a kingdom which, after half a century of instability, wanted him to succeed; and he had also inherited three great earls who together preserved the peace and prosperity of the country. When he made mistakes, his leading subjects' reluctance to allow the country to collapse into civil war enabled him to recover the situation. And he made his fair share of mistakes: his banishment of Godwin, his preferment of Normans, his refusal to act sufficiently vigorously against rebels, and of course his failure to provide for the succession.

---

1 Stigand, he wrote disapprovingly, 'ought either to have been the first to fear, or to give a word of advice'.

Edward's popular image, if he has one, is of a somewhat unworldly king, more interested in the spiritual realm than the one he was supposed to be ruling. This isn't wholly unfair: he might well have made an excellent abbot, and would probably have been happier as the ruler of a monastic house than he was as the ruler of a country. He was not perfectly suited to kingship, and perhaps he was lucky that his reign coincided with the least turbulent period of the eleventh century.

Or perhaps it is too easy to dismiss a quietly effective king as having benefited from unusually propitious circumstances. Edward kept England safe from foreign invasion. He did not harry his own kingdom; nor did he raid the property of the church. He did not raise vast sums in taxation; indeed, when the geld became superfluous he stopped collecting it. He did not have his own subjects executed or mutilated. When he made mistakes, he put them right. When he suffered setbacks, he took pragmatic steps to mitigate their impact. He endured his fair share of indignities, but he remained dignified. He was neither a bully nor a coward. To blame him for his wife's failure to conceive, given that we cannot know the reasons for it, is unreasonable. And once it became clear that he would have no son to succeed him, he brought his nephew and great-nephew back from their Hungarian exile to secure the succession. He compensated for his lack of martial aptitude by giving responsibility for the armed forces to those men who could best handle it. And Westminster Abbey was a greater legacy to England than any military victory could have been.

What else was he supposed to have done?

Edward was canonised in the twelfth century; he remains the patron saint of the royal family, and of difficult marriages.

* * * *

Edward's commending the kingdom to Harold's protection was not quite the same as indicating that he was officially designating the Earl of Wessex as his successor. The Peterborough version of the *Anglo-Saxon Chronicle* is clearer, saying that Harold succeeded Edward 'as the king had granted it to him', though there is no way the Peterborough chronicler was better informed than the author of the *Vita*. Quite why this tale should have been treated with such credulity is not altogether clear. Harold, of course, had every reason to assert it, and the presence of several witnesses, plus the failure of the Norman (or Anglo-Norman) chroniclers to contradict it, might appear to be fairly compelling. But there are a few reasons to be wary.

Firstly, if the *Vita*'s account of Edward's last months is accurate, he had been significantly agitated by the Northumbrian revolt. That he would signal his support for the man who had at the very least thwarted his desire to subdue it, and who had probably instigated it in the first place, is perhaps somewhat unlikely. Edward had never previously indicated any desire to be succeeded by his Earl of Wessex; of course it was only at this point that the issue became a very pressing one, and maybe the drama of a deathbed designation appealed to him, but it's nonetheless perhaps rather implausible that he would finally do so just as the relationship between the two men was at its most fraught.

Secondly, the most prominent witnesses to the alleged designation had good reasons to pretend to believe the story. Neither Queen Edith nor Archbishop Stigand can have expected to have been better treated by William of Normandy than by Harold: Edith, after all, was Harold's sister, while Stigand's position was not only dubious, it had been obtained at the expense of the Norman Robert of Jumièges. If Edward did whisper something in Harold's ear, and Harold reported that it was, in fact, an official designation, they had every incentive to connive in the dissemination of a little white lie.

And thirdly, Harold was going to become king anyway. His deal with Edwin and Morcar had seen to that. It would have taken a brave man indeed to have questioned the story in the witenagemot which elected Harold. (Perhaps it would have taken a brave chronicler to have recorded such doubts for posterity during Harold's reign too.) There was certainly nothing to be gained from challenging Harold's legitimacy in January 1066: the deal was done.

* * * *

On the morning of 6 January, Edward was buried in Westminster Abbey. That afternoon, in the same place, Harold was crowned. The presence of the witan made an immediate coronation practical and sensible: as they were already assembled, they took the opportunity to decide and formalise the succession straight away. In the circumstances this was prudent. Nonetheless, the contrast with Edward's coronation, which had taken place several months after Harthacnut's death, is stark. Edward could take his time and wait for the holiest day of the year. Harold, whose claim to the throne was rather more questionable, could not afford such a luxury. Even so, holding the coronation on the same day as the funeral was unnecessary, unseemly and panicky.

When the Duke of Normandy was told about the events in England, he was predictably furious. He could not, though, have been all that surprised: William was not naïve enough ever to have believed that Harold intended to keep his promises.

And so he began to make preparations. A council was summoned to meet at Lillebonne, where William persuaded his vassals to support his expedition. Matilda, William's wife and therefore the Duchess of Normandy, was appointed as regent of the duchy in her husband's absence. An emissary was sent to the Pope to persuade him to sponsor the enterprise. William offered to carry a Papal banner into battle, an offer which the pontiff accepted: Harold was a usurper and a perjurer, who had broken an oath sworn on holy relics. And he wasn't just not the rightful king: he had not, in the eyes of God, been properly anointed, because his coronation had been carried out by Stigand, whose position as Archbishop of Canterbury was not recognised by Rome.[2]

The council was not just for show, though it was important for William to be seen to be consulting with his barons. A vassal owed his lord service, but this obligation was limited: a vassal was not a lord's servant. Just what the legal position was in the Normandy of 1066 is murky, and perhaps it was murky in 1066. What is clear,

---

2 According to William of Poitiers Harold was crowned by Stigand. This was probably, but not definitely, a fib. The scene in the Bayeux Tapestry puts Stigand at the coronation, but does not show him actually anointing the new king. John of Worcester's account, meanwhile, has Ealdred, the Archbishop of York, officiating, which would certainly have been more proper. In the circumstances Harold would surely have wanted to have been crowned by an archbishop with the right credentials rather than by one without them. And Harold appears to have been sensitive to this consideration: he had Cynsige (Ealdred's predecessor as Archbishop of York) and not Stigand consecrate Waltham in 1060. But although Stigand does appear to have been a bit of an embarrassment, it also appears that the English were not as embarrassed by him as the Normans thought they ought to have been. Stigand was, after all, the beneficiary (and perhaps also the symbol) of Godwin's decisive victory over the Normans in 1052, and the family appears to have taken to him: William of Malmesbury tells a rather charming story of Edith visiting Stigand in prison in the 1070s, after his downfall, and upbraiding him for not taking care of himself. All things considered it was probably Ealdred and not Stigand who performed the ceremony, but there's no contemporary record saying so, and consequently it's impossible to be certain.

though, is that the duke could not insist that his barons follow him for an indefinite period on a campaign abroad.

If the Norman barons weren't convinced by the duke's proposal it's not difficult to see why. It would be risky. By 1066 William had an impressive military reputation: he had secured his own position in Normandy with victory against Guy of Burgundy at the battle of Val-es-Dunes in 1047, he had defeated the King of France's attempt to assert his authority over the duchy at the battle of Varaville in 1057, and he had conquered the neighbouring county of Maine in 1063. But his adversary in England was also a renowned warrior, and even in the best-case scenario of one great battle in which Harold was defeated and killed there would probably be more fighting: one of Harold's brothers might raise another army, or Edgar might, or there might be Scandinavian intervention. Meanwhile their own lands in Normandy might be vulnerable.

'Many magnates,' explained William of Poitiers, 'argued persuasively against the enterprise as too hazardous and far beyond the resources of Normandy.' He added that 'despair made them exaggerate Harold's strength and diminish their own'. But the Duke of Normandy was able to persuade them, and to recruit followers from outside his own territory too: volunteers from Brittany, Flanders, and even Aquitaine (in the south-western corner of France) signed up to fight for him. They were 'all confident in the justice of his cause', asserted William of Poitiers, though even this most partial of historians conceded that they were 'partly attracted by the well-known liberality of the duke'.

They were making exactly the same calculation as their Norman comrades. There was a risk. But under this leader they would have a decent chance in battle, and they expected, if they won, to be handsomely rewarded.

Seven hundred ships assembled, at Dives (near Caen), and by July they were ready to sail. But there was no helpful southerly wind to help them across the English Channel. The wind blew stubbornly from the north, delaying the invasion fleet's departure.

At some point between late July and early September William ordered his ships to proceed despite the unfavourable conditions. It did not go well. The wind blew them, not to England, but back to the coastline of Normandy. Some were shipwrecked, and some men were lost. William tried to cover up the losses by having the dead bodies which weren't lost at sea buried in secret, but word got out, and there were desertions: the affair had done nothing for William's reputation.

But most of the invasion force remained intact. It regrouped 100 miles up the coast at St Valery (just south of Dieppe) and waited for a friendlier wind.

* * * *

Back in England, Harold was trying to calm people down.

The *Anglo-Saxon Chronicle*'s last comment for 1065 is that Harold enjoyed 'little tranquility' once he became king. The same document then records that Harold visited York in the spring of 1066. This was unprecedented for a West Saxon king. It may, of course, have been that these were unusual circumstances and that Harold wanted to do everything he could to unite the country around his rule, and hoped that in making such a trip he would be able to reassure the Yorkshiremen of his honourable intentions. Perhaps he wanted to show the Northumbrians that he was different from his brother as well as from his predecessors: Harold was, of course, a West Saxon king, but his was a new dynasty, and perhaps his brother's misfortunes had taught him the importance of cultivating the Northumbrians.

Or perhaps there was unrest, and Harold went north to deal with it. If there were disturbances, Harold himself might have been their object: presumably most Northumbrians did not appreciate quite how complicit their new king had been in the downfall of his brother, and perhaps they feared potential reprisals. Or perhaps it was directed against Morcar. The 1065 rebels' demand that he be installed as Earl of Northumbria was manifestly not an expression of the will of the people of the north: it almost certainly wasn't even an expression of the preferences of their thegns. If there was discontent among the people of York, maybe it was at having another unsuitable outsider foisted on them.

In any case, Harold made his way to York; and then, in May, the comet returned.

It is tempting to wonder whether it really was seen as a herald of disaster when it appeared in the night sky, or whether this was a post-hoc interpretation. Its arrival does not seem to have been seen as foreshadowing a calamity in Normandy. But the England of 1066 was a jumpy place, nervously waiting for the inevitable invasion. The English were aware that their king might be seen as having usurped the throne; they were also aware that as far as Rome was concerned one of her two archbishops was a fraud. If any people might have looked uneasily at signs which might have indicated divine displeasure it was the English in the spring of that momentous year.

As news of the culmination of the Duke of Normandy's preparations filtered across the English Channel, Harold called out the fyrd. He stationed this army on the Isle of Wight, perhaps in order to intercept a Norman invasion fleet, and waited.

* * * *

Meanwhile, Tostig was on manoeuvres.

Tostig was not a man to sit around at his brother-in-law's court feeling sorry for himself. He was out for revenge on those who had wronged him. In the spring of 1066 he sailed around England's south coast, making the odd incursion into Wessex. He landed at Sandwich and press-ganged local mariners into joining him, before heading northwards and advancing into Mercia. He was repulsed by Edwin and Morcar, probably without any fighting, and was deserted by the sailors who had been coerced into his service. After this he retreated into the North Sea and, with just twelve ships, sailed to Scotland, where he was hosted by Malcolm.

Tostig was testing the country to see if it would support him. The answer, clearly, was that it wouldn't. Perhaps surprisingly, given the vulnerability of England, especially northern England, Malcolm and Tostig did not agree to invade Northumbria together. Presumably Tostig wanted a greater force than Malcolm was willing or able to supply: Malcolm might have been enthusiastic about a raid, but Tostig wanted more: he wanted a full-scale invasion and to restore his own position. For that, he would need a more powerful king than Malcolm. He tried Sweyn Estrithsson, the King of Denmark, and was rebuffed; he then made his way to the court of Harald Sigurdsson, the King of Norway, and offered his services.

Harald Sigurdsson has a good claim to the title of the greatest thug of the eleventh century. A physically imposing figure, the banner he carried into battle was known as the 'Land Waster'. After Cnut's conquest of Norway in 1030 Harald had travelled to Byzantium and served as a mercenary in the Varangian Guard.[3] There he established a fearsome military reputation. He also became extremely rich, both through the spoils of war and through rather more dubious means.[4] In Norway he levied heavy taxation, and enforced its collection not just through 'harrying' but also by mutilating those who would not or could not pay.

When his uncle, Magnus, died in 1047, Harald inherited the kingdom of Norway. And as his uncle's heir, he also had a claim to the throne of England. By the terms of Magnus' 1037 agreement with Harthacnut, should either of them die childless the other would inherit the vacant throne. Sure enough, Harthacnut did die childless, and Magnus could therefore claim to be the rightful king of Denmark and of England; as Magnus' nephew and successor, Harald could do likewise.

It's difficult to believe that a man such as Harald was particularly bothered about this sort of legalistic argument. It was quite clear that England was vulnerable to invasion, and the Norsemen had never needed much encouragement to try their luck.

Tostig told Harald that he would be welcomed by the English. This was rather a stretch: the King of Norway had a reputation

---

3 'Varangian' is the Greek word for 'Viking'. The Varangian Guard was an élite corps in the personal service of the Byzantine Emperor, comprised of warriors of Norse origin. (After 1066 there was an influx of Anglo-Saxons.)

4 The legend is that the custom of *polutasvarf* gave the Varangian Guard the right to take whatever they could carry from the Emperor's treasury on the day of his death. If such a practice existed, it presumably started when heirs to the imperial throne began bribing these élite warriors to support their claims to the succession, and may have developed into a rather unsavoury free-for-all over time. As a commander in the Varangian Guard, Harald would have been able to exploit either scenario to enrich himself.

for ruthless brutality even by the violent standards of Viking Age Scandinavia. According to the Icelandic historian Snorri Sturluson, writing at the beginning of the thirteenth century, Harald was sceptical rather than flattered. But it wasn't the outright lie which it might now appear to have been.

Clearly Tostig himself was unpopular in Northumbria, except perhaps among some of the clergy. Harald was at best unfamiliar, though probably feared as well as respected. Even so, there appeared to be no particular reason for the Northumbrians to prefer Harold Godwinson to Harald Hardrada. In the Danelaw many may have still felt as much kinship with Scandinavians as they did with West Saxons. Many may not have had strong feelings either way, and would, if forced to support one or the other, make a decision based on expediency rather than on any affection for either man, just as had happened half a century previously.

Harald was persuaded. He set off from Norway, stopping in the Norse earldom of Orkney (which included both that archipelago and the Shetland Islands) to pick up more men. The same northerly wind which had kept the Normans in their harbours made the voyage relatively straightforward, and he rendezvoused with Tostig in early September, and together they sailed up the Humber and the Ouse into the heart of Yorkshire. Three hundred longships which carried an army of perhaps as many as 10,000 men disembarked at Riccall, a few miles south of York.[5]

Nearly 300 miles to the south, unaware that this was happening, the fyrd was disbanding.

* * * *

---

5 Viking longships were relatively large, so 300 of them probably carried nearly as many men as the Norman fleet.

Harold reluctantly made the decision to release his fyrdsmen on 8 September. By then he had little alternative. They were becoming restless: they had already served for the customary sixty days, and although they had seen no action, and knew that an invasion at some point was likely, there were other reasons for them to want to go home. They were running out of supplies; and, even more seriously, they were anxious to get back to their farms and bring in the harvest. Harold could not tell them when they would be needed; he didn't know. So he had to allow them to disperse, knowing that he would have to raise another army again soon.

If that wasn't bad enough, Harold and his fleet then sailed for London. But many of the ships did not make it: they were shipwrecked, possibly in the same storm which damaged the Norman fleet on the other side of the English Channel.

The Peterborough version of the *Anglo-Saxon Chronicle* has an enigmatic reference to a naval expedition. Harold, so it reads, 'went out with a fleet against William'. (Henry of Huntingdon, writing in the 1150s, also includes a brief reference to the episode: 'King Harold, who was a fierce warrior, set out to sea with a naval force to oppose Duke William.' The proximity of Huntingdon to Peterborough and the similarity in the choice of words suggest that Henry used the *Chronicle* as his primary source.) So if this happened, when? Was it some time during the summer, while William was waiting for the wind to change and Harold was waiting for William? Or was it at the beginning of September when Harold discharged his army? Might he have sailed back to London via Normandy, and tried to attack the Norman ships in port, or to draw them out into the Channel for a confrontation? It's possible: a more cautious man than Harold might have been reluctant to sail for the Continent again after what had happened to him the last time, but Harold was impetuous and courageous and liked to surprise his enemies.

There is, though, no record of an actual naval battle. Perhaps the weather intervened: if the expedition happened in the first half of September it might have been caught in the aforementioned storm. Or perhaps William refused to be drawn. When the Normans finally did cross the Channel they did so under cover of darkness, maybe because the potential risks of encountering an English patrol were greater than the risks of sailing overnight. If there was an attempt at a pre-emptive naval strike, it did not succeed.

When Harold arrived in London, very bad news was waiting for him. Northumbria was under attack.

* * * *

Harald Hardrada had not hurried from Norway to York. Nor had he taken a direct route, nor was there any attempt to conceal the invasion fleet, which must have made for an intimidating sight as it sailed down the eastern coastline of Scotland and then of Northumbria, making landfall for occasional raids as it made its way southwards. Given the identity of its leaders its objective was fairly predictable, as was the route by which it would be approached. The news that the Norsemen had harried Scarborough and Holderness before returning to their ships and proceeding southbound made an incursion up the Humber the most likely threat to Northumbria's greatest city. There was, therefore, enough warning for Morcar to prepare his defence. Supported by Edwin, he gathered an army of a few thousand men, and when the Norwegians landed at Riccall he stationed them at

Fulford Gate, just a couple of miles south of York. And that was where, on 20 September, the first battle of 1066 took place.

The defenders were probably outnumbered, though probably not heavily. Both armies numbered several thousand men, so to describe the Battle of Fulford Gate as a 'skirmish' (as it is sometimes styled) would be a mistake. The crack troops of Northumbria, Mercia, and Norway were all engaged. And the English did not disgrace themselves. They chose reasonable ground to defend, with a river on one side and marshland on the other, so that they could not be outflanked; they inflicted considerable casualties on the Norwegians; and they fought on despite suffering heavy losses. The English fyrdsmen were not (as it is sometimes erroneously asserted or assumed) pitchfork-wielding peasants. At the core of the army were professional soldiers in the service of the Earl of Northumbria or the Earl of Mercia. They were joined by well-armed thegns, as well as freemen of more moderate means and status.[6] But they were not battle-hardened veterans. They might have fought in the odd campaign against the Scots or the Welsh, but such experience could not prepare them for a pitched battle against an army of several thousand Norsemen. They were no match for the invaders, and they were comprehensively defeated.

Both Morcar and Edwin survived the carnage at Fulford Gate. Both fled the field of battle, and both slunk away, not to be seen again until after the Battle of Hastings. Snorri asserted that Morcar had been killed. This is usually written off as an example of his unreliability, and it's certainly true that he was writing at

---

6 Soldiering was expensive and in general it wasn't for 'ordinary' men, though some must have fought in the desperate circumstances of 1066. A properly equipped soldier needed chain mail, shields, spears, and axes. An underequipped soldier was of little use and might well have been more of a liability than an asset.

some distance (geographical and chronological) from the events described, and relying at least to some extent on oral traditions as well as earlier written histories. He was, though, hardly unique among medieval historians in getting details wrong, and his *Heimskringla*, a collection of sagas which tell the stories of the Norwegian kings, is nonetheless the best Scandinavian source for the events of 1066.[7] It has been suggested that Morcar may have been wounded in the battle, and that he was seen being carried away, which might explain the confusion. Were the wound serious it might also explain Morcar's absence from Stamford Bridge and Hastings (though it wouldn't explain Edwin's). But it is worth remembering that running away from a battlefield was shameful. Perhaps Snorri couldn't quite believe that an Earl of Northumbria would be so dishonourable as to abandon his men to their fate, and gave him the benefit of the doubt.

The Norwegians proceeded into York, where they met no resistance: Harald graciously agreed to accept the submission of the Northumbrians, as long as they agreed to support his bid for the English crown and supply him with men and materiel for a march south. Such an offer no doubt produced a sigh of relief from the inhabitants of that city, who must have been fearing the worst.

So York was not sacked; nor did it become a military base for the invaders, who remained in Riccall. (Harald's army was roughly the same size as the population of the city: there wasn't the space to accommodate them even had they wanted to station themselves there.) The orders were sent out across the region:

---

7 The *Anglo-Saxon Chronicle* entry for 1066 erroneously calls the King of Norway 'Harald Fairhair' (the name of a ruler of that country 130 years previously) and wrongly names his son Edmund (instead of Olaf). Chroniclers can't be dismissed because they get a few details wrong, especially not when those details are of foreigners.

the Northumbrian thegns were to assemble on Monday 25th at Stamford Bridge, a convenient point on the River Derwent a few miles east of York, to pledge their allegiance to the new régime, do homage to their new lord, and provide hostages.

Harold, who was already on his way north, had other plans.

* * * *

There are three dates in September 1066 of which historians can be reasonably sure: Harold disbanded the fyrd on the 8th; the Battle of Fulford Gate took place on the 20th; and the Battle of Stamford Bridge was fought on the 25th. Exactly when Harold found out about the invasion of the north is not known for sure, but it must have been several days after the 8th and several days before the 20th. What happened next is testament to Harold's own vigour and to the country's military organisation. In a few days Harold was able to summon an army of several thousand men, march it northwards, picking up reinforcements *en route*, and arrive in Tadcaster, 10 miles south-west of York, on the evening of the 24th.

Legend has it that Harold and his army did the journey from London to Yorkshire in four days. This is just about possible, though rather unlikely: Tadcaster is nearly 200 miles from London. If the men who left London with Harold were all mounted, as they would have been were they his housecarls, they could possibly have covered the distance in that time. Were they joined by other mounted thegns from the midland counties on their way, and perhaps by infantry from southern Yorkshire on the 24th, they might have managed it (though this region may already have had its best fighting men conscripted to fight for Edwin and Morcar just a few days previously). Some survivors of Fulford Gate might have made their way southwards after the battle and encountered Harold's army heading in the opposite direction (though there is no evidence for this happening). The horses would have been utterly exhausted, but they didn't have to fight; it wouldn't have been easy on the men, but these were England's best soldiers, and perhaps they were up to it.[8]

The origins of the legend lie in the Peterborough version of the *Anglo-Saxon Chronicle*, which reports the result of the Battle of Fulford Gate, followed immediately by the words, 'And it was made known to King Harold how it had happened, and he came with a great army.' This could imply that this was the first he heard about it.

But this quite clearly cannot be accurate. To cover 200 miles in four days is implausible: to cover 400 miles in four days, which is what would have had to have happened if a messenger brought news of the defeat south, and Harold responded by marching north, would have been impossible, even if he had a fully equipped army ready to go immediately.

The Abingdon and Worcester versions of the *Chronicle* tell a more realistic story. They both record that Harold was told about the invasion when his fleet arrived in London. Confusingly both imply that Harold had been on board ship for the journey, even though both also explicitly state that he had ridden from the south coast to London.[9] Still, the timing makes sense. The news reached London, as one might expect, a few days after it had reached York;

---

8 The English did not fight on horseback, but they did use horses for transport. Housecarls and at least some thegns had at least two so that each horse would only spend part of a journey laden.

9 Both Abingdon and Worcester versions report that 'The king rode up ... the ships were dispatched ... the news was made known to King Harold in the south after he had come from the ships.'

and Harold was probably already on his way by the time of Fulford Gate, finding out about the outcome during the journey.

The speed with which the country could respond to invasion is remarkable. There can have been at most a fortnight between Harold being told the news that the kingdom was under attack and the Battle of Stamford Bridge. England was overwhelmingly rural, but clearly the message was efficiently dispatched to the thegns in the countryside who promptly presented themselves for service. History has not recorded quite how the system worked, but a system there must have been: there were probably relays of messengers, presumably on horseback, perhaps using the abbeys as the antecedents of the coaching inns which later made covering long distances at speed possible.[10]

Despite its proximity to York, it appears that no one who noticed an army of perhaps 6–7,000 men on the outskirts of Tadcaster reported it to the men to whom they were due to swear allegiance on the following day. Instead they seem to have tipped off their king as to the whereabouts of his brother. At dawn on the following day Harold marched to York where the location of the Norwegians was confirmed: this was the day on which the Northumbrians were due to submit to their new chiefs.

The English army marched straight through the city and proceeded to Stamford Bridge. According to Snorri, the first that Harald and Tostig knew about the arrival of Harold's men was when they spotted them on the horizon, their armour glinting in the sun.

---

10 To illustrate quite how remarkable it was to get an army confronting the enemy so quickly, here is a comparison. On 4 August 1914, in the age of steam, railways, and telecommunications, Germany invaded Belgium. That evening the UK declared war and dispatched the British Expeditionary Force, which fought its first battle at Mons (also around 200 miles from London) nineteen days later.

This was not just an unwelcome surprise. As soon as the size of the English forces became apparent, it must have been clear to the invaders that they were doomed. Only around two-thirds of the Norwegian army was there at Stamford Bridge: the rest had stayed with the ships at Riccall. Tostig suggested to Harald that they ought to retreat, but the King of Norway refused. It was probably too late for an orderly retreat. Instead, riders were immediately dispatched to summon those who had been left behind that morning, but it was a round trip of more than 30 miles, and it would therefore be several hours before these reinforcements arrived. And there was almost no chance that the men who had been taken by surprise would be able to hold the English off for that long. They were not prepared for battle. 'The weather,' reports Snorri, 'was uncommonly fine, and it was hot sunshine. The men therefore laid aside their armour.' The Norwegians were going to have to fight without their chain mail.

As the English arrayed themselves for battle, and the Norwegians scrambled to prepare to face them, a few housecarls rode out towards the enemy. Posing as his own herald, Harold called out to Tostig, who rode out to meet him.

Tostig was of course fully aware of the dire situation in which he and his men found themselves. But Harold's situation, while happier at that moment, was hardly enviable. He did not need reminding that he had staked his kingship on the support of Edwin and Morcar, for whom he had betrayed his wife as well as his brother, and that this had turned out to have been an enormous error of judgment. They were nowhere to be seen, and perhaps it was already clear that they would not be appearing for the final campaign of the year either.

Harold had an offer to make.

According to Snorri, Harold offered to restore Tostig's earldom, and to give him 'a third of the kingdom' if, instead of fighting against him that afternoon, he brought his men over to Harold's side.[11] It must have been immensely tempting. The alternative, after all, was death on that battlefield on that day.

Tostig turned him down all the same.

He had come to England in the service of Harald Hardrada, he told his brother, and he would not be so dishonourable as to betray him. He would like to return to England. He would like to fight for his country and his family against the Norman invasion which could come at any moment. But he would not abandon the man whom he had promised to serve. Harold would need to offer something so that the King of Norway could return to his country having made a success of his campaign.

So what, asked Tostig, did Harold propose to offer?

'He can have six feet of English soil,' was the reply, 'or as much more as he is taller than other men.'

It was a good line, and it deserves to be remembered. And any other response would have been grossly irresponsible: Harold had to take advantage of his immense good fortune and take this opportunity to inflict a decisive defeat on the Norsemen.

But in delivering it, he also delivered his brother to his tomb. Neither Tostig nor the Norwegians were about to flee. They were facing an army twice the size of their own, and they were without their body armour, but these were tough and principled men who were faithful to the values of the societies into which they had

---

11 It seems unlikely that Harold would have promised to reinstate Tostig as Earl of Northumbria. The vacant earldom of Wessex, though, which covered around a third of the geographical area of England, would have been a logical alternative and is probably what was actually offered.

been born. They had decided to stand and fight, to the death if necessary, and that's exactly what they did.

The Norwegians formed their shield wall in the shape of a circle on the eastern bank of the Derwent, which the English were approaching from the west. The actual bridge after which the site is named was occupied by a soldier sometimes believed to have been a beserker.[12] Henry of Huntingdon takes up the story:

> A single Norwegian, worthy of eternal fame, resisted on the bridge, and felling more than forty Englishmen with his trusty axe, he alone held up the entire English army until three o'clock in the afternoon. At length someone came up in a boat and through the openings of the bridge struck him in the private parts with a spear.

Once the hero was slain, and the bridge seized, the numerically greater and better-equipped English began to overwhelm the enemy. It was not a rout: the battle went on for several hours, and was still underway when the reinforcements from Riccall arrived. These soldiers, already exhausted after spending the afternoon racing to the battlefield, found most of their comrades (including Harald and Tostig) already dead, and yet put up a furious fight: this last phase of the battle became known as 'Orre's Storm' after the man who led the final furious Norwegian charge.

---

12 According to legend, a 'beserker' was a warrior who literally 'went beserk' on the field of battle, hurling himself at the enemy with all his might. It has been suggested that such warriors took drugs in order to give them the energy and attitude required to fight in such a way; it has also been suggested that they never actually existed. This detail of the Battle of Stamford Bridge only appeared in the twelfth century and yet it's sufficiently memorable that it makes its way into most modern accounts.

It was in vain. The Battle of Stamford Bridge is a classic illustration of the military principle of the concentration of force: the English army, in being able to direct all its might against two smaller forces in turn, was thereby able to overwhelm them both.

Eventually, as the sun set, the remnants of the Norwegian army finally began to abandon the battlefield and made for their ships. The English followed them all the way back to Riccall, cutting many of them down as they fled, and when they got there, by which time night had fallen, they burned the invasion fleet.

And then, rather than massacre all the Norwegians they could find, Harold called a halt to the killing. Olaf, Harald Hardrada's sixteen-year-old son, had participated neither in the first phase nor in the second phase of the battle but had remained at Riccall with the longships. Harold extracted a promise from him that he would neither lead nor allow another invasion of England, and then allowed him and the surviving members of the defeated army to sail back to Norway.

Three hundred ships had brought that army to England. Twenty-four took it home.

Olaf kept his promise: he spent the autumn and winter in Orkney, and returned to the Norwegian mainland in the spring of 1067. He succeeded his father as King of Norway, reigned for another twenty-six years, and is known to history as 'the Peaceful'.

Both Scandinavian and English sources agree that the loss of life on both sides was immense. Harold had won an extraordinary victory, but the cost was great: chroniclers record not just rivers flowing with blood but that the bones of the dead lay on the battlefield, acting as a gruesome marker of the location of the slaughter, for years to come. The battle is regarded as marking the end of the Viking Age: there would be raids in the future, but never again would a Great Heathen Army seriously threaten England.

Harald was granted his six feet of English earth, though a year later Olaf was allowed to take his father's body back to Norway. And Tostig's corpse, according to legend, was interred at York Minster.

****

Harold remained in York for a few days after his victory. He rested and feasted and might well have attended his brother's funeral. Perhaps he was disappointed that its citizens had opened its gates to the invaders after Fulford Gate, but there is no hint that he took any action against anyone, and on balance doing so would probably have been unfair. Trying to mount a defence of the city would have been futile: expecting the people of York to put up armed resistance, which would have achieved little, inevitably been overcome, and resulted in the punishment of having the city sacked, seems unreasonable. In any case, on the morning of Stamford Bridge they revealed the Norwegians' presence and plan to their king, not the other way round.

As for the Norwegians, they had only themselves to blame. The division of the army on the day of the battle turned out to be fatal. They had been careless, or reckless, in not posting enough scouts to warn them of the arrival of an army which they must have expected would arrive at some point, even if not quite as soon as it did. And if Harald had believed Tostig's assurances that the people of Northumbria would support him, he made a fatal mistake: on the eve and indeed on the morning of the battle large numbers of Yorkshiremen must have seen Harold's army, and not one of them reported its presence.

The obvious explanation for these elementary errors, which seem extraordinary in the light of Harald's great military reputation and experience, is that after Fulford Gate the idea that another English army would arrive just five days later seemed preposterous. It wasn't carelessness or recklessness: the Norwegians didn't take precautions because they assessed the situation and concluded that there was no prospect of them having to fight another battle so soon. But Tostig of all people knew what his brother, and indeed the English military system, were capable of. Perhaps he warned Harald and was ignored.

Or perhaps they assumed that Harold would prioritise the defence of Wessex over the defence of Northumbria. Again, though, Tostig could surely have put them straight on this point. Harold was confident, he took risks, and he liked to take the initiative. To disregard the possibility that he might try to take the invaders by surprise was immensely unwise.

Fortune, though, had undoubtedly favoured the bold. To say that Harold had seized the moment would not be quite right: learning that the country had been invaded just a few days after disbanding the fyrd was a crisis, not an opportunity. But the way Harold responded to that crisis ensured that the Norwegians were punished for their negligence. He was certainly lucky to arrive in Yorkshire at the exact time he did: a day earlier or later and the story might have turned out differently. But that unexpected appearance was the manifestation of outstanding leadership. It wasn't just that Harold was decisive, proactive, and vigorous: he exploited the potential of England's military organisation to successfully execute an extraordinary operation.

* * * *

Did Harold celebrate his victory, or did he mourn the death of his brother? Did he allow himself to consider what he would do after he repelled the Norman invasion? If he did, he must have pondered his approach to the Earls of Mercia and Northumbria, who had shown themselves to be ineffective and cowardly at best or disloyal at worst.

If his mind drifted on to these long-term considerations, it was soon to be jolted back to the immediate threat. Two days after Stamford Bridge, the wind changed. That evening, the Norman fleet set sail, and the next morning it landed at Pevensey in Sussex.

7

CONQUEST

This England never did, nor never shall, lie
at the proud foot of a conqueror.

William Shakespeare

The Normans crossed the English Channel overnight, leaving St Valery at nightfall and arriving at Pevensey just after daybreak, presumably reckoning that the danger of crossing in darkness was less than the danger of being spotted and intercepted by English patrols. On arrival, they harried the Sussex countryside. They did not move inland, nor attempt to capture Dover or Canterbury, never mind London. Instead they remained in the vicinity of Pevensey, converting the fortifications of that town and Hastings for their own use.

Was this to stay close to their ships, in case the campaign was a failure? Possibly, but probably not: William and his men knew that if they were beaten in the field, the prospect of their defeated army beating an orderly retreat, embarking and sailing for home was unrealistic.

They stayed near the coast because there was a big risk in marching northward, either towards Canterbury or towards London. William probably didn't know the details of Harold's most recent campaign (though he may well have known about Harold's lightning raid on Rhuddlan, in which Harold also demonstrated his ability to catch an enemy unawares). But, much as he might proclaim his right to rule the country, he knew full well that he was in enemy territory. Even William of Poitiers, who was in no doubt about William of Normandy's right to succeed Edward the Confessor, was under no illusions that England's inhabitants shared this view. He acknowledged that, of the English soldiers, 'some were drawn by love for Harold, all by love for their country, which they, albeit misguidedly, wished to defend against aliens'. Were he to march, his movements would be reported to Harold, who could set a trap for him. By advancing into England, his army would make itself vulnerable to a potential attack from any direction.

Whereas by staying on the south coast William ensured that he could have all possible approaches carefully watched. He knew where Harold would be coming from. And he would be ready for him.

* * * *

It is not clear when Harold found out about the Norman landing. Henry of Huntingdon has him being told at dinner in York after Stamford Bridge, which is quite clearly wrong: the Normans did not even set sail for England until at least two days after the battle. The news, whenever it came, was unwelcome but not unexpected. Harold must have hoped that the onset of autumn might persuade

William to call off his operation, or that the Duke of Normandy might encounter similar difficulties in keeping his army together as he had. Having a period of respite over the winter would have been very welcome.

But Harold wasn't that lucky. The news that the Normans had finally disembarked probably reached York in the first couple of days of October. Maybe Harold was still in the city, and departed on hearing the report; maybe he was already underway when it was confirmed that he and England would have one more enemy to face before the end of the campaigning season.

The king was not alone as he rode south, but nor was he accompanied by the bulk of the veterans of Stamford Bridge. That fyrd had done its duty; many of its men were dead, many more were wounded, and it was in no condition to fight another battle. The royal housecarls, of course, remained with their lord, but now England's military organisation was put to the test again. Once more, for the fourth time in as many months, the messengers were sent out to call out the fyrd. This time they mustered at or near London, having been summoned from all over the southern counties. And while they made their way there, Harold plotted how he would lead them to victory.

Before arriving in London, Harold visited Waltham and prayed. He also met with his family, and it was at this reunion that Gyrth, his younger brother, advised him not to lead an army against William.

The story is not recorded in the most contemporary chronicles, and part of the account which emerges later is somewhat improbable: Orderic Vitalis and William of Malmesbury both have Gyrth telling Harold that after breaking the oath he took in Normandy he would be out of divine favour and likely to lose in battle against the man he wronged. Even so, the rest of the story makes sense. Not enough is known about Gyrth to begin to build a picture of his character. If he did offer to lead the army himself, as both those authorities claim, he may well have had his own reasons for doing so: a victory against the Normans would have been a glorious personal achievement. If things had turned out a little differently, if Harold had made different choices in 1065, it is easy to imagine Tostig making such a suggestion, combining as it did an element of self-regard, an element of self-interest, and an element of duty, with sound military strategy.

Because there would have been one tremendous advantage of putting Gyrth in charge of the army. The outcome of victory would have been the same. But the outcome of defeat would have been very different. With Harold still alive, a defeat for an army led by Gyrth would have had the same impact as the Battle of Fulford Gate. It would have been damaging and demoralising, but it would not have destroyed England's capacity to resist invasion. The war would not have been over: Harold could have raised another army and fought another battle, probably against a depleted enemy.

Harold, of course, refused. Did he want the glory for himself? Was he confident that he would defeat the Norman invaders? Of course he did, and of course he was. He had an impeccable military record, and Gyrth's warning, if it were ever delivered, was issued at quite the wrong time: the events of 24 and 25 September had boosted Harold's self-confidence.

The trouble was that Harold had never been lacking that particular quality.

* * * *

Harold responded to the Norman invasion exactly as William had hoped he would. Sussex was the heart of Harold's family's ancestral homeland, the land which Godwin had held even before he became Earl of Wessex. The settlements that the Normans were harrying were not just part of the kingdom of England and the earldom of Wessex: some of them were Harold's personal property.

Did this provoke Harold into a furious, reckless and ultimately catastrophic reaction? Possibly. William of Poitiers says so: 'the enraged king,' he says, 'hastened his march still more when he heard of the devastation of the land around the Norman camp.' It's certainly fair to say that it is unlikely to have dissuaded him from doing what had worked for him in the past.

William's strategy of staying put was probably the least risky approach to take. But there was nonetheless a risk. If Harold resisted the temptation to offer battle straight away, the Normans would be in trouble. Their army probably numbered between 7,000 and 10,000 men. The only way to keep such an army provisioned was to 'live off the land', but that would involve moving from place to place: the environs of Pevensey could not support it indefinitely. And that wasn't the only consideration. William's followers, who had already spent the summer waiting for the wind to change, were ready for action. Expecting them to hang around all autumn too would have been asking for trouble.[1]

Harold knew all this. But there is no hint anywhere that he ever considered using it to his advantage. Instead he chose to do exactly what William wanted him to do. 'He planned,' wrote William of Poitiers, 'to fall upon them unawares by a sudden or a

---

1 And not just because they might mutiny. A perennial problem for armies was, and would be for centuries to come, keeping them free from disease: the longer an army was in the field, the more likely it was that disease would spread.

night attack.' He intended to do to the Duke of Normandy what he had done to the King of Norway: to arrive unexpectedly and catch his enemy off guard.

It was an extraordinarily bad plan.

England was capable of providing Harold with an army of around the same size as William's at a few days' notice. But Harold did not need to throw them straight into battle. He was not going to be able to ambush William, and he must have known it. The Normans had stayed where they were to avoid exactly that scenario. There was to be no element of surprise: they knew that an English army might appear at any time. Without a recurrence of the sort of once-in-a-lifetime luck from which Harold had benefitted just a fortnight previously, there was no prospect of a repetition of Stamford Bridge.

So why hurry to Hastings? Was it absolutely essential to engage the Normans in battle as soon as possible?

No. It wasn't. It was not only unnecessary, but immensely counter-productive.

Perhaps he was thinking of Edmund Ironside's fatal error in not pressing home his advantage fifty years previously. It may be a cliché that generals always fight the last war, but that's all they've got in the way of practical experience to inform their decisions. If that was in Harold's mind, it was a classic example of learning the wrong lesson from history.

Harold was able to summon an army which, as it turned out, was essentially able to match William's in terms of numbers. But given what he managed to raise with a few days' notice, if he had waited just a few more days there could have been significantly more Englishman than Normans on the field of battle. John of Worcester reports that Harold hastened to Hastings even though 'one half of his troops was not yet assembled', and if this is anywhere near true it was grossly irresponsible of him. The Battle of Stamford Bridge had inflicted damaging losses. The fyrdsmen could evidently be replaced more or less immediately. But the housecarls, the core of the royal army, could not. There is no record of how many of them were lost at Stamford Bridge, but as they were the best soldiers, and would therefore have been at the heart of the action, many of those bones which still marked that battlefield decades later must once have been theirs. With them missing, the English army needed greater numbers of men to compensate for their absence.

Harold was not willing to wait until he had greater numbers of men. He was not temperamentally suited to waiting, and he trusted his instinct that it was always best to fall upon the enemy. That, after all, was how he had made his name as a warrior. And so he set off from London with an army which was significantly smaller than it could have been, arriving at a spot 6 miles north of Hastings late on 13 October.

William's scouts had, of course, spotted Harold's army on the move. They had, of course, reported his arrival. And so the Normans, either under cover of darkness or at first light the next day, marched north. If, at daybreak on 14 October, Harold still thought that he might be able to launch a surprise attack on an unsuspecting William, he was in for a very unpleasant shock. Just a mile or so to the south-east, the Norman army was forming up ready for battle.[2]

---

2 William of Malmesbury alleged that the English spent the night before the battle drinking and singing, while 'the Normans passed the whole night in confessing their sins'. This is not substantiated by any other source and was probably an attempt to impart a moral lesson rather than to tell the historical truth.

THE CAMPAIGNS OF 1066

The English scrambled to occupy the closest usable piece of high ground, the strip of territory now known as Senlac (or Senlac Hill, or Senlac Ridge). It might have been the best available territory on which to fight. But it was very far from ideal. It was just far too small: the soldiers were, in the words of William of Poitiers, 'so densely massed that the dead could scarcely fall ... those who were only wounded could not withdraw, but died in the press of their companions'. The shield wall was tightly packed: there would quite literally be no room for manoeuvre. The army would have to stand its ground and hope to wear the enemy down.

Instead of fighting a bold, attacking campaign on his own terms, Harold had found himself arraying his forces in preparation for the sort of defensive battle which did not suit him at all. He hoisted his banners, the red dragon of Wessex and his own personal standard, the Fighting Man, while the approaching Normans carried the banner which had been presented to them by the Pope. They would have to attack uphill. They would have to find a way to break the shield wall. But William would be able to dictate how the battle unfolded. He would choose how and where to attack, and when, while Harold and his men would just have to take what was hurled at them. In defiance, the English army stood ready, and shouted a simple chant at the warriors who had come to conquer their country.

'Ut, Ut, Ut.'[3]

* * * *

The battle began at around nine o'clock in the morning with Norman archers firing at the English position. (Interestingly, Orderic Vitalis reports that 'King Harold was slain in the first onset.' His source for this was probably William of Jumièges, who states that 'Harold himself fell in the first shock of battle'. Most other authorities describe Harold as dying towards the end of the battle, but if he was killed by an arrow in the eye, which the Bayeux Tapestry, while ambiguous, seems to indicate, then this is consistent with his death happening at the beginning.)[4]

---

3 The Old English word for 'out'.

4 In the scene portraying Harold's death, the caption 'Harold Rex Interfectus Est' – 'King Harold Is Killed' – appears at the top. 'Harold Rex' is directly above a figure who has been struck by an arrow in the eye; 'Interfectus Est' is directly above a figure being hacked to death.

The Norman cavalry rode up the hill to attack, with infantry in support, but were unable to break the defensive line.

The shield wall was holding. Neither arrows nor knights nor foot soldiers could make a decisive breakthrough. William himself, who led the army into battle from the front and spent much of the battle at the heart of the action, had three horses killed under him. And as his men launched themselves at the English shields, and found themselves repelled, the advantage of the higher ground began to tell. It seemed that this was to be an attritional battle, not one in which the genius of either general would be the deciding factor.

Several hours after the battle had begun, with no sign of the shield wall weakening, one section of the Norman army found itself not just failing to make any dent in the English defensive formation, but actually falling back. And this wasn't a unit being gradually pushed backwards, or even an orderly retreat: a part of the Norman force turned and ran away down the hill, pursued by the English. A rumour had spread through the Norman ranks that William had been killed. This was an acutely dangerous moment for his army: William of Poitiers explains that 'the Normans now believed that their leader had fallen', and excuses their retreat on the basis that it 'was not an occasion of shameful flight, but of grief'.

Clearly even Norman warriors were susceptible to losing their nerve at crucial moments; clearly there was a significant wobble in their ranks. It was at this crucial instant that the duke, dramatically and bravely, removed his helmet to show his men that he was still alive, and gave the order for a counter-attack.

The English pursuit had given the retreating warriors an opportunity. By rushing down the hill they had broken up their own line. No longer packed together behind their shields, they were now themselves vulnerable; and, having been in ignominious flight just moments previously, the Normans took full advantage. The foot soldiers stopped and turned, while the knights wheeled their horses around, and, suddenly benefitting from the advantage of towering above their enemies, they cut them down.

And this, at least according to William of Poitiers, gave the Normans an idea.

'They remembered how,' he explains, 'a little while before, flight had been the occasion of success,' and they immediately incorporated a feigned retreat into their battle plan. Three more times, sections of the Norman army pretended to have been battered, and fell back, as though beaten, only to turn and fall upon their enemies.

Deliberately feigning flight in order to tempt an enemy out of an impregnable defensive position, while possibly regarded as incompatible with the Anglo-Saxon warrior code, cannot have been an entirely unexpected battlefield ploy. So why did the English fall for it? One occasion might be understandable, but several times?

There isn't a satisfactory answer. Harold's army was quite clearly not an undisciplined rabble: it held its position all day on suboptimal ground despite mounting losses.

Perhaps William of Poitiers was exaggerating when he said that it happened on three occasions. Perhaps it was tried, but only with very limited success. Perhaps these operations only involved a small number of men on each side, and if they were targeted at different parts of the English front line it's plausible that those warriors, themselves in the midst of battle, might not have known what was going on a few hundred metres away.

Or perhaps it was just the natural reaction of soldiers scenting victory. As dusk fell over the battlefield of Hastings, and the English began to abandon their positions, the Normans chased them too. The fleeing warriors, who were probably just trying to find somewhere to hide from their enemy, picked their way through some difficult terrain, a wooded area with some natural pitfalls; a contingent of knights on horseback vigorously and perhaps recklessly went after them, and stumbled or fell into an 'evil ditch', or (in the original Norman French) *malfosse*. Some died instantly; others were not killed by the fall, but were set upon by the men whom they had just been pursuing and met their ends that way. (Eustace of Boulogne, who had fought for William, was wounded but not killed in this encounter.)

It does, therefore, seem a little unfair to blame Harold's leadership, or his generalship, for his men's falling into the trap. (It would, of course, be particularly unfair to do so if William of Jumièges and Orderic Vitalis were right, and that while all this was going on he was already dead.) Even so, if the Battle of Hastings was a contest between the Duke of Normandy's attack and the King of England's defence, and at least to some extent it was, Harold's military inadequacies were painfully exposed. Harold was very, very good at what he did best. But William, who was conscious of these strengths, had outsmarted him, and he was unable to adapt. And it wasn't just that William had manoeuvred his army into a better position before the battle began. In the midst of battle, William gave the right orders and his army was disciplined enough to carry them out. If Harold ordered his men to resist the temptation to chase the fleeing Normans down the hill, they did not obey him.

Did that change the course of the battle? Maybe not. The feigned retreats were not decisive. The English line, though worn down, continued to hold. The battle raged on, even as the afternoon turned into the evening.

But finally, after an entire day's fighting, the shield wall weakened. Leofwin and Gyrth were killed. And then, most authorities agree, Harold himself fell. Whether or not the cause of death was an arrow in the eye, it seems clear that after several long hours of fighting the English position had been so damaged and depleted that the Normans were finally able to break through, to overwhelm even the royal housecarls, and to hack the king's body to pieces.

As night fell, the surviving English began to abandon the field of battle. Some paused to inflict that one last blow against the invaders in the *malfosse*. Others made for whatever safety they could find, leaving their dead comrades, and their king, in the hands of the victors.

In the aftermath of the battle, Harold's mother, Gytha, who had lost four sons in three weeks, and three in one day, approached the victorious Duke of Normandy to ask for her son's body. William refused, even when she offered his weight in gold. Having caused all this slaughter, William is supposed to have said, Harold did not deserve an honourable burial. Instead, in a piece of mocking disrespect which nonetheless now, perhaps because of the passage of time, feels somehow almost appropriate, his corpse was interred atop a cliff on the south coast, so that he might guard England's shore forever.

That's one tale of what happened to the last Old English king. There is, though, an alternative legend, one cherished by the monks of Waltham, who had as much cause as anyone in England to revere Harold and his memory. Accompanied by two monks of that religious house, Edith Swan-Neck made her way to the battlefield. Picking her way through the carnage, she identified her husband's mutilated body by marks known only to her. It was taken back to Waltham, where it was given a secret but decent and worthy Christian burial.

Maybe Harold did not deserve such tender loving care from the woman he had so cynically discarded. And maybe he does not deserve to be regarded fondly by history. It was, after all, his casual betrayal of some of those closest to him which had brought England to the brink of disaster, and his bad decisions in October 1066 which tipped the country into the abyss of catastrophe.

Nothing could save England now.

* * * *

After his victory, William did not make straight for London. Instead he proceeded to Dover and took the submission of that town, before heading along the old Roman road to Canterbury and thence to Southwark. He did not meet any sustained opposition, but his army nonetheless laid waste to the countryside as they advanced through it: according to John of Worcester 'he ceased not from burning villages and slaughtering the inhabitants'.

At this time, London consisted only of the square mile on the north bank of the River Thames which now constitutes the City of London. (Westminster Abbey was therefore not part of the city, but a couple of miles upstream.) Directly opposite, on the south bank, was the village of Southwark. When William arrived there, he did not attempt to cross the river.

London, stubborn, obstinate London, was not ready to accept him. The witan had proclaimed Edgar as England's new king, and this last show of defiance was clearly taken seriously in some parts of the country: yet another English army was being mustered, and a significant force had evidently already gathered in or around that city.[5]

London was protected by city walls to the north, west and east as well as the river to the south. Even with much of the rest of the country defeated it would be difficult to take by force (as Sweyn and Cnut had found half a century earlier). An opposed crossing of Thames would have been perilous: whether they used the one bridge (on or near the site of London Bridge) or boats, there was no way for the Normans to get several thousand men from one bank to the other without their being very vulnerable on arrival, even to a numerically far smaller force. A well-organised defence could have inflicted heavy casualties even if it was eventually overwhelmed. So instead William followed the course of the river inland, his men continuing to devastate everything in their way, until they reached Wallingford, the first point at which the river could be forded.

Instead of being able to make a stand to defend the country's greatest city, the surviving earls, thegns, housecarls and fyrdsmen were bypassed. They, and their king, could only follow the progress of the Norman army through fearsome reports of the sacking of

---

5 It was at this point that the Abbot of Peterborough died. This required the monks of that abbey to elect a replacement, and to apply to the King to have the decision ratified. They duly requested that Edgar confirm their appointment. This infuriated William, who refused to recognise the decision and demanded forty gold marks before he would be prepared to give his assent to their choice. (Once the money was paid, though, he did not insist on a different abbot.)

towns and villages, and await their turn. And as they did, and the stories filtered back, morale steadily ebbed away.

At Wallingford the Normans crossed the Thames, where they were met by Archbishop Stigand, who formally submitted to William.

As far as the Normans were concerned, of course, Stigand was irrelevant: he might have called himself Archbishop of Canterbury but he was not recognised as such by the Papacy under whose banner they had just fought. Even so, if anyone might have been expected to defy William it was Stigand, who had everything to lose and nothing to gain from régime change. Presumably he hoped that in return for breaking with those still hoping to resist the inevitable he would receive better treatment. His defection did not make London surrendering without a fight inevitable, but it was somehow symbolic. If even he preferred to take his chances with the Normans, the outcome was surely beyond doubt.

After fording the Thames, the Norman army swung back towards London. Even now there was still some appetite for a fight, although there was also palpable panic as the citizens prepared themselves for a battle, or for a siege, or for the worst.

Edwin and Morcar had plunged the kingdom into turmoil at the end of Edward the Confessor's reign. They had fled the battlefield of Fulford Gate, and they had been conspicuous by their absence from Stamford Bridge and Hastings. Too late they had made their way to London; and now, as King Edgar contemplated the prospect of a final showdown, they made the same calculation as Stigand and slunk away. 'While many were preparing to go forth to battle,' wrote John of Worcester, 'the earls withdrew their support, and returned home with their army.'

So there would be no repeat of London holding out for its king against the invader as it had done for Edmund Ironside against Cnut. Accompanied by what was left of the English élite, including Ealdred, the Archbishop of York, and 'some Londoners of the better sort', Edgar made his way to Berkhamsted, which William had just entered, and 'giving hostages, made their submission, and swore fealty to him'.[6]

The campaigns of 1066 were over. The witan rescinded its choice and elected William. There was despair, and in some quarters there was dread, but there was also relief: the harrying would surely now stop, and although William was no Englishman's ideal king, many told themselves that it might not be so bad after all. England had been ruled by foreigners before, and it had not been catastrophic; there might even be opportunities for different men from different families. Had not the great House of Godwin emerged under the rule of Cnut?

If that's how the English were reasoning, they were about to be disillusioned.

For a while the harrying did not stop. The witan may have elected him, but the Normans did not consider their duke as the King of England until he was crowned; and until the coronation, which was held on Christmas Day, they continued to view themselves as an occupying force in enemy territory. William had won a decisive battle, but there were large parts of the country which he had not subdued: the witan had assented to his accession,

---

6 John of Worcester adds Edwin and Morcar to the list of those who did so, suggesting that after deserting Edgar they learned that there was to be no fighting after all, and so hurried back to participate in the surrender. This implies rather a lot of movement in a short period of time, and while (as we've seen) this was quite possible, perhaps on this matter William of Poitiers, who has the earls submit a few months later, is closer to the truth.

but grudgingly, and only after exhausting all other options. His position was not, in December 1066, precarious; but nor was it indefinitely unassailable.

The ceremony took place in Westminster Abbey, just as Harold's had; and it was conducted by Archbishop Ealdred, just as Harold's had been. But the Normans' unfamiliarity with English customs created a deadly misunderstanding. William, like his predecessors, was crowned in the presence of the English élite. There was no room for the victorious army, which had to wait outside while their lord was anointed with the holy oil which would elevate him into his new position. Towards the end, as was normal, the new king was presented to his leading subjects; and, as was normal, they acclaimed him with loud cheers.

Unfortunately, the assembled warriors, hearing only the noise, assumed that this had instead been a roar of disapproval, that proceedings had been disrupted, and that there might be trouble. They raised the alarm, and for a while there was a dangerous tumult, with the enraged Normans setting fire to houses. Inside, as Orderic Vitalis describes, there was panic:

> The flames quickly spreading, the people in the church were seized with panic in the midst of their rejoicings, and crowds of men and women, of all ranks and conditions, eagerly struggled to make their escape from the church, as if they were threatened with immediate danger. The bishops only, with some few of the clergy and monks, maintained their post before the altar, and trembling with fear completed the coronation office with some difficulty, the king being much alarmed.

It was an inauspicious start to the new reign.

8

COLONISATION

This will be the manner of the king that shall reign over you...
He will take your fields, and your vineyards, and your oliveyards,
    even the best of them, and give them to his servants.
And he will take the tenth of your seed, and of your vineyards,
    and give to his officers, and to his servants.
And he will take your menservants, and your maidservants, and
    your goodliest young men, and your asses, and put them
    to his work.
He will take the tenth of your sheep: and ye shall be his servants.
And ye shall cry out in that day because of your king...
and the LORD will not hear you.

The Prophet Samuel

The new king had plenty of loyal followers to reward. But he also had plenty of resources with which to do so. The deaths of Harold, Leofwin and Gyrth, as well as the many housecarls and thegns who had died at Fulford Gate, Stamford Bridge and Hastings, had made plenty of land available for redistribution, and had created plenty of vacancies for royal officials.

William did not try to dismantle the English élite straight away. Earls Edwin, Morcar, and Waltheof, along with Archbishops Ealdred and Stigand, kept their positions and their titles. The women of the Godwin dynasty were not persecuted: Gytha held on to her estates around Exeter, while Edith was treated honourably, as befitted the relict of Edward the Confessor: she retired to her lands in Wessex, and when she died, in 1075, she was buried near her husband in Westminster Abbey. Even Edgar remained at liberty, though when William returned, in the spring of 1067, to Normandy, he took the ætheling, as well as the earls and archbishops, with him. (When they came back to England, Edgar took his family and sought refuge in Scotland, where his sister Margaret married King Malcolm.)

Why was William so reasonable? If he had ever been under any illusion that England might welcome him as its rightful monarch, the events of 1066 persuaded him otherwise. The high-ranking English survivors of that year had shown him no loyalty: why not replace them with men who had?

There are several possible answers. One is that while William's 'official' position was that Harold had always been an illegitimate usurper, to regard Englishmen who had supported him as traitors to their true king was an unreasonable position to hold. Cnut had respected men who had served his adversaries loyally, and distrusted men who hadn't; it was a logical and prudent position to take as well as a moral one.

Another is that while the Normans were not as war-weary as the English, nor did Normandy have England's potential military resources. William would rather not have to deal with resistance or rebellion, but if he immediately dispossessed the earls, there was a good chance that, rather than go into exile never to be heard of again, they would raise the country, or at least the north and the midlands, in their support. They would have nothing to lose; and while their military reputation was unlikely to inspire much enthusiasm, Mercian and Northumbrian thegns who had survived the carnage of 1066 might nonetheless be persuaded to back an uprising. If their new king was going to treat earls who had submitted to him without fighting in such a way, those thegns might reasonably fear that they and their property would be next.

There was a further potential problem. No doubt William could find better lieutenants than Edwin and Morcar, neither of whom had distinguished themselves in any way in their brief careers as earls. But replacing them would not necessarily be straightforward. Theirs were powerful positions, and could become even more so under William, who had Normandy (and Maine) to rule too. Under Cnut, who had also combined ruling England with ruling lands in continental Europe, the great earls had been given great responsibilities and had become great men in their own right. Now Edwin was no Leofric, and Waltheof was no Siward. But who was? Did William have, among those who had campaigned alongside him, men of their ability and judgment and loyalty?

It didn't look like it. And replacing Edwin, Morcar, and Waltheof with Normans was fraught with difficulty. Whoever was elevated to those earldoms could become dangerously strong; whoever was not might well become dangerously disaffected. William had an early warning of this when Eustace of Boulogne, who had fought alongside him at Hastings, decided that he had received insufficient reward and, in spring 1067, attacked Dover. The affair turned out to be a fiasco: Eustace himself escaped, but many of his followers were killed, some of them by being chased off the famous White Cliffs. But if William needed a reminder of the fickleness of men's loyalties, this would do. Even the king's (half-) brothers, Odo of Bayeux and Robert of Mortain, who were to take on great responsibilities in England, could not be trusted, at least not in the way that Edward the Confessor had trusted Harold: while Odo did not fall from favour until several years later, his own personal ambition was his eventual downfall, and perhaps William could see the potential threat there all along.

And so William decided that it would be best to allow two of the incumbents to retain their earldoms for the time being. They might appreciate his magnanimous generosity. Or they might not. He probably suspected that betrayal was rather more likely: neither Edwin nor Morcar had shown any loyalty to their previous lords. But he could deal with that as and when it happened. If such a scenario was inevitable, and it probably was, better to delay it until such time as Wessex, East Anglia and London had been digested and his position in England firmly secured. There was, after all, plenty to be done outside Mercia and Northumbria. The south was William's priority. It was what made England a prize: this was where much of the wealth was. And because of the demise of Harold and his brothers it was also where new leaders were most urgently needed. Edwin and Waltheof held on to their titles.

Morcar, though, did not. There is no record of his having been removed from office, but William appointed several Earls of Northumbria in the 1060s (none of whom turned out to be a success) so he must have been. Perhaps Harold did so after Fulford Gate, though that raises the question of why he did not treat Edwin in the same way. Perhaps Morcar was only appointed Earl of Northumbria after Edward the Confessor's death, in which case William might have chosen not to recognise that he had ever been a legitimate earl. Or perhaps William replaced Morcar but not Edwin because Edwin was older, and at least in theory able to discharge the duties of an earl, whereas Morcar, as the younger brother, was not. (Though *that* raises the question of why he did not treat *Waltheof* in the same way. Perhaps because Northumbria was different: one thing that the Conquest did nothing to change was the particular character of that earldom, with its particular challenges, which demanded a strong man and not a feckless wastrel like Morcar. In any case, although Edwin and Waltheof appear to have retained their titles as earls, they did not exercise the sort of powers that Edward the Confessor's earls did. William would not be allowing any of his subjects to have that amount of influence.

The great earldoms were, after all, only half a century old. They had been created by Cnut to suit his particular circumstances and had survived because none of his successors had been strong enough to abolish them. Apart, perhaps, from Northumbria, William had no need for them. He appointed Ralph 'the Staller,' a Breton who had served Edward the Confessor, Earl of East Anglia, and then allowed his son, also named Ralph, to succeed him, but abolished the earldom after the younger Ralph rebelled in 1075. Thereafter William's earldoms were smaller, and based on the traditional counties of England.

But conquest was not the limit of William's ambition, nor indeed that of most of his followers. Unlike the warriors who had sailed from Scandinavia with Cnut half a century previously, they were not seeking to gather as much treasure as they could before enjoying a glorious return to their homes. They were intending to settle in England and to become part of its ruling élite.

The Norman Conquest was over. The Norman Colonisation was about to begin.

* * * *

William was, according to Orderic Vitalis, 'a very wise man, and very rich, more splendid and powerful than any of his predecessors were'. He took a robust approach to law and order. 'A man of any account might go over his kingdom unhurt with his bosom full of gold', and 'no man dared slay another'. His men were disciplined. 'He forbade their oppressing the conquered', warning them that 'they must be cautious not to excite revolt by their unjust treatment of those whom they had fairly subdued'. While 'he restrained the people by force of arms', he also 'set bounds to arms by the laws'. You could walk the streets at night in William's England: 'If any ceorl lay with a woman against her will, he soon lost the limb that he played with', while 'taxes and all things concerning the royal revenues were so regulated as not to be burdensome to the people'.

Orderic was well placed to assess the Norman record. From the vantage point of the first half of the twelfth century, he had the advantage that what he was writing about was within living memory, but equally enough time had passed between the events and his putting quill to parchment that he could take a cooler, less partisan approach than, say, William of Poitiers or the author of the *Anglo-Saxon Chronicle*. And it might have helped that he had one Norman and one English parent. The Norman régime may have had its benefits, but Orderic did admit that at its heart was the fact that 'strangers were enriched with English wealth, while her sons were iniquitously slain, or driven into hopeless exile in foreign lands'.

Orderic was also well aware that even his nuanced defence of Norman rule would test his readers' credulity, and he had an answer ready for those who might observe that the conduct of the Norman occupiers had not always conformed to the lofty standards he ascribes to them. He was too serious an historian to pretend that the English were not subjected to lawless violence and rapacious taxation by their conquerors. But he had someone to blame for it. This was not the king's fault, he explained, but that of his ambitious chief adviser, Odo, the Earl of Kent. The royal forces were supposed to obey the law. But Odo, who, in his half-brother's absence, was 'issuing his orders everywhere like a second king', allowed them to disregard the law: he protected men who 'robbed the people and ravished the women' from any consequences.

This is unlikely to have been of much consolation to the régime's victims. Orderic wasn't the first commentator to blame 'wicked counsellors' rather than the monarch for bad government, and he wouldn't be the last. These 'loyal fictions' could be convenient, but they rarely identify responsibility for political decision-making accurately.

An obvious example of William's contempt for the people he conquered, and of the impact of the Conquest on the English, was his creation of royal forests. 'Ejecting the inhabitants,' explains William of Malmesbury, 'he let a space of many miles grow desolate, that he might there pursue his pleasures.' Areas officially designated as 'forest' were not all actual forests, but rather land in which the natives were forbidden to clear or cultivate the land, to keep animals, to hunt, to carry hunting equipment (this even extended to dogs, which were banned from royal forests) or to chop down trees for firewood. Forest law was, of course, unpopular. 'His rich men bemoaned it,' the *Anglo-Saxon Chronicle* lamented, 'and the poor men shuddered at it.' It was enforced through harsh penalties: the same source records that anyone caught hunting deer was blinded.

****

The Godwin dynasty had been destroyed by the events of 1066, though there were still some individual survivors. The only son of Godwin to survive, Wulfnoth, remained a prisoner for all of William's life. (He was briefly released on William's death in 1087 but the Conqueror's son and successor as King of England, William Rufus, then imprisoned him again.) Of Hakon there is no trace. Tostig had two young sons, Kjetil and Skuli, both of whom settled in Norway.

Of Harold's wives, the last we hear of Edith of Mercia is her being sent north to Chester after Hastings. Edith Swan-Neck was a major landowner in 1066, but there is no record of her after that. Perhaps she followed her husband's family into exile, or perhaps she was dispossessed by the Normans, though that wasn't usually William's style: his prominent English subjects were usually given the benefit of any doubt and allowed to remain in possession of their lands until they died or forfeited it by rebellion. But there is no way of knowing what happened to her.

As well as Godwin, Edmund and Magnus, his sons by Edith Swan-Neck, Harold appears to have had two more, both born in 1066, possibly posthumously. One of them, Harold, was the son of Edith of Mercia; the other, Ulf (or Wulf), may have been

Harold's twin, or he may have been the son of Edith Swan-Neck.[1] Wulf (or Ulf) was in William's custody along with Wulfnoth in 1087; Harold, meanwhile, eventually joined his cousins in Norway, where he was welcomed by King Olaf, who had not forgotten how the boy's father had spared him after Stamford Bridge. Harold's daughter Gytha also went into exile, and eventually married Vladimir of Kiev, bearing him seven sons and three daughters. Her sister Gunhild remained in England, eventually leaving Wilton Abbey, where she spent most of her life, in the 1090s, to marry, scandalously, Alan the Red, a Breton who had fought for William at Hastings.

Neither Godwin nor Edmund nor Magnus had fought at Hastings. It's unlikely that they were too young: presumably their absence was intended to ensure the continuity of the dynasty. (This consideration presumably explains why Olaf, the teenage son of Harald Hardrada, travelled with his father from Norway to Northumbria, but did not fight at Stamford Bridge). Harold's election had been slightly dodgy, and his legitimacy a little dubious, in a way that Edward's had never been. But his accession was also undeniably the will of the witan, which did after all constitute the leading constitutional experts of the age, and there was little if any appetite for any of the alternatives. Still, support for Harold's individual claim to the throne did not extend to his sons. After his death the witan had (briefly) turned to Edgar, not to any of Harold's sons, who went into exile in Ireland.

In the spring of 1068 the young men did as their father had done fifteen years previously and set sail for their homeland from

---

1 If they were twins, their early separation is difficult to explain. If Edith of Mercia was able to keep one son out of William the Conqueror's hands, why not the other?

their Irish exile. They too sought to rouse the West Saxons in their support. But unlike their ancestors they were to be disappointed. They approached Bristol, only to find that the citizens there were not interested in welcoming them: far from finding support, they found themselves barred from the city, which preferred to demonstrate its loyalty to King William. There was a skirmish, and the commander of the city's defences, Eadnoth, was killed, but there was quite clearly no enthusiasm for their cause, and they withdrew to the Emerald Isle. A year later they tried again, this time targeting Exeter, but with no more success. Eventually they left Ireland for Scandinavia, and thereafter they too disappear into historical oblivion.

If any part of the country was going to support them it should have been the south-western corner. This was the heartland of the old kingdom of Wessex, which had held out against the Danes; it was part of the earldom which had been ruled by their father and their grandfather. But it was, from a Norman perspective, remote: it was a long way from London and the southern counties which faced Normandy across the English Channel. So it was not swarming with Normans: indeed the aforementioned Eadnoth was an Englishman who had been Harold's Master of the Horse. The matriarch of the House of Godwin, Gytha, still held land there.[2] And, most promisingly, there had already been some opposition to the Normans in Exeter, which had initially refused to allow them to enter the city. Yet support for Harold's sons was negligible.

---

2 There is no evidence for Gytha having been involved in her grandsons' activities, but she too went into exile, fleeing to St Omer in Flanders, perhaps because she expected reprisals, though there is no clue as to whether this is because she had participated in their treachery or whether she just feared for her safety afterwards.

Perhaps this was because at the time of this incident the Normans had handled Exeter carefully. Instead of sacking the city, they had pardoned its citizens, and instead of looting they had satisfied themselves by erecting and garrisoning a castle. If this was intended to convince the inhabitants that Norman rule would not be so bad, while at the same time emphasising that resistance would be futile, it appears to have succeeded.

But Harold's sons were unable to persuade the English, or even the West Saxons, that they had a case. Harold's marriage to Edith Swan-Neck does not appear to posterity to have significantly differed from some earlier royal marriages. Both Edmund Ironside and Harold Harefoot, who were born into very similar unions, were considered legitimate. Even so, Harold seems to have accepted that his children by Edith Swan-Neck were not bona fide æthelings. As king, the earldom of Wessex had been at his disposal, but he had neither appointed his eldest son as his successor there nor divided it between him and his brothers. This recognition might or might not have been part of the deal when he married Edith of Mercia. But even if it was, perhaps that was just an acknowledgement of what was already clear. Harold may have been the rightful king. The desperate times of 1066 had called for desperate measures. But royal blood really mattered, and neither Harold nor his offspring had any of it.

Would England, or Wessex, have put up more of a fight for a scion of the ancient ruling house? The experience of Edgar's attempts to raise an army during his brief reign suggests not. *Pace* Shakespeare, this England had indeed lain at the foot of a conqueror, several times. She had done so at the end of the ninth century, when Alfred the Great had preserved the kingdom of Wessex against the Great Heathen Army. She had done so at the beginning of the eleventh century, when Sweyn had crushed Æthelræd, before Edmund Ironside then rallied the country against Cnut. There is, of course, a danger in ascribing the different outcomes to the characters of the different kings of England. In retrospect, Alfred and Edmund look heroic while Æthelræd looks weak, and it was somewhat more complicated than that. But it wasn't really *that* much more complicated. England would have fought had she had a leader who could inspire his countrymen to follow him. Harold, like Alfred and Edmund, had been one such leader. Edgar, and Harold's sons, like Æthelræd, were not.

This might not have been due to their personal failings, though Edgar does not appear to have impressed his contemporaries. Orderic describes him as 'handsome in person' and 'a good speaker' but 'slow in action', while William of Malmesbury attributes his lack of support to 'indolence or simplicity'. All of them, though, were young and unproven, and few Englishmen can have fancied their chances against William. Rather than risk their lives and fortunes on such adventures, most preferred to make their accommodation with the new order. 'Some of the most discreet citizens of the towns, and noble knights of distinguished name and wealth,' wrote Orderic, 'espoused the cause of the Normans against their own countrymen with great zeal.' Before long, he explained, 'the English and Normans lived amicably together in the villages, towns and cities, and intermarriages between them formed bonds of mutual alliance'.

****

Castles, like the one built at Exeter, had several functions. They were residences, garrisons and administrative centres; they provided places to safely keep money, arms, and prisoners.

They were architectural assertions of power and dominance. And they were military bases from which towns and their surrounding areas could be controlled. The idea of a fortified military base was not a new one, but Anglo-Saxon kings did not erect fortifications to keep their own subjects in line. The Norman castle, whether it be a forbidding stone structure such as the Tower of London, or the more common and more modest motte-and-bailey building, was essentially a tool of oppression. As a fortress it enabled the Normans to secure themselves against the native population and to monitor the landscape over which it loomed. And as a base it provided all the materiel they would need to launch operations, on whatever scale. Resistance, a castle seemed to proclaim, was futile.

For some, though, there could be no collaboration with the occupying power, or at least not straight away, and so, however futile, resistance was their only option. In the West Midlands, there was a resurgence of the old Mercian–Welsh alliance against royal authority. A Mercian thegn by the name of Eadric, a nephew of the treacherous Eadric Streona, refused to abase himself before the Conqueror. Instead he and Bledwynn, a brother of Gruffydd, defied the Normans in the same way that Gruffydd and Ælfgar had defied Edward: outright disobedience and sporadic raiding. Interestingly, especially given Edward's reputation for weakness and William's for ruthlessness, William appears to have responded to Eadric in the same way that Edward had responded to Ælfgar: instead of attempting to root him out and make an example of him, he offered his forgiveness in return for future loyalty. And Eadric evidently accepted, because by 1070 he was with the royal forces at Chester.

While Harold's sons were trying to capitalise on discontent in the south-west, there was trouble in the north. William's first appointment as Earl of Northumbria, Copsi, appears to have been a particularly unwise one: Copsi had been Tostig's loyal lieutenant in the north, and as such was unlikely to command the support of the Northumbrians. When, just a few weeks after his appointment, he was murdered, William replaced him with a native Northumbrian by the name of Gospatric, who promptly rebelled; the third earl, a Norman named Robert, did not even survive his first night in Durham before he too was assassinated. Northumbria was, yet again, in open rebellion: and Edwin, again, was involved.

Edwin was no doubt irked by having been taken off to Normandy and by his obvious decline in status. He had also asked to marry one of William's daughters and been rebuffed. (The Conqueror had several, but evidently he did not consider Edwin worthy of any of them.) He too sought the support of the Welsh, but neither was able to raise much of a force. William responded by marching north, stopping to erect castles in Warwick and Nottingham to impose a permanent presence in the heart of Mercia. The rebels submitted rather than face the wrath of their king, and Edwin successfully begged for pardon.

But there was no sign that the English were ready to settle down and accept their new masters, and this state of ongoing hostility made life uncomfortable for the conquerors as well as for the conquered. The England of the late 1060s was a dangerous place. It was dangerous for the English, who were vulnerable to the impredations of their new rulers. But it was also dangerous for the Normans. As members of a marauding horde they were predators. However, once they were dispersed around the country they became potential prey. Estimating eleventh-century population sizes is very difficult, but it's unlikely that there were fewer than 2 million people in England, and it's very unlikely that there were anywhere near 20,000 Normans in the country. They couldn't all live in castles and only leave under armed guard. That they were vulnerable is graphically shown by the introduction of the 'murdrum' fine. If a corpse was discovered, and could not be identified, it was legally presumed to be Norman, and a financial penalty was imposed on the natives.

Clearly relations between the Normans and the English were not everywhere as harmonious as Orderic suggested, and this had consequences for family life. The same chronicler recorded disapprovingly that 'some of the Norman women were so inflamed by passion that they sent frequent messages to their husbands, requiring their speedy return, adding that, if it were not immediate, they would choose others'. The prospect of following the conquerors across the English Channel clearly did not appeal, and perhaps it's not surprising that several Norman men 'returned obsequiously to their lascivious wives'.

The unrest was far from over. The next year saw another outbreak, this time with the Danes and the Scots involved as well as Edgar and Waltheof. Northumbria rose against the Normans again, but this time it all seemed rather more serious. Malcolm intervened on the side of the rebels; Danish longships sailed up England's eastern coastline, and there were landings in Kent, East Anglia, Lincolnshire, and Yorkshire, with some warriors entering the city of York. But the raiders avoided meeting William's forces in battle, and although they remained in the country for some time, they were an irritating nuisance rather than a threat. Sweyn Estrithsson, the King of Denmark, had learned to respect the King of England's military abilities, and preferred not to risk Harald Hardrada's fate: he was not with the fleet, and without royal leadership there was a distinct lack of direction among the raiders.

There was no question that the royal forces were far stronger than their enemies. But by 1069 Northumbria seemed to be ungovernable. William could march into York and Durham and enforce obedience at the point of a sword, but outside the cities, and once his men had withdrawn, it may as well not have been part of England for all the respect its inhabitants showed to the king. This was intolerable, and William was determined to put an end to it. He had tried being reasonable. He had tried moderation and conciliation. Now it was time for a show of brute strength, not just by way of retaliation but also to set an example, to show that he would not be defied indefinitely.

And so, that winter, the Normans harried the North. William led the expedition to hunt down and punish the rebels himself. But his punitive campaign was not limited to those who had rebelled. Instead it encompassed the entire region, which he ruthlessly ravaged. Orderic was not impressed:

To his lasting disgrace, he yielded to his worst impulses and set no bounds to his fury, condemning the innocent and the guilty to a common fate. In the fullness of his wrath he ordered the corn and cattle, with the implements of husbandry and every sort of provisions, to be collected in heaps and set on fire until the whole was consumed, and thus destroyed at once all that could serve for the support of life in the whole country lying beyond the Humber. There followed, consequently, so great a scarcity in England in the ensuing years, and severe famine involved the innocent and unarmed population in such misery, that in a Christian nation more than a hundred thousand souls, of both sexes and all ages, perished.

One prominent (and indisputably guilty) man, though, was spared: Waltheof, who was captured but granted mercy and pardoned; just a few months later he married William's niece, Judith. Edgar, meanwhile, managed to escape. He returned to Scotland, but in 1072 William sent a force northwards to punish Malcolm for his part in the rising, and in return for peace Malcolm agreed to stop harbouring Edgar, who therefore left Scotland for Flanders, where enemies of the Duke of Normandy were always welcome.

William of Malmesbury concurred that the Conqueror's actions were indefensible. 'Unbecoming such great majesty' is his restrained judgment, accompanied by the damning addition, 'I have here no excuse whatever to offer.' The desolation, though, achieved what it had set out to do: William was to have no more serious trouble from Northumbria.

Amid the smouldering ruins of York, and the carnage and wreckage of the Yorkshire countryside, William feasted, celebrating the Christmas of 1069 and the crushing of his enemies.

* * * *

A few remaining rebels remained at large, unwilling to surrender despite the hopelessness of their cause. William wrapped up his northern campaign as the winter of 1070 came to an end. Pockets of resistance remained, and were crushed. By 1071 both Edwin and Morcar, who had not been involved in the rebellion of 1069, had joined the scattered outlaws roaming the countryside: Edwin was, in the words of the *Anglo-Saxon Chronicle*, 'treacherously slain by his own men'.

Morcar ended up in East Anglia, where the last resistance to the Normans was being orchestrated by a dispossessed Englishman by the name of Hereward. Little is reliably known about Hereward, who came to be known to history as 'the Wake' (though only a couple of centuries later). He first appears in 1070, looting Peterborough Abbey, possibly in alliance with the Danes who were still desultorily sailing along the English coastline. This might not be an auspicious start to an heroic story, but the justification – that he was taking the valuables in order to prevent the Normans from seizing them – is not wholly unbelievable. According to John of Worcester, 'William commanded that the monasteries of all England were to be searched' so that 'the money which rich Englishmen had deposited there' could be seized. This sounds rather like a euphemism for stealing valuables from religious houses, and it is consistent with both Orderic's and William of Malmesbury's references to the confiscation of property from the English Church.

Once the might of William's forces were turned on Hereward's band of men, of course, they had no chance, and if Hereward was counting on Danish support, he was to be disappointed: they returned home in that year. The rebels were surrounded on the Isle of Ely, where they held out into 1071, but eventually they were forced to surrender. Morcar was captured, and spent the rest of his life in custody.

Hereward, though, was not found among the defeated men. He had managed, somehow, to sneak away, and although legend has it that he was reconciled with William, there is no historical evidence for this. More likely he survived, for a while, as an outlaw, though the life expectancy of someone who lived outside the law, and therefore without its protection, was not very high.

The legend of Robin Hood is traditionally dated to the reign of Richard the Lion Heart at the end of the twelfth century.

But the tale, of a dispossessed midland landowner, alienated from the régime, retreating into the greenwood to take his chances with other outlaws, harassing and stealing from the hated barons, and winning the loyalty of ordinary people by sharing some of the proceeds with them, is unmistakably rooted in the Norman Conquest.

* * * *

When it was all over, there was one last farcical attempt at a rebellion. In 1075 Roger, Earl of Hereford, and his brother-in-law, Ralph, Earl of East Anglia, began plotting against William. According to John of Worcester, 'they compelled Waltheof, who was won over by their treachery, to join', which is a quite remarkable example of an account trying to have it both ways in just one sentence. The last English earl, having just been persuaded to join, then wrecked the plot by blabbing about it. The rebels asked for Danish assistance, and Sweyn did send some ships, but their occupants (again) were only interested in plundering (including breaking into York Minster) and returning home. The plot was easily crushed. Ralph escaped back to Brittany in disgrace; Roger was deprived of his lands and exiled. Waltheof also fled overseas, but he begged for pardon, and offered to buy the forgiveness of the king. William, reported the *Anglo-Saxon Chronicle*, 'made light of it until he came to England', whereupon he was arrested, tried, and, after a few months, executed.

The difference in their treatment is sometimes explained as the consequence of Waltheof, an Englishman, being treated according to English law while Roger, a Norman, was treated according to Norman law. This is unconvincing. Morcar, after all, was not executed for his treachery. If John of Worcester was telling the truth, Waltheof could count himself unlucky. He hadn't, after all, taken up arms. It is not out of the question: William had no doubt had enough of troublesome English subjects, and it's quite conceivable that the way the English had abused his leniency had exasperated him to the point where he had Waltheof executed for the slightest involvement in what turned out to be a fiasco. However, it seems more likely that Waltheof (for whom this was not a first offence) had been a more important figure in the abortive rising than the accounts suggest. By the twelfth century he was becoming a cult figure, a symbol of a lost England, and maybe that's why he is portrayed as a victim rather than as someone who abused the king's mercy.

Orderic was unable to resist giving Waltheof an impressive end. He met his death reciting the Lord's Prayer, but had only reached 'and forgive us our trespasses' when he was decapitated. But the last English earl wasn't quite finished. 'The head,' Orderic tells us, 'after it was severed, uttered with a loud and distinct voice, in the hearing of all present, "But deliver us from evil. Amen!"'

* * * *

In 1069, Ealdred, the Archbishop of York, died. This left England without a 'proper' archbishop and so, once William had crushed Northumbria, he needed to turn his attention to the Church. He was conscious, though, that as king his powers were limited, and so he invited the Pope to send a papal legate (a representative who would have the authority of the Papacy) to impose some overdue reforms on the English Church. According to Orderic (himself, of course, a clergyman) many English bishops were men whose 'sinful lives and ignorance of pastoral care made them unworthy of episcopal office'. This had been part of William's pitch to the Pope before the Conquest, but he had not acted straight away, preferring to wait for official dispensation to go ahead and remove some of the more egregious examples.

The delegation arrived in England in 1070. Predictably, Stigand was deposed: not only had he never been properly consecrated, but he had continued to hold Winchester 'in plurality' with Canterbury. He was incarcerated, his property was seized, and he died in prison in February 1072. Several bishops (and several abbots too) were also removed from office, including Stigand's brother Æthelmær, the Bishop of Elmham (in East Anglia); Æthelwin, the Bishop of Durham; and Leofwin, the Bishop of Lichfield. Their replacements were all Normans, with one exception: Lanfranc, the new Archbishop of Canterbury, was an Italian by birth, though he had spent the previous thirty years in Normandy.

Straight away, even before all the new appointments could take effect, there was a dispute. Lanfranc insisted that the new Archbishop of York, Thomas, should acknowledge the supremacy of Canterbury. Thomas was reluctant to do so, and there was a stalemate: Lanfranc refused to consecrate Thomas without it. Eventually the dispute was taken to Rome, where the Pope ruled in favour of Lanfranc and Canterbury.

Orderic described these successors as 'prudent, full of gentleness and humanity, venerated and loved by men, and venerating and loving God'. They were 'men of letters, of excellent character, and zealous promotors of religion', and a welcome improvement on the natives. It's certainly true that there were some obvious deficiencies among the English clergy. Leofwin was married, and Lanfranc was a zealous advocate of clerical celibacy. Meanwhile Æthelwin was almost certainly involved in the Northumbrian uprisings of 1068 and 1069, and when, after their failure, he was caught trying to escape from Durham, he was found in possession of Church property.

Whether Æthelmær was targeted because of his record rather than because of his family tree isn't clear. It's interesting, though, that Leofwin was a member of the House of Mercia, being a nephew of Leofric (and therefore a cousin of Edwin and Morcar); and that Herfast, who succeeded Æthelmær as Bishop of Elmham, was himself married. Now this doesn't necessarily indicate hypocrisy: the principle that Christian clergymen ought not to be married was centuries old, but throughout Christendom it was widely flouted, and it was probably unrealistic to expect to fill all of England's bishoprics with suitable celibate clerics. Even so, it does look like this was a purge of the Old English 'establishment', in which men with connections to the great families of Edward's England were replaced by men whom William could trust.

The Normans were vigorous builders of monasteries. William of Malmesbury acknowledged that 'monasteries arose, ancient in their rule, but modern in building'. But he added, somewhat caustically, 'I perceive the muttering of those who say it would have been better that the old should have been preserved in their original state than that new ones should have been erected from their plunder.' That well over fifty years after the Conquest those mutterings were still audible does rather suggest that there was still some resentment that the Normans 'gave many possessions in England to foreign churches', whose 'poverty was mitigated by the riches of England'. For many abbeys, the Norman Conquest involved the destruction of their buildings, the theft of their property, and the replacement of their abbot, and evidently for many Englishmen this was not a price worth paying for updating their architecture.

No doubt there were plenty of genuinely pious Normans. But the cynicism of their ecclesiastical leaders was remarkable. Take Odo, the Bishop of Bayeux, who remained in that post throughout his time as Earl of Kent. Now this wasn't, strictly speaking, pluralism, which involves the holding of more than one *ecclesiastical* office, but it's safe to assume that he wasn't effectively ministering to his flock in Bayeux from Kent. His record and reputation were already far from admirable by 1082, when his half-brother had him incarcerated. The exact circumstances of Odo's fall are murky, but there is a story that he was caught attempting to raise money and muster his own army, allegedly to support a bid for the Papacy. This may sound preposterous, and it was indeed unlikely, but at the time of Odo's arrest there was an ongoing crisis in Rome, and the idea of a Norman army marching in, restoring order, and installing a Pope wasn't completely outlandish: the Normans were militarily mighty, and they already controlled Sicily. If they could seize that island, why not Rome too?

Dealing with Odo wasn't straightforward for William: imprisoning a clergyman, even one who had behaved in so dubious a manner, was controversial. Lanfranc, though, had an elegant solution: 'You will not seize the Bishop of Bayeux, but confine the Earl of Kent.' There was, of course, an element of poetic justice to this. Odo had been present at the Battle of Hastings; as England's 'second king' his rule had been tyrannical; and his pastoral care in Bayeux was non-existent: he could hardly complain that he was being treated like someone who had never taken Holy Orders.

Even so, Lanfranc's behaviour is hardly emblematic of a deeply religious man. His enjoyment of political power is evident. Far more evident, indeed, than the alleged improvements which the Normans made to the English Church. Appointments to ecclesiastical office in Edward's England were undoubtedly nepotistic, but the same was quite clearly true in William's England too: as late as 1085 the *Anglo-Saxon Chronicle* drily observed that the newly appointed bishops of London, Norfolk and Chester were all royal clerks. Perhaps the monasteries were still failing, twenty years after the Conquest, to produce men of sufficient quality to take on these offices, but there can have been fewer worse abbots than the Norman from Caen whom William foisted on Glastonbury, the richest monastery in the country, in the late 1070s.

In 1083, explains John of Worcester, there was 'a dreadful quarrel between the monks of Glastonbury and their abbot, Thurstan, a man unworthy of the dignity', who 'attempted to force the monks to relinquish the Gregorian chant' in favour of a Norman version. The monks were 'much aggrieved at this', and Thurstan's response was to burst in on them at the head of an armed gang. The monks took refuge in the abbey church, perhaps because they could barricade the doors, perhaps because they thought that their abbot would draw the line at allowing or ordering them to be harmed in that location. If that was what they believed, they were about to be disillusioned. Thurstan's men (described by the *Anglo-Saxon Chronicle* as 'Frenchmen', suggesting that these were not local toughs recruited to rough up the monks, but Norman soldiers) broke in and attacked the monks. According to John of Worcester, they 'even speared to death one of the monks as he was clinging to the altar; another was shot by arrows on the altar-steps'. The monks defended themselves with benches and candlesticks. It was, according to the *Chronicle*, gruesome: 'The blood came from the altar upon the steps, and from the steps on the floor.'

William's response was equivocal. According to John of Worcester, Thurstan was sent back to Caen, but 'a great number of the monks were, by the king's command, dispersed among the cathedrals and abbeys, where they were confined'. Clearly they were seen as dangerous troublemakers.

After William's death, 'the abbot repurchased the abbey'. The Norman Conquest had not eliminated simony from the English Church either.

* * * *

The system of landholding which the Normans introduced to England was based around the principle that ultimately the entire country belonged to the Crown, and that the king would then 'enfeoff' his barons, or grant them land in return for military service. Those barons would then, in turn, enfeoff knights, again in return for military service.[3] This 'feudal system' (as it wasn't called at the time) was based on this relationship. It is sometimes characterised as a pyramid, with the king at the pinnacle, his barons one step down, the knights one level below that, and anyone beneath the rank of a knight at the bottom. But this is a misleading way to think about the structure of society. There was one king at the top, yes. And he did enfeoff a relatively small number of men: William the Conqueror had fewer than two hundred tenants-in-chief (as men who held land directly from the

---

3 A 'fief' (or 'fee'), therefore, was the land with which a tenant was enfeoffed; the amount of land needed to sustain one knight was known as a 'knight's fee'.

king were known). But the tidy structure implied by pyramidical diagrams was not how Norman England was arranged.[4]

In theory no one except the Crown owned land (which was, of course, an unwelcome change for Englishmen who had hitherto considered their land to be their private property). Every landholder was a tenant-in-chief or, if he did not hold land directly from the king, a sub-tenant. But in practice landholding was very close to landownership. Men held their fiefs for a lifetime, but their sons inherited them. Kings could impose 'entry fines', a kind of inheritance tax, on heirs; if those heirs were underage, the Crown would exercise 'wardship' over their fiefs, which included keeping any profits from the land, until the heirs were of age. If there were no male heirs, the Crown could allocate the fief to someone else: widows and daughters might not be ejected from the land, but they might be required to marry its new holder. (This was not popular with the 'young women of high rank', who, in Orderic's words, 'were subject to the insults of grooms, and mourned their dishonour by filthy ruffians'.)

Land was still a commodity, and once it had been granted there was nothing to stop it from being bought and sold. After all, the king's tenants-in-chief were *supposed* to use it to enfeoff sub-tenants: a baron was expected not just to turn up for military service, but to bring with him as many knights as his fief would support. And those knights did not farm the land themselves: instead they sub-let it to men who would. At each level, some would prosper and some wouldn't; and those who

---

4 Barons weren't the only people to be tenants-in-chief. Bishops and abbots also held land directly from the Crown, and although they were forbidden to fight themselves, they were also required to provide the king with knights in accordance with the amount of land which they held.

prospered would be in a position to buy land from those who didn't. Some would find themselves with more land and less money than they wanted, and some would find themselves in the opposite situation. And some would find themselves in possession of property which was inconveniently sited. The first land to be distributed was that which had belonged to men who had been killed in the events of 1066. This land, naturally, was scattered all over the country, and it was in this form that it was parcelled out. A fief did not necessarily consist of one territorially contiguous piece of land, but might be made up of several strips, sometimes in different counties. Transfers between landholders were inevitable.

Now such transfers could, in 'feudal' terms, be untidy. Sometimes transfers were between two tenants-in-chief or two sub-tenants. Often a sub-tenant might hold some land from one tenant-in-chief, and some from another. Occasionally, indeed, a tenant-in-chief might hold some land from a sub-tenant. What happened if a man held land from more than two people? Well, theoretically he owed military service to both, which was clearly unworkable, though the phenomenon gave rise to the concept of the 'liege lord', or the man from whom a tenant held most of his land and to whom he therefore owed his primary allegiance.

Fortunately there was a convenient way around this. A sub-tenant in this situation might well agree to pay a lord in cash rather than with military service. That would suit both. And in reality even when relationships were straightforward the payment of money instead of the performance of military service was often preferable for all concerned. Sometimes kings did not need knights, and sometimes knights would rather not be in the field, and sometimes those coincided. By the end of the eleventh century these payments had been formalised into a tax, called 'scutage', which funded professional warriors, who in this period as in others were usually a better bet than conscripts.

These tenants-in-chief and sub-tenants were overwhelmingly Norman. The Conquest liquidated the thegns as a class. Many were killed in the cataclysm of 1066. Many went into exile, sometimes to serve the Byzantine Emperor as Harald Hardrada had done. Those who survived and remained found themselves downgraded in wealth and in status. Some of their daughters married Norman barons; many others sank without trace into the ranks of English freemen.

For the lower end of society, the impact is more difficult to assess. Slaves remained slaves; or, perhaps more accurately, given that people passed in and out of it, slavery was not eliminated, despite official Norman distaste for the practice. The ceorls disappear from the historical record, with some being reclassified as freemen and those who were required to work for their lords being described as 'villeins', but it seems unlikely that such a change of status had significant implications for the people themselves, especially the villeins, who lived on the edge of destitution in Anglo-Saxon and Norman England alike.

That isn't to say, though, that the Norman Conquest was an irrelevance to the English freeman. It certainly wasn't. Even if he had been left untouched by rampaging knights, even if he hadn't stored his money in a monastery, and even if he lived nowhere near the north, or a royal forest, he was nonetheless liable to pay tax. And, unlike Edward the Confessor, William levied a lot of tax.

England and Normandy remained entirely separate throughout William's reign. He was both Duke of Normandy and King of England, but Normandy did not annexe England, and when William died his eldest son, Robert, inherited Normandy, while his second son, William Rufus, inherited England. Still, William was of course determined to defend both territories, and this wasn't cheap. (Nor, indeed, were castles, which needed maintaining as well as building.)

England already had an efficient system of tax collection, and William exploited it: he continued to levy the *geld* as his Anglo-Saxon predecessors had done, and a new generation of reeves collected it just as their Anglo-Saxon predecessors had done. But it didn't yield enough revenue for his purposes, and he was not a man to shrug and accept that he would have to get by on less money.

The problem became urgent in 1085. The Danes were preparing another invasion, and for a while it looked dangerous. Denmark's new king, Cnut the Holy (who is now the patron saint of that country), gathered a considerable fleet which would, had it sailed, have constituted a serious threat. In response, William hurried back from Normandy, bringing with him 'a larger force of mounted men and infantry than had ever come to this country'. England had to pay for it. 'People had much oppression that year,' complained the *Anglo-Saxon Chronicle*. The only way to keep his warriors supplied was to allow them to take what they required from the natives, 'who fed them, each according to his quota of land'. And even that wasn't all. To prevent the expected invaders from using it to supply themselves when they arrived, 'the king had the land near the sea laid waste'.

In the end, the Danes never came. Henry, the King of the Germans, began menacing the southern border of Denmark, and Cnut had to turn his attention to that threat; a year later he was murdered by rebels. But the affair had persuaded William that he needed a better way of exploiting England's wealth.

At first, his approach was simply to be tougher and more ruthless. 'There was little righteousness in this country in anyone,' wrote the (monastic) author of the *Anglo-Saxon Chronicle*, 'except in monks alone.' He went on to deplore William's avarice. He needed money and 'did not care how sinfully it was obtained'. The Chronicler gave examples. 'The king sold his lands on very hard terms, as hard as he could. Then came somebody else, and offered more than the other had given, and the king let it go to the man who had offered him more.' The Normans also 'imposed unjust tolls, and did many other injustices'.

And this at a time of pestilence and famine. 'Such a disease came on people that very nearly every other person was ill,' reported the *Anglo-Saxon Chronicle*, and then 'there came so great a famine over England that many hundreds of people died a miserable death'.

It's not surprising that the Chronicler was unimpressed. 'The more just laws were talked about,' he commented caustically, 'the more unlawful things were done.'

William, needless to say, was not aroused to sympathy by the plight of his subjects. England wasn't providing him with what he wanted. But he was unwilling to conclude that this was because it didn't have the resources to do so. There was, he suspected, plenty of wealth not being tapped: the question was where.

To find out, he dispatched commissioners all over the country. According to the *Chronicle*, they 'so thoroughly surveyed it that there was not a hide of land in England that he knew not who had it, nor what it was worth, and afterwards set it down in his book'. 'Not an ox, nor a cow, nor.' The process was so comprehensive that it became known as the Domesday Survey: it was as inescapable as the Day of Judgment. 'It is a shame to relate,' commented the *Chronicler*, 'but it seemed no shame to him to do it.' The findings were written up into a two-volume book, which has survived.

Immensely helpfully for historians, the surveyors recorded not just the details of the land and who held it at the time the survey was carried out, but also who held it 'on the day when King Edward was living and dead' – that is, on 5 January 1066. So it is thanks to the Domesday Book that we know, for instance, that in Edward's time the landholdings of the Earl of Wessex were greater than those of the King of England. It is thanks to the Domesday Book that we know that Stigand's bishoprics of Canterbury and Winchester were both very wealthy, and that he was therefore one of the richest men in the country.

It is thanks to Domesday that we can estimate that there were around five thousand thegns in Edward's England, and that around a tenth of the population were slaves. But most of all Domesday illustrates the extent to which the English landowning class was eliminated as a result of the Norman Conquest. That thegnly class was more or less entirely wiped out. This does not mean that they were slaughtered (though many of those who were significant landowners in January 1066 were indeed killed in the battles of that year, and more went into exile). But their heirs were dispossessed. There are very few English names in the Domesday Book. At best the sons of those who had been Edward's aristocrats found themselves in much-reduced circumstances, sub-tenants of the new Norman ruling élite.

It is also thanks to Domesday that we know the grim extent of the Harrying of the North. Much of the region between the Humber and the Tees was recorded as 'wasta est', or 'it is waste'. This had a particular meaning: land which had been farmed in the past, but was no longer being cultivated. This didn't necessarily mean that someone had laid waste to it – sometimes, of course, land fell out of use for other reasons – but the extent of wasteland in Northumbria over sixteen years later paints a clear picture. It is not credible to write off the accounts as exaggeration: the Normans really did reduce the region to wasteland.

By August 1086, thanks to Domesday, William knew who all the sub-tenants of his tenants-in-chief were, and he took the opportunity to summon them to Salisbury, where he demanded that they do homage and swear fealty to him personally. This personal oath did not change the structure of obligation: such men were still required to serve their feudal lords, who were of course still required to serve their king. It is perhaps evidence of a certain jumpiness though. The threat from the native English had dissolved, but the loyalty of the barons could not be relied on, and maybe William wanted to remind all concerned that his knights were ultimately there to serve him, not the men from whom they held land directly. That he thought this reminder was necessary suggests some insecurity, even after twenty years on the throne.

Domesday was William's last great project. A few months later, in the summer of 1087, at sixty years of age, he was stricken with the painful bowel disease which would kill him. Finding the noise of Rouen intolerable, he retired to a priory just outside the city. On his deathbed, he issued a general pardon of his prisoners, including Morcar and Wulfnoth. (He wanted to exclude Odo from the amnesty, but according to Orderic Vitalis, 'friends of the bishop' pressed the dying king to release him along with the rest. William told the assembled notables that 'whether I will it or not, your petition shall be granted', which was no doubt true, and reluctantly agreed.) He confessed his sins, including those committed against the English.

And then, on 9 September, William died, surrounded by the great and the good of Normandy. As soon as he was dead, recounted Orderic, 'the wealthiest of them mounted their horses and departed in haste to secure their property' while 'the inferior attendants, observing that their masters had disappeared, laid hands on the arms, the plate, the robes, the linen, and almost all the royal furniture, and leaving the corpse almost naked on the floor of the house hastened away'.

Eventually William's body was retrieved, and taken to St Stephen's Abbey in Caen, which he had founded in 1063, for the funeral. It was a fiasco. As the hearse was proceeding through the city a fire started to blaze, inducing panic and prompting the crowd to abandon their mourning in favour of firefighting. Then, before the burial could take place, the service was interrupted by a man claiming that the land on which the abbey stood had been unlawfully seized from him a quarter of a century previously. And then it turned out that the stone sarcophagus which had been prepared for William's corpulent frame was too small. The body had to be forced into the coffin, but that burst the diseased intestines, which unleashed a foul odour throughout the building. Those who could, left; the remaining priests and monks hurried through their duties.

'His death,' commented Orderic, 'was worthy of his life.'

EPILOGUE

The twelfth-century historians from whom we know so much about the Norman Conquest were, in some ways, very distant from the times they were writing about. But one connection with the past was still alive. The rightful King of England had been chased out of Northumbria and then sent away from Scotland to continental Europe. After a few years William forgave him and allowed him to return, but Edgar's was a restless soul, and he did not stay: in 1086, still in his early thirties, he sold most of his English lands and sought adventure with a small band of followers in Apulia, in southern Italy. Once more he found exile no more congenial than living in Norman England, and before long his native land had drawn him back. Later he was to travel to the Holy Land, perhaps as a crusader but more likely as a pilgrim visiting Jerusalem.

Eventually, as he aged, he did settle in England. There is no record of his having married or had children, but he was still alive in 1125, by which time he would have been in his seventies. William of Malmesbury recorded that 'he now grows old in the country, in privacy and quiet'.

Perhaps he allowed himself to wonder what might have happened had Edward lived just a few more years. Perhaps William would have recoiled from challenging a man with so indisputable an hereditary right to the throne. Perhaps Harold would have been unable to persuade the witan that the country needed a man of his experience and stature if Edgar had been almost a grown man himself. Perhaps there would have been no need for Harold to have connived in the dispossession of his brother, and so perhaps there would have been no invasion from Scandinavia. Perhaps Harold and Tostig would have continued as England's sacred oaks into the late eleventh century. And perhaps, when the time came, their sons would have risen in their turn. Perhaps England would once more have had a Godwin as Earl of Wessex. Perhaps Kjetil or Skuli would have risen to become Earl of Northumbria. Indeed, Edgar may have told himself, had things turned out differently he might have spent his last years deciding which of Godwin's great-grandchildren should succeed their fathers as his earls.

Edgar had never fully captured his country's imagination. Perhaps he came closest to it in old age. Perhaps the few people who came into contact with him were reminded of what might have been, had history turned out differently. Perhaps those who had no memory of the days of Edward the Confessor, but who lived with the oppressive indignities of Norman rule, indulged themselves in looking back ruefully, wishing that England had been spared what it had endured.

Appendix I

ARCHBISHOPS

Canterbury

bef. 988	Dunstan
988–990	Æthelgar
990–994	Sigeric the Serious
995–1005	Ælfric
1006–1012	Ælfheah
1013–1020	Lyfing
1020–1038	Æthelnoth
1038–1050	Eadsige
1051–1052	Robert of Jumièges
1052–1070	Stigand
1070–1089	Lanfranc

York

bef. 992	Oswald*
995–1002	Ealdwulf*
1002–1023	Wulfstan*
1023–1051	Ælfric
1051–1060	Cynisge
1061–1069	Ealdred
1070–1100	Thomas of Bayeux

Appendix II

EALDORMEN & EARLS

Northumbria

bef. 994	Thored
994–1002	Ælfhelm
1002–1006	vacant
1006–1016	Uhtred
1016–1023*	Erik
1023*–1055	Siward
1055–1065	Tostig
1065–1066	Morcar
1067	Copsi
1067	Osulf
1067–1068	Gospatric
1068–1069	Robert

Mercia

bef. 983	Ælfhere
983–985	Ælfric
985–1007	vacant
1007–1017	Eadric Streona
1017–1023	Leofwin
1030–1057	Leofric

1057–1062*	Ælfgar
1062*–1071	Edwin

* dating is inexact; there was quite possibly a period in which the earldom was vacant

East Anglia

bef. 992	Æthelwin
993–1002	Leofsige
1002–1017	vacant
1007–1021	Thurkill the Tall
1020s–1040s	poss. Osgod Clapa, poss. vacant
1045–1053	Harold*
1053–1057	Ælfgar
1057–1066	Gyrth
1066–9	Ralph 'the Staller'
1069–75	Ralph

* during Harold's exile in 1051–2 the earldom of Mercia was briefly held by Ælfgar

Wessex

There was no Earl of Wessex until Godwin, who held the office from around 1020 until his death in 1053, with a brief hiatus during the crisis of 1051–1052; Harold was then Earl of Wessex from 1053 until he became King of England in 1066, after which the earldom was abolished.

Appendix III

THE EDICT WHEN THE GREAT ARMY CAME TO ENGLAND

All of us have need eagerly to labour that we may obtain God's mercy and his compassion and that we may be able through his help to withstand our enemies.

Now it is our will that all the nation shall fast as a general penance for three days on bread and herbs and water, namely on the Monday, Tuesday and Wednesday before Michaelmas.

And every man is to come barefoot to church, without gold and ornaments and to go to confession.

And all are to go out with the relics and to call on Christ eagerly from their inmost hearts.

And one penny or the value of one penny is to be paid from each hide, and it is to be brought to church.

And if anyone does not perform this, then he is to compensate for it as it is legally ordained: the freeman with thirty pence, the slave with a flogging, the thegn with 30 shillings.

And wherever that money has to be paid, every penny is to be distributed for God's sake.

And the food also, which each would have consumed if the fast had not been ordained for him, is all to be willingly distributed for God's sake after the fast to needy men and bedridden persons and men so afflicted that they are unable to fast thus.

And each member of a household is to pay a penny as alms, or his lord is to pay it for him, if he has not got it himself; and men of rank shall pay a tithe.

And slaves during those three days are to be freed from work, in order to go to church, and in order that they may the more willingly observe the fast.

And in every minster all the community are to sing their psalter together during those three days.

And every priest is to say mass for our lord and for all his people. And in addition one mass is to be said every day in each minster with special reference to the need which is now urgent for us, until things become better.

And at each of the canonical hours the whole community, prostrate before God's altar, is to sing the psalm: 'Why, O Lord, are they multiplied' and the prayers and collects.

And all in common, ecclesiastics and laymen, are to turn eagerly to God and to deserve his mercy.

And every year henceforth God's dues are to be paid at any rate correctly, to the end that Almighty God may have mercy on us and grant that we may overcome our enemies.

God help us. Amen.

Appendix IV

THE SERMON OF THE WOLF
TO THE ENGLISH

Beloved men, know that which is true: this world is in haste and it nears the end. And therefore things in this world go ever the longer the worse, and so it must needs be that things quickly worsen, on account of people's sinning from day to day, before the coming of Antichrist. And indeed it will then be awful and grim widely throughout the world. Understand also well that the Devil has now led this nation astray for very many years, and that little loyalty has remained among men, though they spoke well.

And too many crimes reigned in the land, and there were never many of men who deliberated about the remedy as eagerly as one should, but daily they piled one evil upon another, and committed injustices and many violations of law all too widely throughout this entire land. And we have also therefore endured many injuries and insults, and if we shall experience any remedy then we must deserve better of God than we have previously done. For with great deserts we have earned the misery that is upon us, and with truly great deserts we must obtain the remedy from God, if henceforth things are to improve.

Lo, we know full well that a great breach of law shall necessitate a great remedy, and a great fire shall necessitate much water, if that fire is to be quenched. And it is also a great necessity for each of men that he henceforth eagerly heed the law of God better than he has done, and justly pay God's dues. In heathen lands one does not dare withhold little nor much of that which is appointed to the worship of false gods; and we withhold everywhere God's dues all too often. And in heathen lands one dares not curtail, within or without the temple, anything brought to the false gods and entrusted as an offering. And we have entirely stripped God's houses of everything fitting, within and without, and God's servants are everywhere deprived of honour and protection. And some men say that no man dare abuse the servants of false gods in any way among heathen people, just as is now done widely to the servants of God, where Christians ought to observe the law of God and protect the servants of God.

But what I say is true: there is need for that remedy because God's dues have diminished too long in this land in every district, and laws of the people have deteriorated entirely too greatly, since Edgar died. And sanctuaries are too widely violated, and God's houses are entirely stripped of all dues and are stripped within of everything fitting. And widows are widely forced to marry in unjust ways and too many are impoverished and fully humiliated; and poor men are sorely betrayed and cruelly defrauded, and sold widely out of this land into the power of foreigners, though innocent; and infants are enslaved by means of cruel injustices, on account of petty theft everywhere in this nation. And the rights of freemen are taken away and the rights of slaves are restricted and charitable obligations are curtailed. Free men may not keep their independence, nor go where they wish, nor deal with their property just as they desire; nor may slaves have that property which, on their own time, they have obtained by means of difficult labour, or that which good men, in Gods favour, have granted them, and given to them in charity for the love of God. But every man decreases or withholds every charitable obligation that should by rights be paid eagerly in Gods favour, for injustice is too widely common among men and lawlessness is too widely dear to them.

And in short, the laws of God are hated and his teaching despised; therefore we all are frequently disgraced through God's anger, let him know it who is able. And that loss will become universal, although one may not think so, to all these people, unless God protects us. Therefore it is clear and well seen in all of us that we have previously more often transgressed than we have amended, and therefore much is greatly assailing this nation. Nothing has prospered now for a long time either at home or abroad, but there has been military devastation and hunger, burning and bloodshed in nearly every district time and again. And stealing and slaying, plague and pestilence, murrain and disease, malice and hate, and the robbery by robbers have injured us very terribly. And excessive taxes have afflicted us, and storms have very often caused failure of crops; therefore in this land there have been, as it may appear, many years now of injustices and unstable loyalties everywhere among men.

Neither has anyone had loyal intentions with respect to others as justly as he should, but almost everyone has deceived and injured another by words and deeds; and indeed almost everyone unjustly stabs the other from behind with shameful assaults and with wrongful accusations – let him do more, if he may. For there are in this nation great disloyalties for matters of the Church and the state, and also there are in the land many who betray their lords in various ways. And the greatest of all betrayals of a lord in the world is that a man betrays the soul of his lord. And a very great betrayal of a lord it is also in the world, that a man betray his lord to death, or drive him living from the land, and both have come to pass in this land: Edward was betrayed, and then killed, and after that burned; and Æthelræd was driven out of his land.

And too many godparents and godchildren have been killed widely throughout this nation, in addition to entirely too many other innocent people who have been destroyed entirely too widely. And entirely too many holy religious foundations have deteriorated because some men have previously been placed in them who ought not to have been, if one wished to show respect to God's sanctuary. And too many Christian men have been sold out of this land, now for a long time, and all this is entirely hateful to God, let him believe it who will. Also we know well where this crime has occurred, and it is shameful to speak of that which has happened too widely.

And it is terrible to know what too many do often, those who for a while carry out a miserable deed, who contribute together and buy a woman as a joint purchase between them and practice foul sin with that one woman, one after another, and each after the other like dogs that care not about filth, and then for a price they sell a creature of God – His own purchase that He bought at a great cost -- into the power of enemies. Also we know well where the crime has occurred such that the father has sold his son for a price, and the son his mother, and one brother has sold the other into the power of foreigners, and out of this nation. All of those are great and terrible deeds, let him understand it who will. And yet what is injuring this nation is still greater and manifold: many are forsworn and greatly perjured and more vows are broken time and again, and it is clear to this people that God's anger violently oppresses us, let him know it who can.

Full shameful laws and disgraceful tributes are common among us, through God's anger, let him understand it who is able. And many misfortunes befall this nation time and again. Things have not prospered now for a long time neither at home nor abroad, but there has been destruction and hate in every district time and again, and the English have been entirely defeated for a long time now, and very truly disheartened through the anger of God. And pirates are so strong through the consent of God, that often in battle one drives away ten, and two often drive away twenty, sometimes fewer and sometimes more, entirely on account of our sins. And often ten or twelve, each after the other, insult the thegn's woman disgracefully, and sometimes his daughter or close kinswomen, while he looks on, he that considered himself brave and strong and good enough before that happened.

And often a slave binds very fast the thegn who previously was his lord and makes him into a slave through God's anger. Alas the misery and alas the public shame that the English now have, entirely through God's anger. Often two sailors, or three for a while, drive the droves of Christian men from sea to sea, out through this nation, huddled together, as a public shame for

us all, if we could seriously and properly know any shame. But all
the insult that we often suffer, we repay by honouring those who
insult us. We pay them continually and they humiliate us daily;
they ravage and they burn, plunder and rob and carry to the ship;
and lo! what else is there in all these happenings except Gods anger
clear and evident over this nation?

It is no wonder that there is mishap among us: because we
know full well that now for many years men have too often
not cared what they did by word or deed; but this nation, as
it may appear, has become very corrupt through manifold sins
and through many misdeeds: through murder and through evil
deeds, through avarice and through greed, through stealing and
through robbery, through man-selling and through heathen vices,
through betrayals and through frauds, through breaches of law
and through deceit, through attacks on kinsmen and through
manslaughter, through injury of men in holy orders and through
adultery, through incest and through various fornications. And
also, far and wide, as we said before, more than should be are
lost and perjured through the breaking of oaths and through
violations of pledges, and through various lies; and non-
observances of church feasts and fasts widely occur time and
again. And also there are here in the land Gods adversaries,
degenerate apostates, and hostile persecutors of the Church and
entirely too many grim tyrants, and widespread despisers of divine
laws and Christian virtues, and foolish deriders everywhere in
the nation, most often of those things that the messengers of God
command, and especially those things that always belong to God's
law by right.

And therefore things have now come far and wide to that
full evil way that men are more ashamed now of good deeds

than of misdeeds; because too often good deeds are abused with derision and the God-fearing are blamed entirely too much, and especially are men reproached and all too often greeted with contempt who love right and have fear of God to any extent. And because men do that, entirely abusing all that they should praise and hating too much all that they ought to love, therefore they bring entirely too many to evil intentions and to misdeeds, so that they are never ashamed though they sin greatly and commit wrongs even against God himself. But on account of idle attacks they are ashamed to repent for their misdeeds, just as the books teach, like those foolish men who on account of their pride will not protect themselves from injury before they might no longer do so, although they all wish for it. Here in the country, as it may appear, too many are sorely wounded by the stains of sin. Here there are, as we said before, killers and murderers of their kinsmen, and murderers of priests and persecutors of monasteries, and traitors and notorious apostates, and here there are perjurers and murderers, and here there are injurers of men in holy orders and adulterers, and people greatly corrupted through incest and through various fornications, and here there are harlots and infanticides and many foul adulterous fornicators, and here there are witches and sorceresses, and here there are robbers and plunderers and pilferers and thieves, and injurers of the people and pledge-breakers and treaty-breakers, and, in short, a countless number of all crimes and misdeeds. And we are not at all ashamed of it, but we are greatly ashamed to begin the remedy just as the books teach, and that is evident in this wretched and corrupt nation.

Alas, many a great kinsman can easily call to mind much in addition which one man could not hastily investigate, how wretchedly things have fared now all the time now widely throughout this nation. And indeed let each one examine himself well, and not delay this all too long. But lo, in the name of God, let us do as is needful for us, protect ourselves as earnestly as we may, lest we all perish together. There was a historian in the time of the Britons, called Gildas, who wrote about their misdeeds, how with their sins they infuriated God so excessively that He finally allowed the English army to conquer their land, and to destroy the host of the Britons entirely. And that came about, just as he said, through breach of rule by the clergy and through breach of laws by laymen, through robbery by the strong and through coveting of ill-gotten gains, violations of law by the people and through unjust judgments, through the sloth of the bishops and folly, and through the wicked cowardice of messengers of God, who swallowed the truths entirely too often and they mumbled through their jaws where they should have cried out; also through the foul pride of the people and through gluttony and manifold sins they destroyed their land and they themselves perished. But let us do as is necessary for us, take warning from such; and it is true what I say, we know of worse deeds among the English than we have heard of anywhere among the Britons; and therefore there is a great need for us to take thought for ourselves, and to intercede eagerly with God himself.

And let us do as is necessary for us, turn towards the right and to some extent abandon wrongdoing, and eagerly atone for what we previously transgressed; and let us love God and follow God's laws, and carry out well that which we promised when we received baptism, or those who were our sponsors at baptism; and let us order words and deeds justly, and cleanse our thoughts with zeal, and keep oaths and pledges carefully, and have some loyalty between us without evil practice. And let us often reflect upon the great Judgment to which we all shall go, and let us save ourselves from the welling fire of hell torment, and gain for ourselves the glories and joys that God has prepared for those who work his will in the world. God help us. Amen.

Appendix V

THE PENITENTIAL ORDINANCE

The Normans have always had their defenders and their apologists. There can, though, be no doubt that by the standards of the eleventh century their conduct in England was regarded as unbecoming of Christians. The Norman bishops, well aware that the army's behaviour fell a long way short of what might be expected of men fighting under the banner of the Pope, drew up a document which was conveyed to England by papal legate Bishop Ermenfrid of Sion, and which became known as the 'Penitential Ordinance'.

This document sets out penances for those who had sinned during the campaign, and it is therefore an interesting insight into what the eleventh-century ecclesiastical mind regarded as acceptable during war, and what it didn't. Not much fell into the first category: interestingly, just participating in the Battle of Hastings was regarded as inherently sinful. As far as the Norman bishops were concerned, that the campaign had papal blessing did not absolve anyone involved in it: men who took up arms were committing sins, even if they were doing so in what the Church regarded as a just cause, and were required therefore to do penance for them.[1]

This extended, as was logical, to members of the clergy. They were, as the Ordinance sternly reminded them, forbidden to fight in any case, but clearly some had done so anyway. The bishops were less concerned with imposing a specific penance on them than with establishing that in taking up arms they were indeed committing sins. There is a story that Odo of Bayeux, William's half-brother and the most famous clerical warrior at Hastings, wielded a club or a mace rather than a sword so that he would not violate the injunction not to shed any blood. If that is true, it's clear that he did not thereby escape the moral censure of his fellow bishops, who deliberately produced a document which indicted almost everyone who had taken part in some way and left no loopholes for clever clerks to cite in their own defence.

Just how the Penitential Ordinance was received by its intended audience is not known, though it is difficult to imagine the adventurers who had joined the Duke of Normandy's mission taking it particularly seriously. Whether any of them admitted to themselves that they had been 'looting' rather than 'in search of supplies', or to have been 'motivated only by gain' rather than by the more acceptable reasons of feudal obligation or zeal for a righteous cause is impossible to answer; these were questions for men's consciences and for the priests to whom they confessed their sins.

And what of the implications of the Penitential Ordinance for William himself? Even his most vigorous advocates would struggle to portray him as selflessly fighting the good fight to rescue the

---

1 That is, to confess, repent, and atone for one's sins.

English people and their Church from the tyranny of the House of Godwin. Nor could he shrug and say that he was only discharging his feudal obligation to his lord. If anyone was 'motivated only by gain', it was him.

Perhaps, it has been suggested, the foundation of Battle Abbey, which William had built on the site of the Battle of Hastings (with the altar of the abbey church supposedly placed in the spot where Harold met his end) somehow counted as his penance. Certainly it would be characteristic of the man to erect a monument to his greatest victory and claim it an atonement for his sins.

The Penitential Ordinance

Whoever knows that he has killed in the great battle is to do one year's penance for each man slain.

Whoever struck another but does not know if that man was thereby slain is to do forty days' penance for each case, if he can remember the number, either continuously or at intervals.

Whoever does not know the number of those he struck or killed shall, at the discretion of his bishop, do penance for one day a week for the rest of his life, or, if he is able, make amends either by building a church or by giving perpetual alms to one.

Those who struck no one yet wished to do so are to do penance for three days.

Clerks who fought, or were armed for the purpose of fighting, because they are forbidden to fight are to do penance according to the institutions of canon law as if they had sinned in their own country. The penance of monks is to be determined according to their rule and the judgment of their abbot.

Those who fought motivated only by gain are to know that they owe penance as for homicide; but because they fought in public war the bishops out of mercy have assigned them three years' penance.

Archers who do not know how many they killed or wounded are to do penance for three Lents.

That battle aside, whoever before the consecration of the king killed anyone offering resistance as he moved through the kingdom in search of supplies, is to do one year's penance for each person so slain. Anyone, however, who killed not in search of supplies but in looting, is to do three years' penance for each person so slain.

Whoever killed a man after the king's consecration is to do penance as for wilful homicide, with this exception, that if the person killed or struck was in arms against the king the penance shall be as above.

Those who committed adultery or rape or fornication shall do penance as though they had thus sinned in their own countries.

Similarly concerning the violations of churches. Things taken from a church are to be restored to the church from which they were taken if possible. If this is not possible they are to be given to some other church. If such restoration is refused, the bishops have decreed that no one is to sell or buy the property.

BIBLIOGRAPHY

Primary Sources

Byrhtferth of Ramsey, *The Life of Saint Oswald*

Eadmer of Canterbury, *The History of Recent Events*

Henry of Huntingdon, *The History of England*

John of Wallingford, *The Chronicle of John of Wallingford*

John of Worcester, *The Chronicle of Chronicles*

Orderic Vitalis, *The Ecclesiastical History*

Snorri Sturluson, *Heimskringla*

Sulcard of Westminster, *Prologue Concerning the Building of Westminster*

Symeon of Durham, *History of the Church of Durham*

The Anglo-Saxon Chronicle

The Encomium Emmae Reginae

The Vita Ædwardi Regis

William of Jumièges, *Deeds of the Norman Dukes*

William of Malmesbury, *Deeds of the English Kings*

William of Poitiers, *Deeds of William, Duke of Normandy and King of England*

Secondary Sources

Abels, Richard, *Æthelræd: the Failed King* (Allen Lane, 2018)

Barlow, Frank, *Edward the Confessor* (Yale University Press, 1997)

Barlow, Frank, *The Feudal Kingdom of England* (Routledge, 1999)

Barlow, Frank, *The Godwins* (Routledge, 2003)

Bates, David, *William the Conqueror* (The History Press, 2004)

Bolton, Timothy, *Cnut the Great* (Yale University Press, 2007)

Campbell, James, *Anglo-Saxon England* (Penguin, 1991)

Carpenter, David, *The Penguin History of Britain: The Struggle for Mastery: Britain 1066–1284* (Penguin, 2004)

Douglas, David, *William the Conqueror: The Norman Impact Upon England* (University of California Press, 1992)

Freeman, E. A., *The History of the Norman Conquest of England: Its Causes and Its Results* (1867–1879)

Golding, Brian, *Conquest and Colonisation: The Normans in Britain 1066–1100* (Palgrave, 2013)

Howard, Ian, *Harthacnut: the Last Danish King of England* (Tempus, 2008)

John, Eric, *Reassessing Anglo-Saxon England* (Manchester University Press, 1997)

Jones, Charles, *The Forgotten Battle of 1066: Fulford* (Tempus, 2006)

Keynes, Simon, *Charters and Diplomas of Æthelræd the Unready* (Cambridge University Press, 1980)

Lacey, Robert & Danny Danziger, *The Year 1000: An Englishman's Year* (Abacus, 2003)

Lavelle, Ryan, *Æthelræd II: King of the English 978–1016* (The History Press, 2008)

Lavelle, Ryan, *Cnut: the North Sea King* (Allen Lane, 2017)

Lawson, M. K., *Cnut: England's Viking King* (The History Press, 2011)

McLynn, Frank, *1066: The Year of the Three Battles* (Pimlico, 1999)

Morris, Marc, *The Norman Conquest* (Windmill Books, 2013)

Rex, Peter, *Edward the Confessor: King & Saint* (Amberley Publishing, 2013)

Rex, Peter, *Harold: The King Who Fell at Hastings* (Amberley Publishing, 2017)

Rex, Peter, *The English Resistance* (Amberley Publishing, 2014)

Roach, Levi, *Æthelræd the Unready* (Yale University Press, 2016)

Stenton, Frank, *Anglo-Saxon England* (Oxford University Press, 1970)

Walker, Ian, *Harold II: the Last Anglo-Saxon King* (The History Press, 2010)

Williams, Ann, *Æthelræd: the Ill-Counselled King* (Hambledon Continuum, 2003)

Wood, Michael, *In Search of the Dark Ages* (BBC Books, 2006)

INDEX

Ælfgar 127 (fn), 136, 142-7, 151, 152, 171, 176, 177, 236, 261
Ælfgifu of York 45, 46, 84, 107
Ælfgifu of Northampton 109-11, 119, 121, 151 (fn)
Ælfheah, Archbishop of Canterbury 70-1, 81, 259
Ælfhelm, ealdorman of Northumbria 56-7, 63, 72, 82, 85, 109, 260
Ælfhere, ealdorman of Mercia 15, 22, 260
Ælfmaer, abbot of St Augustine's Abbey, Canterbury 69-70
Ælfric, ealdorman of Mercia 22-3, 28, 34 (fn), 260
Ælfric of Hampshire 34-5, 36, 53, 56, 57, 97-8
Ælfstan, Bishop of Rochester 23-4
Ælfthryth 14, 18, 20-1
Ælfwin of Mercia, son of Ælfric 28-9
Æthelmaer, bishop of Elmham 244-5
Æthelræd the Unready 37, 42, 54, 55, 69, 71, 93, 96, 97, 100, 104, 105, 106, 110, 117, 122, 123, 127, 146, 155 (fn), 165 (fn), 178, 235, 267
parentage 14; candidature after Edgar's death 15; part in Edward the Martyr's murder 17-20; accession 21; 'invasion' of Rochester 23-5; offering tribute to Danes 29-32, 37-8, 67-8, 72; treaty with Normandy 32-4; and naval failures 34-5, 63; treaty with Olaf 38-40; taxation 40-1; takes the initiative in Irish Sea 43-4; campaign in Normandy 44-5, 47; marriage to Emma of Normandy 45-7; Viking raids of 1002 48; and St Brice's Day massacres 49-52; strength of English government under 55-6; political assassinations 56-8, 82-4; campaign of 1006-7 59-61; law codes 63-4, 76-8; campaign of 1009 63-7; issues Lamb of God coin 66; goes

into exile 72-3; return 74-5;
relationship with Wulfstan
79-82; and Edmund's rebellion
84-5; Cnut's invasion 85-8;
death 89; assessment 89-91
Æthelric 132, 134
Æthelstan, king 8, 46 (fn)
Æthelstan ætheling, son of
Æthelræd 46 (fn), 115
Æthelwin, bishop of Durham 244,
245
Æthelwin, ealdorman of East
Anglia 15, 261
Alan the Red 232
Alexander II, Pope 171, 185, 243,
244
Alfred the Great 8, 16, 32, 37, 40,
46 (fn), 60, 101, 137, 178,
234, 235
Alfred, son of Emma & Æthelraed
46, 84, 110, 122, 123 (fn),
131, 135
Alney Island, Gloucestershire 100,
101
Anglo-Saxon Chronicle 16-17,
18, 21, 22, 23, 25, 26 (fn),
34, 35, 36, 37, 42, 47, 48, 49,
52, 53, 56, 58, 59, 60, 63, 64,
67, 68, 69, 72, 74, 86, 88, 90,
93, 104, 107 (fn), 121, 123,
124, 128, 135, 137, 140, 141,
143, 144, 147, 156, 171, 183,
187, 192, 195 (fn), 197, 229,
231, 240, 242, 247, 248, 252,
253-4
Assandun 97-8, 100
Battle of Maldon 26-30
Bayeux Tapestry 125, 126, 162,
164, 166, 167, 185 (fn), 214,
Bedfordshire 67, 68 (fn), 88
Beorn 128
Berkhamsted 222
Berkshire 59, 68 (fn)
Bledwynn 236

blood feud 20, 83
Brihtric 63
Bristol 147, 233
Buckinghamshire 67, 68 (fn), 88
butsecarles 152 (fn)
Byrhtferth of Ramsay 16, 17
Byrhtnoth 26-8, 30 (fn), 31 (fn)
Calne 17
Canterbury 64, 69, 70, 125, 132,
167, 206, 207, 219
   archbishop & see of 14, 17, 21,
26, 34, 70, 111, 132, 133,
138, 139, 180, 185, 221, 244,
254, 259
castles 234, 235-6, 238, 252
ceorls 52, 53, 58 (fn), 85, 107-8,
229, 251
Charles the Simple of France 33
charters 49, 55, 155 (fn),
Cheshire 88
Chester 8, 9, 22, 231, 236, 247
Cirencester 22
Cnut, king of England, Denmark
and Norway 69, 85, 121, 123,
126, 127, 130, 138, 151 (fn),
154, 190, 220, 222, 225, 226,
228, 235
   marries Ælfgifu of Northampton
72; acclaimed king by Danes
74; withdrawal from England
75; negotiates with brother
76; invades England 86-8;
elected king 92; campaign
against Edmund Ironside
93-8; treaty with Edmund
100-2; becomes king of all
England 103; reorganisation
of government 105-6;
pilgrimage to Rome 107 (fn);
marries Emma of Normandy
108-9; expedition to Denmark
111-13; law code 113-15,
172-4; appointment of earls
114-5; relationship with

Godwin 115-6; Christianity
117-8; holding back the tide
118-9; death 119
Cnut the Holy, king of Denmark
252
collaborators 235
Copsi 237, 260
Cornwall 22, 60
Council of Lillebonne 185-6
Cuckamsley Hill 59-60
Cumbria 43-4
Danegeld see geld
Danelaw 36, 37, 50, 72, 90, 101,
174, 191
Danes 8, 30, 32, 36-8, 44, 47, 48,
49-52, 52-6, 59-61, 64-7, 68
(fn), 69-71, 73, 74-5, 81, 82,
83, 85-6, 90, 91, 93-8, 101,
103, 106, 108, 111, 114, 117,
233, 238, 241, 252
Denmark 37, 38, 43, 44, 53, 55,
71, 75, 76, 85, 87, 96, 105,
111–19, 121, 122, 126, 128,
130, 156, 189, 190, 238, 252
designation 16 (fn), 20, 76, 163,
168, 181, 183-4
Devon 22, 25, 48, 52
Domesday Survey 253-5
Dorset 22, 51
Dover 134-5, 166, 206, 219, 227
Drogo of Mantes 46 (fn), 165 (fn)
Dunstan, St, Archbishop of
Canterbury 14, 15, 16, 21, 26,
84, 259
Durham 57, 161, 237, 239, 244,
245
Eadmer 167-8
Eadric Streona 56-8, 63, 64-6, 81,
82-3, 85, 86, 87, 88, 90, 93,
95, 96, 97, 98, 102-6, 115,
155 (fn), 236, 260
Eadric the Wild 236
Eadwig, son of Aethelraed 46 (fn),
84, 107

Eadwig, King of the Ceorls 107-8
Eanham Codes 61-2, 70
East Anglia 7, 15, 35 (fn), 48, 54,
55, 56, 67, 68 (fn), 88, 97, 98,
106, 114, 127, 136, 138, 142,
143, 144, 145, 151, 227, 238,
240, 242, 244, 261
Eadnoth 233
Eadwulf, earl of Bernicia 123
Ealdred, Archbishop of York 154,
161 (fn), 185 (fn), 222, 223,
225, 243, 259
Edgar, king 8-9, 14, 15, 16, 20
Edgar ætheling 154-5, 159, 178,
186, 220, 221, 222, 225, 232,
234, 235, 238, 240, 257, 258,
265
Edith of Wessex, Queen 127, 130,
135, 137, 138, 149, 162, 180,
181, 183, 185 (fn), 225
Edith of Mercia 145, 177, 231,
232 (fn), 234
Edith Swan-Neck 151, 177, 179,
219, 231, 232, 234
Edmund Ironside 46 (fn), 84, 105,
110, 154, 178, 211, 222, 234,
235
  defiance of Æthelræd 84-5;
  dispute with Eadric Streona
  86-7; campaign as father's
  aetheling 87-9; election by
  London & acclamation by
  Wessex 92; campaigns of 1016
  93-8; relations with the witan
  99-100; negotiations with
  Cnut 100-2; death 102; legacy
  102-3
Edmund, son of Edmund Ironside
102-3, 154
Edmund, son of Godwin 151 (fn),
231, 232
Edward the Confessor 46, 75, 84,
122, 150, 151, 152, 161, 166,
179, 184, 207, 221, 225, 227,

228, 232, 236, 245, 247, 251, 254, 258

accession 123-4; relationship with Emma of Normandy 124-5; appearance & character 125-6, 148-9; dismissal of fleet 126-7; relationship with Godwin 127-30; relationship with Sweyn Godwinson 127-8; relationship with Edith 130-1; religious policy 131-4, 149; and the Normans 132-4; crisis of 1051-2 134-8; offer of the succession to William of Normandy 138-42; appointment of Harold as Earl of Wessex 142; appointment of Tostig as Earl of Northumbria 142-3; relationship with Ælfgar 142-7; killing of Gruffydd 147-8; relationship with Harold 151-3, 162-4, 168-9; and Edward the Exile 154-6; and the succession 157-9, 162-4; 168-70, 183; and the Northumbrian rebellion 171-3; decline & death 176, 178, 180-1; assessment 181-2; burial 184

Edward the Elder 8

Edward the Exile 105, 154-6

Edward the Martyr 14, 15, 16, 17, 18, 19, 20, 21, 23, 62, 267

Edwin, earl of Mercia 147, 171, 175, 176, 177, 178, 179, 184, 189, 193, 194, 195, 196, 199, 221, 222 (fn), 225, 226, 227, 228, 237, 240, 245, 261

Eilmar of Malmesbury 11 (fn), 84

Emma of Normandy 45, 46, 47, 52, 71, 72, 75, 84, 108-10, 121, 122, 123, 124, 125

Encomium Emmae Reginae 47, 71, 75, 76, 87, 93, 94, 97, 98, 108, 117, 118, 125

enfeoffment 166, 169, 248, 249

entry fines 249

Erik Bloodaxe 36

Erik, earl of Northumbria 88, 106, 111, 114, 115, 119, 260

Essex 26, 27, 37, 68 (fn), 97

Eustace of Boulogne 46 (fn), 134-35, 217, 226-7

Exeter 52, 225, 233, 234, 235

feudalism 248-50, 255, 274, 275

fief 248 (fn), 249, 250

Five Boroughs 72, 82, 85, 86

Fleet (river) 37

forest law see royal forest

Freeman, EA 89

Fulford Gate, battle of 193-5, 196, 197, 198, 203, 204, 209, 221, 224, 227

fyrd 48, 53, 55, 59, 64, 66, 67, 72, 83, 87, 88, 93, 96, 97, 108, 111-12, 189, 191, 192, 194, 196, 204, 208, 212, 220

gafol 40, 41, 106

Gainsborough 72, 74

geld 40-1, 72, 106, 110, 127, 182, 252

Glastonbury 111, 247

Godgifu, daughter of Aethelraed & Emma 46, 134 (fn)

Godgifu, wife of Leofric of Mercia 115

Godwin, earl of Wessex 115-6, 122, 123 (fn), 127-8, 130-1, 132, 134, 135-8, 139, 140-2, 145, 146, 148, 150, 151, 152, 157, 158, 162, 179, 181, 185 (fn), 210, 228, 231, 232, 258, 261

Godwin, son of Harold 151 (fn), 231

Gospatric, earl of Northumbria
237, 260
Great Heathen Army 7, 37, 60,
202, 234
Gruffydd 144, 145, 147, 148, 164,
168, 176, 177, 236
Gunhild, sister of Sweyn
Forkbeard 48, 50
Gunnhild, daughter of Harold
151, 232
Guy of Burgundy 186
Guy of Ponthieu 164-5, 170
Gytha, wife of Godwin 116, 130,
218, 225, 233
Gytha, daughter of Harold 151
(fn), 232
Gyrth 145, 152, 208, 209, 218,
224, 261
Hakon, governor of Norway 119
Hakon, son of Sweyn Godwinson
140, 141, 163, 165, 231
Halley's Comet 11, 26, 84, 188
Hampshire 34, 37, 53, 59, 61, 64,
68 (fn), 97, 98
handfasting 110, 151 (fn)
Harald Bluetooth 117
Harald, King of Denmark 75, 76,
111
Harald 'Hardrada' 126, 189-91,
193, 195, 198-9, 200, 201,
202, 203-4, 232, 238, 251
Harold Harefoot 121-3, 124,
Harold Godwinson 127, 128, 136,
138, 142, 143 (fn), 144, 145,
146 (fn), 186, 188, 223, 224,
225, 227, 231, 232, 233, 234,
235, 236, 258, 261, 275
Welsh campaign 147-8; character
149-50; first marriage
150-1; political dominance
151-2; and Edward the Exile
155-6; plotting to succeed
Edward 158-9, 178-9; trip
to Normandy 161-71; and
the Northumbrian rebellion
175-7; second marriage
177; presence at Edward the
Confessor's death 180-1;
designation by Edward 183-4;
coronation 184-5; visits York
187-8; dismissal of fyrd 192;
naval expedition against
Normans 192-3; Stamford
Bridge campaign 196-205;
returns south 207-8; considers
Gyrth as commander for
Hastings campaign 208-9;
summons fyrd & advances on
Hastings 210-12; at Hastings
213-18; death 218; burial
legends 218-9
Harold, son of Harold Godwinson
231-2
harrying 45, 48, 61, 63, 66, 75,
86, 88, 92, 97, 135, 136, 147,
182, 190, 210, 222, 254
Harrying of the North 239-40,
254-5
Harthacnut 110, 114, 121, 122,
123, 124, 129, 140, 184, 190
Hastings, battle of 214-8
Henry I, king of France 186
Henry IV, Holy Roman Emperor
252
Henry of Huntingdon 19, 49, 100,
102, 114, 116, 118, 192, 201,
207
Herefordshire 132, 144, 145, 242
Hereward the Wake 240-1
Herfast, bishop of Elmham 245
hide (unit of land) 25, 30 (fn), 31
(fn), 63, 253, 262
Holderness 193
hostages 38, 72, 113, 139-42, 148,
163-4, 165 (fn), 168, 196, 222
housecarls 152, 196, 197 (fn),
199, 208, 212, 218, 220, 224
Hugh of Normandy 52-3

Humber 57, 72, 191, 193, 239, 254

Huntingdon 192

Huntingdonshire 68 (fn), 175

Ireland 22, 136, 232, 233

John XV, Pope 34

John of Wallingford 50

John of Worcester 18, 19, 20, 23, 24, 36, 49, 50, 52, 56, 58, 60, 64, 69, 86, 93, 107, 127 (fn), 172, 185 (fn), 211, 219, 221, 222 (fn), 241, 242, 243, 247, 248

Judith of Flanders 136, 161 (fn)

Judith, niece of William of Normandy and wife of Waltheof 240

Kent 37, 60, 63, 64, 67, 68, 70 (fn), 85, 95, 125, 230, 238, 246

Kjetil 231, 258

Lady Godiva, see Godgifu, wife of Leofric of Mercia

Lanfranc 244, 246, 259

Leo IX, Pope 132

Leofric of Mercia 115-6, 127, 128, 136, 137, 142, 143, 145, 151, 179, 226, 245, 260

Leofsige 48, 54, 56, 58, 261

Leofwin, earl 136, 146, 152, 218, 224

Leofwin, bishop of Lichfield 244-5

Lincolnshire 36, 72, 75, 85, 238

London 22, 34, 35 (fn), 37, 63, 66, 67, 72-3, 82, 86, 88, 92, 93, 95, 101, 111, 132, 134, 136, 147 (fn), 192, 193, 196, 197, 198 (fn), 206, 207, 208, 212, 219-22, 227, 233, 236, 247

longships 34, 37, 52, 63, 72, 85, 191, 202, 238

Macbeth 114, 146 (fn)

Magnus 'the Good,' king of Norway 119, 121, 126, 130, 190

Magnus, son of Harold 151 (fn), 231, 232

Malcolm, king of Scotland 146 (fn), 161, 189, 225, 238, 240

Maldon 26, 28, 30, 32, 34

Man, Isle of 44

marriage more danico see handfasting

Marx, Karl 55

Matilda 185

mercenaries 40, 48, 51, 71, 75, 87, 111, 190

Mons, battle of 198 (fn)

Morcar, earl of Northumbria 171, 172, 173, 175, 176, 177, 178, 179, 184, 188, 189, 193, 194, 195, 196, 199, 221, 222 (fn), 225, 226, 227, 228, 240, 241, 242, 245, 255, 260

murdrum 238

natural disasters 17, 25, 55, 78, 84, 239, 253

Northamptonshire 67, 68 (fn) 171, 175

Northumbria 7, 25 (fn), 34, 36, 37, 45, 56, 57, 72, 81, 82, 85, 88, 106, 115, 116, 119, 123 (fn), 127, 137, 142, 143, 145, 151, 152, 159, 160, 161, 171-9, 181, 183, 187, 188, 189, 191, 193, 194, 195, 196, 198, 200 (fn), 203, 204, 205, 226, 227, 228, 232, 237, 238, 239, 240, 243, 245, 255, 257, 258, 260

Northumbrian rebellion of 1065 171-6

Norway 37, 39, 43, 44, 75, 88, 119, 121, 126, 130, 144, 156, 189, 190, 191, 193, 194, 195

(fn), 199, 200, 202, 203, 211, 231, 232
Norwegians 38, 39, 44, 106, 119, 144, 193, 194, 195, 198-204
Nottingham 72 (fn), 237
Odda of Deerhurst 136
Odo of Bayeux 125, 227, 230, 246, 255, 274
Olaf Tryggvason 37-40, 42, 43,
Olaf, St, king of Norway 75, 106, 118-9
Olaf 'the Peaceful', king of Norway 195 (fn), 202-3, 232
Olof, King of Sweden 103
Orderic Vitalis 19, 166, 208, 214, 217, 223, 229, 230, 235, 238, 239, 241, 243, 244, 249, 255, 256
Orkney 22, 106, 191, 202
Orre's Storm 201
Osgod Clapa 114, 261
Oswald, Archbishop of York, 15, 16, 259
Ouse, river 191
outlawry 115, 143, 144, 171, 173, 240, 241, 242
Pallig 48, 50, 51
pallium 34, 118, 161 (fn)
Penitential Ordinance 273-6
Penselwood 93
Pevensey 205, 206, 210
pluralism 77, 133, 246
polutasvarf 190 (fn)
Portland 22
Ralph of Mantes, earl of Hereford 132, 144, 145
Ralph the Staller, earl of East Anglia 228, 261
Ralph de Gael, earl of East Anglia 228, 242, 261
Rhuddlan 147, 207
Riccall 191, 193, 195, 199, 201, 202

Richard I of Normandy 33 (fn), 34, 109
Richard II of Normandy 33, 45-7
Ridgeway Hill, Dorset 51
Robert Curthose 251
Robert, earl of Northumbria 237, 260
Robert of Jumieges 132, 134, 138, 139, 183, 259
Robert of Mortain 227
Robert the Magnificent, Duke of Normandy 138 (fn), 169
Robin Hood 241-2
Rochester 23-4, 37, 81, 117
Roger, earl of Hereford 242
Rolf see Rollo
Rollo of Normandy 33
Rouen 164, 166, 255
royal forest 230-1, 251
St Bertin's Abbey 47 (fn), 125 (fn)
St Brice's Day Massacre 49-52, 77, 155 (fn)
St Frideswide, Priory of 49, 51, 77, 155 (fn)
St John's College, Oxford 51
St Omer 47 (fn), 125 (fn), 233 (fn)
St Stephen's Abbey, Caen 256
St Valery 187, 206
Salisbury 53, 255
Salisbury Oath 255
Sandwich 59, 63, 66, 86, 189
Scarborough 193
Scots 8, 57, 146, 160, 194, 238
Scotland 22, 146 (fn), 189, 193, 225, 240, 257
scutage 250
seax 94, 104
Senlac 213
Sermon of the Wolf 77-9, 80, 264-72
Sherston, battle of 93-5
Shetland 22, 191
shield wall 94, 201, 213, 214, 215, 218

Shrewsbury 56

Shropshire 60, 88

Sigeric the Serious, Archbishop of Canterbury 34

Siward 115, 116, 123 (fn), 127, 128, 137, 142, 146 (fn), 151, 159, 160, 175, 226, 260

Skuli 231, 258

slavery 53, 61, 70, 79-81, 251, 254, 262-3, 265-6, 268

Snorri Sturluson 191, 194, 195, 198, 199, 200

Southampton 22, 38, 92

Southwark 136, 219

Spearhavoc 132, 134

Staffordshire 88

Stamford Bridge 195, 196, 198-202, 203, 205, 207, 208, 211, 212, 221, 224, 232

Stigand 138 (fn), 180-1, 183, 185, 221, 225, 244, 254, 259

Strathclyde 8, 43, 44

Sulcard of Westminster 23, 24

Sussex 37, 63, 64, 68 (fn), 115, 205, 206, 210

Sweyn, son of Cnut 106, 109, 110, 119

Sweyn Estrithsson 126, 156, 130, 189, 238, 242

Sweyn Forkbeard 37, 39, 40, 42, 43, 48, 52, 53, 54, 71-3, 74, 75, 76, 83, 87, 88, 90, 96, 100, 104, 117, 119, 123, 220, 235

Sweyn Godwinson 127-8, 140, 150, 163, 165 (fn)

Symeon of Durham 161 (fn)

Tadcaster 196, 198

tax 15, 31, 40, 41, 55, 63, 66, 68, 78, 111, 112, 123, 174, 182, 190, 229, 230, 249, 250, 251, 252, 266

Thames, river 35 (fn), 37, 60, 63, 66, 67, 95, 96, 97, 136, 147 (fn), 219, 220, 221

Thanet 22

thegns 25, 36, 37, 54, 58 (fn), 72, 79, 82, 83, 87, 88, 93, 108, 115, 159, 160, 171-6, 188, 194, 196, 197 (fn), 198, 220, 224, 226, 236, 251, 254, 262, 268

Thetford 54

Thomas of Bayeux, Archbishop of York 244, 259

Thored of Northumbria 34, 36, 45, 260

Thurkill the Tall 64, 67, 69, 70, 71, 72, 73, 75, 87, 93, 106, 111-14, 261

Thurstan 247-8

Tostig 128, 136, 142, 143, 145, 147, 149, 150, 151, 152, 159, 160, 161, 171-7, 179, 189-91, 198-201, 203, 204, 209, 231, 233, 258, 260

Tower of London 236

tribute 31, 32, 40, 48, 54, 67, 68, 71, 72, 79, 82, 102, 172, 174, 268

Uhtred of Northumbria 57, 72, 88, 106, 260

Ulf 231, 232

Ulfcytel 54, 56, 67, 85, 88, 97, 98

Val-es-Dunes, battle of 186

Varaville, battle of 186

Vikings 7-8, 21-2, 25-7, 29-35, 37, 40-4, 46-8, 50, 55, 56, 63, 66, 70, 78, 117, 190, 191, 202

Vita Aedwardi Regis 124, 127, 130, 131, 134, 135, 136, 146 (fn), 148, 149, 152, 160, 162, 172, 173, 175, 176, 181, 183

Vladimir of Kiev 232

Wales 144, 145 (fn), 147-8, 168, 176, 178

Wallingford 59, 60, 220, 221

Walter of the Vexin 165 (fn), 170

Waltheof 142, 175, 176, 177, 225, 226, 227, 228, 238, 240, 242-3

Waltham 151, 185 (fn), 208, 218, 219

wardship 249

Warwick 237

welsh 8, 144, 145 (fn), 147, 160, 168, 171, 175, 176, 194, 236, 237

wergild 20 (fn)

Wessex 7, 8, 25 (fn), 32, 36, 37, 38, 48, 54, 59, 60, 84, 86, 87, 92, 93, 95, 96, 101, 106, 116, 127 (fn), 136, 137, 142, 145, 147 (fn), 150, 159, 166, 170, 179, 189, 200 (fn), 204, 210, 214, 225, 227, 233, 234, 254, 261

Westminster Abbey 149, 180, 182, 184, 219, 223, 225

Wight, Isle of 48, 59, 64, 66, 73, 189

William, bishop of London 132

William of Jumieges 45, 47, 122 (fn), 166, 167, 169, 214, 217

William of Malmesbury 11 (fn), 19, 21, 23 46, 47, 48, 50, 64, 68 (fn), 79, 80, 86, 90, 93, 101, 102, 114, 126, 133, 164, 166, 185 (fn), 208, 212(fn), 230, 235, 240, 241, 245, 257

William of Poitiers 101 (fn), 139, 140, 162, 164, 165 (fn), 166, 167, 168, 185 (fn), 186, 207, 210, 213, 215, 216, 222 (fn), 229

William I 101 (fn), 125, 138, 139, 140, 141, 155, 157, 161, 162, 163, 164, 169-71, 177, 178, 183, 192-3, 208, 210-2, 232, 233, 235; 257, 258, 274, 275

and Harold's trip to Normandy 165-7; invasion preparations 184-7; invasion 206-7; at Hastings 214-9; advance on London 219-22; coronation 223; treatment of English magnates 224-9, 236-7; and Norman excesses 229-31; treatment of rebels 236, 241-2; harrying of the North 239-40; and the English Church 243-8; and tax 252-3; and Domesday 253-5; death 255-6

William Rufus 231, 252

Williams, Ann 89-90

Wilton 53, 149, 232

Winchester 70, 72, 138 (fn), 147 (fn), 244, 254

witan 13, 14, 16, 17, 21, 22, 29, 48, 49, 57, 60, 61, 68, 69, 74, 75, 79, 82, 83, 85, 92, 102, 104, 107, 110, 111, 121, 140, 157, 159, 169, 170, 173, 177, 178, 179, 180, 184, 220, 222, 232, 258

Wulf, see Ulf

Wulfnoth, ealdorman of Sussex 63, 115

Wulfnoth, son of Godwin 140, 141, 163, 231, 232, 255

Wulfstan, Archbishop of York 61, 77-82, 113-4, 133, 174, 259

York 88, 171, 187 188, 191, 193, 194, 195, 196, 197, 198, 203, 207, 208, 238, 239, 240, 242

York, archbishop & see of, 15, 16, 61, 77, 79, 82, 106, 116, 161, 185 (fn), 222

Yorkshire 171, 187, 191, 196, 203, 204, 238, 240, 243, 244, 259